ENDANGERED WILDLIFE
of the World

Volume 5
IGU ~ MAR

Marshall Cavendish
NEW YORK • LONDON • TORONTO • SYDNEY

Published by Marshall Cavendish Corporation
2415 Jerusalem Avenue
North Bellmore, New York 11710
USA

Endangered wildlife of the world.
     p.   cm.
     Includes bibliographical references and index.
Summary: Describes various endangered or threatened species around
the world, covering their habitat, behavior, and efforts to protect
them.
  ISBN 1-85435-489-2 (set) :
  1. Endangered species—Juvenile literature. 2. Wildlife
conservation—Juvenile literature. [1. Rare animals. 2. Rare
birds. 3. Wildlife conservation.] I. Marshall Cavendish
Corporation.
QL83.E55 1993
591.52'9—dc20   92-14974
                           CIP
                           AC

Produced by the Creative Spark
General editor: Gregory Lee
Art direction: Robert Court
Design: Mary Francis, Robert Court
Photo research, production coordination: Elayne Roberts
Page layout: Elizabeth Sirimarco
Maps: Thomas Colandrea
Production: Beverly Escarrega, Melody Nickerson
Illustrations: Barbara Emmons

Marshall Cavendish editorial consultant: Marylee Knowlton

Printed in Malaysia by Times Offset (M) Sdn Bhd
Bound in the United States by Lake Book Manufacturing

Photo Credits
584 (Ken Lucas), 672 (Edward Ely) Biological Photo Service; 586 (Bob
McKeever), 612 (Larry Tackett), 613 (Dave Watts) Tom Stack & Associates; 587,
630 (Ken Kelley), 592 (Craig W. Racicot), 641, 646, 656, 662, 679, 680, 711, 713
(Ron Garrison), 681, 699 Zoological Society of San Diego; 588, 636, 639, 640,
652, 654, 685, 687 Warren D. Thomas; 594, 666, 684, (John Cancalosi), 596, 664,
715 (Kevin Schaffer), 655 (Ted Schiffman), 658 (David Harinn), 659 (BIOS), 665
(S. Asad), 683 (Yann Arthus-Bertrand), 707 (Fred Bavendam), 717 (C. Allan
Morgan), 719, 720 (Luiz Claudio Marigo) Peter Arnold, Inc.; 599 (C. Heidecker),
623 (H. Cruickshank) VIREO; 615 (Hans Reinhard), 632 (Frank W. Lane), 645
(Kenneth W. Fink), 705 (M. Freeman) Bruce Coleman, Inc.; 620 (D. Demello),
710 New York Zoological Society; 625 Glen Smart; 660 Robert and Linda
Mitchell; 669 (Stephen J. Krasemann) DRK Photo; 671 B. "Moose" Peterson;
676 (William N. Roston), 690 (Bauer), 693, 694 (J.R. Shute) American Fisheries
Society; 692 Suzanne L. Collins & Joseph T. Collins; 696 Noel Burkhead

Cover: A male mandrill. Photograph courtesy New York Zoological Society.
Title page illustration: Kiwi.

Glossary

albino

any organism lacking color in the skin or fur; albino species have pink eyes, while albino fish often have no functioning eyes

amphibia

the Latin scientific name for amphibians

arboreal

living in or adapted for living in trees; arboreal animals prefer living in trees and seldom, if ever, descend to the ground (see *terrestrial*)

arthropoda

the Latin scientific name for crustaceans and spiders

aves

the Latin scientific name for birds

barbels

a slender growth on the mouths or nostrils of certain fishes, used as a sensory organ for touch

bipedal

any organism that walks on two feet

buff

in bird species, a yellow-white color used to describe the plumage

captive breeding

any method of bringing several animals of the same species into a zoo or other closed environment for the purpose of mating; if successful, these methods can increase the population of that species

carnivore

any flesh-eating animal

carnivorous

flesh eating

carrion

the decaying flesh of a dead organism

class

a biological ranking of animals who share a common set of traits, below the rank of phylum and above the rank of order

classification

how a species is ranked biologically in relation to other species (see *taxonomy*)

clear cutting

a method of harvesting lumber that eliminates all the trees in a specific area rather than just selected trees

clutch, clutch size

the number of eggs laid during one nesting cycle

contiguous

touching, meeting, joining at a surface or border; the home of an animal is contiguous if it is uninterrupted by natural or artificial boundaries

deciduous

dropping off, falling off during a certain season or at a regular stage of growth; deciduous trees shed their leaves annually; a deciduous forest contains these trees

decurved

curving downward; a bird's beak is decurved if it points toward the ground

defoliate

to strip trees and bushes of their leaves

deforestation

the process of removing trees from a particular area

diurnal

active during the day; some animals are diurnal, while others are active at night (see *nocturnal)*

dominance

the ability to overpower the behavior of other individuals; an animal is dominant if it affects others of its own species in a way that benefits itself; also, the trait of abundance that determines the character of a plant community: grasses dominate a prairie, and trees dominate a forest

dorsal

pertaining to or situated on the back of an organism; a dorsal fin is on the back of a fish

ecology

the relationship between a living organism and its environment

ecosystem

a community of animals, plants, and bacteria and its interrelated physical and chemical environment

endangered species

any species on the verge of becoming extinct;

disappearing from the wild forever

endemic

native to a particular geographic region

estrous

the time period when female mammals can become pregnant

exotic species

any plant or animal species that is not native to a particular habitat

extinct species

any species that has not been located in the wild for 50 years and is presumed to have disappeared forever

family

a biological ranking of species that share specific traits, below the rank of order and above genus; *subfamily* is a narrower classification of species within the same family

feral

a wild animal that is descended from tame or domesticated species

fishery, fisheries

any system, body of water, or portion of a body of water that supports finfish or shellfish; can also be used as an adjective describing a person or thing (for example, a fisheries biologist)

forest

a plant community in which trees grow closely enough together that their crowns interlock to form a continuous overhead canopy

fry

young fish

gene pool

the total hereditary traits available within a group; when isolated from other members of their species, individual organisms may produce healthy offspring if there is enough variety in the genes available through mating

genus

a biological ranking of species that share many specific traits, below the rank of family and above species; *subgenus* is a narrower classification of species within the same genus

gestation

the period of active embryonic growth inside a mammal's body between the time the embryo attaches to the uterus and the time of birth; some mammals carry dormant embryos for several weeks or months before the embryo attaches to the uterus and begins to develop actively, and this dormancy period is not part of the gestation period; *gestation*

period is the time length of a pregnancy

granivore

any seed-feeding animal

granivorous

seed feeding

guano

manure, especially of sea birds and bats

habitat

the environment where a species is normally found; *habitat degradation* is the decline in quality of a species' home until it can no longer survive there

herbivore

any plant-eating animal

herbivorous

plant eating

hierarchy

the relationships among individuals of the same species or among species that determine in what order animals may have access to food, water, mates, nesting or denning sites, and other vital resources

hibernate

to spend the winter season in a dormant or inactive state; some species hibernate to save energy during months when food is scarce

home range

the area normally traveled by an individual species during its lifespan

hybrid

the offspring of two different species who mate; see *interbreed*

hybridization

the gradual decline of a species through continued breeding with another species; see *interbreed*

immature(s)

a young bird that has not yet reached breeding maturity; it usually has plumage differing from an adult bird of the same species

in captivity

a species that only exists in zoos or other captive breeding programs, and is no longer found in the wild

incubation

the period when an egg is kept warm for the time necessary for an embryo to develop to hatching age

indigenous species
    any species that is native to its habitat

insecta
    the Latin scientific name for insects

insular species
    a species isolated on an island or islands

interbreed
    when two separate species mate and produce offspring; see *hybrid*

invertebrate(s)
    any organism without a backbone (spinal column)

juvenal
    a bird with an intermediate set of feathers after its young downy plumage molts and before growing hard, adult feathers

juvenile(s)
    a young bird or other animal not yet mature

litter
    the animals born to a species that normally produces several young at birth

lore(s)
    the irregularly shaped facial area of a bird between the eye and the base of the beak

mammalia
    the Latin scientific name for mammals

migrate, migratory
    to move from one range to another, particularly with the change of seasons; many species are migratory

milt
    the reproductive glands of male fishes; also, the breeding behavior of male fishes

mollusca
    the Latin scientific name for mussels, clams, and snails

montane forest
    a forest found in mountainous regions

natural selection
    the process named by Charles Darwin (1809-1882) to describe how species evolve by such methods as adapting to their environment and evading predators

nocturnal
    active at night; some animals are nocturnal, while others are active by day (see *diurnal*)

nomadic species
    a species with no permanent range or territory; nomadic species wander for food and water

offal
    waste products or leftovers; usually the internal organs of a slain animal

old growth forest
    a forest that has not experienced extensive deforestation

omnivore
    any species that eats both plants and animal flesh

order
    a biological ranking of species sharing certain characteristics, below the rank of class and above family

ornithologist(s)
    a scientist who specializes in the study of birds

osteichthyes
    the Latin scientific name for fish

pelage
    the hairy covering of a mammal

pelagic
    related to the oceans or open sea; pelagic birds rarely roost on land

phylum
    one of several broad, biological rankings of organisms of the plant and animal kingdoms, above the rank class and below kingdom

plumage
    the feathers that cover a bird

prairie
    a plant community without trees and dominated by grasses; a grassland; often incorrectly used synonymously with *plain* or *plains*, which is a landform feature and not a plant community

predator
    a species that preys upon (hunts) other species

predation
    the act of one species hunting another

primary forest
    a forest of native trees that results from natural processes, often called *virgin forest*

primate(s)
    a biological ranking of species in the same order,

including gorillas, chimpanzees, monkeys, and human beings (*Homo sapiens*)

range
the geographic area where a species roams naturally

rare
any animal with a small worldwide population (or local population) that is at risk but not yet threatened or endangered

recovery plan(s)
any document that outlines a public or private program for assisting an endangered or threatened species

relict
an isolated habitat or population that was once widespread

reptilia
the Latin scientific name for reptiles

riffle(s)
a shallow rapid stretch of water caused by a rocky outcropping or other obstruction in a stream

riparian
relating to plants and animals that dwell close to and are influenced by rivers

roe
fish eggs

rufous
in bird species, an orange-brown color with some pink used to describe the plumage

secondary forest
a forest that has grown back after cutting, forest fire, or other types of deforestation; secondary forests may or may not contain exotic tree species, but they almost always differ in character from primary forests

sedentary species
a species that does not migrate

siltation
the process of sediment clouding and obstructing a body of water

species
a distinct kind of plant or animal; the biological ranking below genus; a *subspecies* is an isolated population that varies somewhat from its own species

taxonomy
the science of biologically ranking plants and animals,
arranging the relationships between species

terrestrial
living in or adapted for living principally on the ground; some birds are terrestrial and seldom, if ever, ascend into trees (see *arboreal*)

territory
the area occupied more or less exclusively by an organism or group, usually defended by aggressive displays and physical combat

threatened species
any species that is at risk of becoming endangered

tribe
a more specific classification within the biological rankings of family or subfamily

tubercles
a prominent bump on a fish's body connected to a spine

tussocks
a thick bunch of twigs and grass, often found in swamps

veldt
a grassland region with some scattered bushes and virtually no trees; other terms are *steppe, pampas,* and *prairie*

ventral
on or near the belly; the *ventral fin* is located on the underside of a fish and corresponds with the hind limbs of other vertebrates

vertebrates
any organism that has a backbone (spinal column)

water column
the zone of a pond, lake, or ocean below the surface and above the bottom that holds free-swimming or free-floating fish and other animals and plants

watershed
the area of land that contributes water to a single stream or stream system, usually including the soil and plants in that land area because they have the capacity to store water and thereby affect water flow and water cycling in that landscape

weir
a dam or other obstruction of a stream that diverts water from its natural path

woodland
a plant community in which trees grow abundantly but far enough apart that their crowns do not intermingle, so no overhead canopy is formed

IGUANAS

Class: Reptilia
Order: Squamata
Family: Iguanidae

The genus Iguana *contains two species:* Iguana delicatissima, *found only in the Lesser Antilles, and* Iguana iguana, *the common or green iguana found in tropical and subtropical regions from Mexico to Paraguay and the Lesser Antilles.* Iguana *is also the common name given to several related lizards of the family* Iguanidae. *They are all relatively large lizards and herbivorous, meaning that they feed on plants. These lizards also lay eggs.*

Lizards of the family Iguanidae *are known as Iguanids. The family was once distributed throughout the world but is now found primarily in the New World. The remaining Old World genera can be found on the Fiji and Tonga islands, and on the island of Madagascar. These are rough-scaled lizards with color-changing ability. While most lizards can change their color slightly to reflect heat and light, the iguana is able to achieve more obvious color change, helping it become inconspicuous to predators. However, only true chameleons can change their color in response to mood or environment. They abound in rain forests and desert regions of the Old World and in tropics and subtropics.*

Like all lizards, iguanas are ectotherms—that is, they are animals whose body temperatures are controlled by their environment. Therefore, behavioral mechanisms are used to maintain body temperatures. These diurnal animals derive heat from exposure to the sun and regulate heat by alternately sunning themselves and withdrawing to shaded areas.

The skin of iguanas is often used for leather goods such as handbags, wallets, and shoes. They are also taken as pets, and in agricultural areas they are often desired for insect control. As with many other types of lizards, they are used for food among impoverished people.

*In addition to the iguanas mentioned here, several other species are in trouble: the Barrington Island iguana (*Conolophus pallidus*) is considered rare; two other species are also considered threatened, the Cuban ground iguana (*Cyclura nubila*) and the Fiji crested iguana (*Brachylopuus vitiensis*). Two species of iguana are considered endangered, the Anegada ground iguana (*Cyclura pinguis*) and the Jamaican ground iguana (*Cyclura collei*).*

GALAPAGOS LAND IGUANA
(Conolophus subcristatus)

Status: Threatened

Description:

Clutch size: Up to 9 eggs
Diet: Herbivorous
Habitat: Arid or transitional zones with sparse or moderate vegetation and soil for burrowing
Range: Galapagos Islands

Darwin's Island

The Galapagos land iguana is placed in its own genus. It is a big-headed, stout-bodied lizard with yellowish coloration on the head and a rusty-brown colored body. It was originally found on six islands of the archipelago: Fernandina, Isabela, Santiago, Santa Cruz, Baltra, and South Plaza. Apparently it is now extinct on Santiago. Charles Darwin found the reptile very common on this island in his exploration in 1835, but it may have been extinct there by 1905, when only bones were found by a California Academy of Science expedition. On this island, it was probably destroyed by pigs. On Baltra, it was destroyed by United States military personnel who were stationed there during World War II. There is now a small population on Seymour Island, which was introduced in the 1930s from Baltra.

There are no accurate estimates made for most populations, but the

The Galapagos Islands are an archipelago rich in flora and fauna, as biologist Charles Darwin discovered in the nineteenth century. But as humans put greater and greater stress on the island wildlife, species like the Galapagos land iguana suffered greatly.

South Plaza group is thought to be made up of between 200 and 300 lizards. Since the discovery of the islands in 1535, large numbers of the land iguanas have been slaughtered. The tail became a food source for various visitors to the islands, including whalers, hunters and colonists. But this was not the major cause of the iguana population's decline.

The land iguanas have suffered much the same fate as the giant tortoises found on the islands. They have been reduced by human predation for skins, predation by introduced cats, and habitat reduction by farmers who are destroying natural nesting areas. Young lizards on Isabela are being killed in large numbers by feral cats; young and perhaps even adults are being destroyed by feral dogs and pigs. Rats are a major predator of both tortoise and iguana eggs and hatchlings.

Galapagos Land Iguana
South America

Predation of this nature is also a problem on Santa Cruz. Another significant problem has been the grazing of goats on the islands, which clears the vegetative cover of the iguana, exposing the vulnerable young to birds of prey and other predators. Scientists are careful not to make casual observations when studying the Galapagos land iguana because the animal, particularly the juveniles, are very elusive and rarely seen, even in stable populations.

Conservation

Since 1959, all uninhabited areas of the Galapagos have been a national park, and it is now illegal to hunt, capture, or remove any species of plant or animal, as well as rocks and minerals, from the islands. This includes the land iguanas. Fernandina is the largest uncolonized and least penetrable island, and a stable but unmeasured population apparently persists there. Isabela was once thought to have few iguanas, but the island was difficult to explore. Now it seems that this largest island of the Galapagos archipelago may have the largest surviving population. A detailed study of the distribution, population dynamics, reproductive potential, general ecology, and the threats caused by predators needs to be conducted to establish a feasible recovery plan for the Galpagos land iguana.

MONA IGUANA
(Cyclura stejnegeri)

Status: Threatened

Description:

Length: 3-4 feet (1.3 m)
Clutch size: Average, 12 eggs
Diet: Herbivorous-omnivorous; prefers the toxic Manzanillo fruit
Habitat: Most common along major escarpments and slopes
Range: Mona Island, Greater Antilles

Largest on the Island

The Mona iguana is the largest Puerto Rican lizard. It is a heavy-bodied lizard, with a proportion-ately large head and a robust, laterally compressed tail. It has a jowl under the jaw that can be quite pronounced in large, mature males, and a small horn on the snout just in front of the eyes. There is a crest on its back,

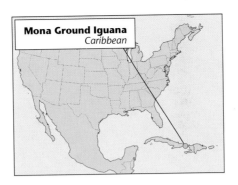

Mona Ground Iguana
Caribbean

extending from head to tail, and the general color of the lizard is olive to olive gray with some individuals displaying intermitent blue and brown hues.

This iguana is restricted to Mona Island, a small, limestone island located midway between Puerto Rico and Hispaniola in the Greater Antilles. Large parts of the island are covered by outcrops of solid limestone, where mostly dry and semideciduous scrub vegetation of low trees and shrubs or cacti grow.

` The Mona iguana eats both plants and animals. Fecal samples determined that at least 71 plant species and 12 animal species make up its diet. A favored food is the fruit from the toxic Manzanillo tree. All the plant species that iguanas eat are also eaten by goats, and consumption by goats reduces the amount of food available to iguanas.

Mona iguanas do not need to use much energy to forage. They are most apt to eat what is readily available, and tend to be slow movers who stay close to their burrows. Outside of mating season, almost all of their time—an estimated 94 percent—is spent resting. The remaining time is spent foraging and eating; distant travel is reserved for food searching, although the female will travel to hunt for nesting grounds.

Reproduction

The breeding season begins in mid-June and ends in November when the eggs hatch. Males begin the process by establishing a territory that includes female retreat burrows. Males will defend their territory aggressively, and fights usually involve head-bobbing, tossing, or pushing, although biting rarely occurs. Females seldom move from retreat burrows within male territories during breeding. Afterward, they migrate to nesting grounds, and egg laying occurs two to four weeks after mating.

Only a small portion of Mona island offers soils deep enough for iguana nesting, and pregnant females are often forced to migrate great distances searching for optimal nesting sites. These sites are at a premium. Sometimes females will inadvertently destroy the nest and eggs of a prior nesting female in their own attempts to nest. Once a spot has been located, females will dig for about two hours, retreating occasionally to cool off, and continuing to dig until a hole large enough to accommo-date the whole animal has been excavated. Once the nest is ready, she lays her eggs, and the clutch size averages 12. The female covers the egg chamber once the eggs have been laid, but leaves an air space above them. She will guard the nest for 10 days. Three months later, the young emerge by digging out from the nest chamber. The young receive no parental care.

Status

Prior to 1972, little was known about the populations of the Mona iguana. Threats to the species have

The Mona iguana has probably been considered food by native aborigines on Mona island since pre-Colombian times.

laying of the iguana, and human activities interfere with this. For example, humans have trampled nest chambers. Iguanas are also killed by vehicles as they attempt to cross roads.

Little was done for the Mona iguana until the Department of Natural Resources was established in 1973. This department has managed the island since then, protecting its natural wildlife and vegetation. From 1973 to 1976, one resident biologist was assigned to the island, improving the enforcement of protective legislation.

SOUTH PACIFIC BANDED IGUANA
(Brachylophus fasciatus)

Status: Endangered

Description:

Clutch size: Unknown
Diet: Probably herbivorous
Habitat: Secondary forest and coconut plantations along the coast
Range: Fiji and Tonga islands, South Pacific

Old World Iguanid

The South Pacific banded iguana was apparently not uncommon at the beginning of the twentieth century. Studies conducted as recently as 1915 indicated relatively sizable populations, but it must now be considered exceptionally rare. There is some concern that the

probably been introduced relatively recently. These would include predators such as cats, dogs, mice, and rats introduced by early colonists. Animals such as goats, burros, and pigs have also had adverse effects on the iguana because of changes they cause to the native vegetation. Pigs are a serious threat, as they are known to

dig up nests and eat iguana eggs. One estimate suggests that there are about 2,000 iguanas on Mona island but with an apparent scarcity of immature individuals. Human-related activities are the major cause of decline. Introduction of mammals, hunting, agriculture, and deforestation, and recreational activities have all posed threats to iguana adults, juveniles, and eggs, limiting the population growth and stability of the species. Privacy is crucial to the mating and egg

species may, in fact, be extinct on many of the islands in the chain and very scarce on Fiji.

As has been the case with many other species in regions around the world, exotic animals presented an immediate threat to the South Pacific banded iguana. The mongoose devoured both eggs and young for many years. Other introduced animals, including poisonous toads and mynah birds, greatly reduced the potential habitat of this iguana.

Humans have also done their share to hurt the species. Iguanas are often persecuted by native Fijians. Deforestation and development have greatly reduced the potential habitat of an already vulnerable species.

Recovery and Conservation

In order to protect the banded iguana, protection from introduced predators and food competitors must be a priority. Individuals could be transferred to islands where there are no exotic species, allowing the populations to increase. Public education alerting people to the scarcity of the lizard and the creation of national parks which include suitable habitats and no predators are viable options in creating a recovery plan for the South Pacific banded iguana.

—*Elizabeth Sirimarco*

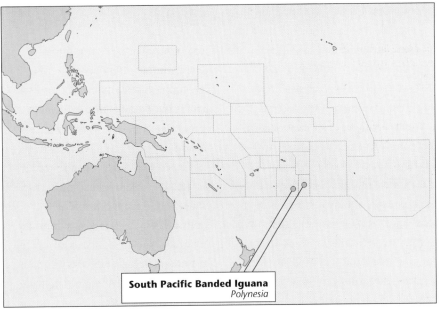

South Pacific Banded Iguana
Polynesia

BLACK-FACED IMPALA

(Aepyceros melampus petersi)

Status: Endangered

Class: Mammalia
Order: Artiodactyla
Family: Bovidae
Subfamily: Bovinae
Tribe: Alcelaphini

Description:

Weight: 88-176 lb (40-80 kg)
Shoulder height: 29.5-37 in (75-95 cm)
Diet: Leaves, twigs, and grasses
Gestation period: 195-210 days
Longevity: 12-15 years
Habitat: Open woodland to scrub bush
Range: Southwest Angola and northwest Namibia

The black-faced impala is the only form of impala that is endangered. Unfortunately, few of the species exist in captivity.

The Elegant Impala

The impala is one of the most graceful four-legged animals. It is an antelope, part of the same group of animals that includes hartebeestes and wildebeestes. An impala's fawn-colored coat and lyre-shaped horns give it a beautiful appearance. When watching the African antelope, its beauty seems heightened by its graceful leaps across the open range.

While the impala does live in scrub bush country and open grassland, it prefers areas that have some cover near a constant water source. An impala is quite sociable, and is often found in the company of other African plains animals. Its social habits, however, are very fixed, with two common groupings: male bachelor groups, or families consisting of one dominant male and 15 to 20 females. While this may seem like a pleasant situation for the male, it is actually one of constant work; he must round up the females continually, because they tend to wander. And he is always fighting off other males who would take over his harem. A male usually maintains his dominant status for only a few years until he is replaced by a younger, stronger male. Once a male is cast out, it tends to be solitary and is preyed upon by leopards, lions, cheetahs, and hyenas.

The impala is a browser, eating leaves, twigs, young shoots, and especially the acacia plant. It has excellent vision and smell and is

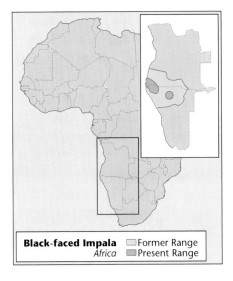

Black-faced Impala
Africa   ☐ Former Range ■ Present Range

wary of humans who approach too closely, unless it is accustomed to the presence of humans (for instance, in a wildlife park).

One in Danger

The one form of impala that is endangered is the black-faced impala. The black-faced impala gets its name from a dark-colored patch on its face. Otherwise, its coloration is much the same as the common impala. It is found in Angola and Namibia, and its numbers in Angola are seriously diminished because of competition with domestic animals, heavy hunting, and the devastation caused by a lengthy civil war. This impala is fairly stable in Namibia's Etosha National Park, but elsewhere in that country its numbers have dwindled. There are perhaps 1,000 to 2,000 of these animals left.

Impalas do well in captivity and there is a healthy population of the common impala. A few black-faced impalas exist in captivity, but the gene pool (the number of unrelated individuals) is too small and needs to be broadened if captive breeding is ever going to help this species recover in the wild.

—*Warren D. Thomas*

IMPERIAL-PIGEONS

Class: Aves
Order: Columbiformes
Family: Columbidae

Imperial-pigeons grow quite large and heavy, many of them sporting knobs at the base of the upper half of the beak. Two species inhabit portions of eastern India and range into Southeast Asia, while two others live in northern and eastern Australia. Otherwise, the imperial-pigeons are birds of the Pacific islands and East Indies. They are closely related to the fruit-doves, and their genus (Ducula) accounts for the third largest number of species in the pigeon family. Those species that live in areas easily accessible to ornithologists have been moderately well studied. Some of the more remote species have not been studied at all.

GIANT IMPERIAL-PIGEON
(Ducula goliath)

Status: Threatened

Description:

Length: 20 in (50.8 cm)
Weight: Unknown
Clutch size: 1 egg
Incubation: Unknown
Diet: Fruits
Habitat: Montane forests
Range: New Caledonia, South Pacific

A Thunderous Call

A great booming call thunders down through the trees of New Caledonia. To the uninitiated, the call sounds like the bellow of a bull or some other great mammal. It is, however, the call of the giant imperial-pigeon, a unique bird of

the New Caledonian forests.

A large, dark bird, the giant imperial-pigeon has a blackish head, back, wing, tail, and breast band. A band around the throat and neck is more slate gray. A chestnut band across the mid-tail and a chestnut belly patch highlight an otherwise drab bird. Its bright red foot, toe, and beak add a splash more color. A fruit-eating bird, the giant imperial-pigeon offers a sweet, juicy meat that has made it a favorite with hunters.

For many years the species held its own in the primary forests of remote mountain slopes and valleys. No observations or research evidence indicate the bird uses secondary forest or other habitat types. So the effects of human progress on New Caledonia now threaten the giant imperial-pigeon.

New Caledonia's 6,530 square miles (16,978 square kilometers) hold almost 200,000 people. They grow coffee, tobacco, bananas, and pineapples; but nickel mining is the most important part of their economy. Mining activity directly destroys imperial-pigeon habitat. Mining roads built into remote mountain areas also open new access roads for people. The improved access has intensified hunting pressure on the giant imperial-pigeon. Hunting is allowed only one month each year, but illegal hunting is not vigorously discouraged.

If the giant imperial-pigeon is to survive, measures to preserve its habitat must be enacted now. Someday, New Caledonia will mine its last nickel deposits. Without foresight, the New Caledonian people will have no nickel, no forests, and no giant-imperial pigeons.

MARQUESAS IMPERIAL-PIGEON
(Ducula galeata)

Status: Threatened

Description:

Length: 22 in (55.9 cm)
Weight: Unknown
Clutch size: 1 egg
Incubation: Unknown
Diet: Large fruits
Habitat: Forests and woodlands
Range: Nukuhiva Island in the Marquesas Archipelago, French Polynesia

Land of Cannibals

The people of Nukuhiva Island once fed themselves on the flesh of other people. So long as the people lived as cannibals, the Marquesas

imperial-pigeon thrived. As Western civilization overtook the people of Nukuhiva, the imperial-pigeon and cannibalism both declined. The two phenomena may not be clearly connected, but they undoubtedly share a common cause.

The Marquesas imperial-pigeon is a large, stout bird with broad wings and long tail. It has a dark, shiny green back and tail that contrast slightly with a dark gray head, neck, and underparts. The undertail is reddish brown. The cere, a fleshy area at the base of the beak, extends forward to near the beak tip and is covered with small, white feathers. This bird may have once lived on other islands in the Marquesas group, but it now survives only in the valleys of Nukuhiva's west end.

The Marquesas are an archipelago of 11 islands in French Polynesia, part of France's Overseas Territories in the South Pacific. Together the islands cover about 1,544 square miles (4,014 square kilometers). Once called Marquesas Island, Nukuhiva is the largest island at 127 square miles

(330 square kilometers). Oceanic explorers of Melanesian ancestry settled the islands, probably around 200 A.D. Thirteen centuries passed before Spanish sailors discovered the islands in 1595. The first meeting of the two cultures was violent and disastrous for the native islanders. Captain Cook rediscovered the islands in 1774. During the many European struggles for power in the eighteenth and nineteenth centuries, France won control over many South Pacific islands, the Marquesas among them.

Europeans seeking territorial conquests carried with them the burdens of modern peoples. They introduced smallpox, tuberculosis, syphilis, and leprosy into a human culture that had never known these diseases. A native population of more than 100,000 people plummeted to less than 3,000 by the 1960s. The native people on some Marquesas Islands disappeared altogether. Intent on using distant territories as a source of wealth for the mother country, the French brought African and Asian laborers to the Marquesas to

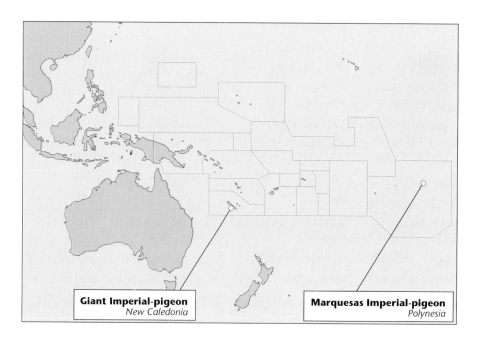

Giant Imperial-pigeon
New Caledonia

Marquesas Imperial-pigeon
Polynesia

work the sugar cane plantations.

As modern culture replaced the indigenous culture, enormous changes were imposed. Primarily, forests and woodlands were cut for wood building materials and to make room for agriculture and livestock grazing.

The Marquesas imperial-pigeon is unique to the Marquesas Archipelago if not to Nukuhiva. This species had no outlying populations on other atolls or island groups where it could survive if catastrophic events occurred on Nukuhiva. Population estimates in the 1970s ranged from a low of 75 birds to a high of 400. Despite the low numbers and a hunting ban imposed by France in 1967, islanders still hunt the birds as food. The human population growth on Nukuhiva, the continued emphasis on agriculture, the persistent grazing by both livestock and feral pigs, goats, sheep, and cattle, and the lax enforcement of the hunting ban, all spell trouble for the imperial-pigeon. If anything, conditions will steadily worsen.

Ornithologists have invested much hope in the prospect of saving endangered island birds by establishing them on other islands where they do not encounter such severe problems. While this idea is attractive, it also threatens other species. Many island birds are endangered because exotic animals have out-competed them in their own habitat. If these birds were moved to other islands, similar problems might ensue. The potential for such an effect does exist. The Marquesas imperial-pigeon has, however, been recommended as a candidate for such a relocation program.
—*Kevin Cook*

Imperial-pigeons belong to the genus Ducula, *a group that makes up the third largest number of species in the pigeon family.*

SIMIEN JACKAL
(Canis simensis)

Status: Endangered

Class: Mammalia
Order: Carnivora
Family: Canidae

Description:
Weight: 15-33 lb (7-15 kg)
Shoulder height: 15-24 in (38-60 cm)
Diet: Birds, eggs, locusts, rabbits, small mammals, rodents
Gestation period: 60-65 days
Longevity: Up to 10 years, 16 in captivity
Habitat: Mountainous plateaus
Range: The Simien and Bale Mountains, Ethiopia

Animal of the Underworld?

Anubis, a god of ancient Egypt, was depicted as having the head of a jackal. That he was the god responsible for leading human souls to the underworld makes sense. As highly visible carrion eaters, jackals must have seemed like logical escorts to the spirit world, where Egyptians believed they would go after death. Since then, people have come to understand the role of jackals a little differently. But humans still have an uneasy feeling about this animal.

Surprisingly little is known about the Simien jackal. Until recently, it seemed to be a creature of too many names and too few appearances. It was called the Abyssinian wolf, the Simien fox, and the Simien dog—everything, in short, but a jackal.

Only the brink of extinction has sparked some scientific agreement. The Simien jackal is too small and light to be a wolf, too high at the shoulder and too long-legged to be a fox, and its face is too pointed to be a true dog. Increasingly rare, it is still believed by many to be a subspecies of the similar and more numerous golden jackals found

Until recently, the jackal was called by a variety of names, including the Abyssinian wolf, the Simien fox, and the Simien dog. Scientists did not agree that it was, indeed, a jackal, until the animal became endangered.

throughout much of northern and eastern Africa and southwestern Asia.

Appearance

The Simien jackal has a long slender muzzle, and a light yellowish-to-reddish brown coat that becomes darker toward the middle of the animal's back. The tail is black with a white tip.

Where once the animal was visible at lower elevations, increased persecution by humans (and perhaps by hyenas and other carnivores) has driven it into remote areas of the Simien and Bale Mountains of Ethiopia. These mountain ranges are separated by several hundred miles of flat, developed land over which the animals do not range. This

suggests that the jackals represent the last survivors of two disappearing population groups.

The Simien Mountains jackals are smaller in size and their coats are red to reddish yellow in pigmentation. The jackals in the Bale Mountains are larger, with darker red coats.

Its favorite prey, grass rats, are hunted mainly by patrolling, investigating holes and burrows, lying in wait for the rodents to appear, and then dashing after and pouncing on them. Rodent hunting tends to be a solitary activity, although other prey is hunted in cooperative packs. Larger game is usually located by scent, pursued to exhaustion, then brought down by the more powerful adults.

While most jackals are somewhat nocturnal, the Simien jackal is diurnal, preferring to hunt grass rats by day when they are easily seen and their escape routes can be easily cut off. Unlike many of its fellow jackals, *Canis semensis* often sleeps in the open or in places with slightly longer grass, even under cold conditions. Generally, the Simien jackal appears to tolerate the presence of others of its kind very well.

Social Carnivores

This jackal seems to have a clan-based society. Usually around dawn and dusk, adult jackals gather together in groups of up to seven members. On such occasions, there is much friendly action and noise. The strange utterances of jackals do not closely resemble those of wolves or foxes. In seeking contact with one another they often seem to employ high whining howls repeated at short intervals. Other vocalizations include a bark of

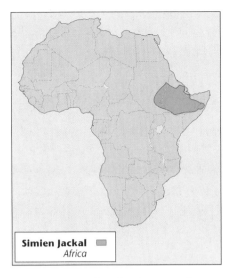

Simien Jackal
Africa

annoyance and a yipping cry. Short barks and whines in the presence of pups have also been reported.

Pair groups appear to form in January, but births do not occur until May or June. The sexes mature after about one year, but sexually mature pups often stay on with family groups as helpers, remaining with the group to help parents raise a second litter. This behavior enables the jackals to combat what seems to be a high rate of pup mortality. Pups are nursed for about eight weeks and then introduced gradually to solid food through regurgitation. At about six months pups are introduced to hunting practices.

Researchers who have examined this jackal's droppings have found no traces of wool or livestock remains, yet native shepherds and others continue to kill these animals they consider pests, sometimes shooting them on sight. Farmers and shepherds have increasingly brought domestic dogs into the jackals' habitat, applying further pressures to a diminishing population. Eagles also prey upon jackals. Granted minimal protection by the Ethiopian government, even national park lands have been made available for

grazing. The animal is protected by law and is classified as endangered by the IUCN and the U.S. Fish and Wildlife Service, but its numbers continue to dwindle. An authority in the mid-1980s suggested that as few as 500 Simien jackals remained in the wild.
—*Renardo Barden*

JAGUAR
(Panthera onca)

Status: Threatened

Class: Mammalia
Order: Carnivora
Family: Felidae

Description:

Size: 44-61 in (112-185 cm)
Tail length: 17.7-29.5 in (45-75 cm)
Shoulder height: 27-30 in (68-76 cm)
Weight: 79.4-348.4 lb (36-158 kg)
Gestation period: 93-105 days
Litter size: 1-4 kittens
Diet: Deer, monkeys, peccaries, tapirs, agoutis and aquatic animals such as capybaras, turtles, crocodilians, and fish
Habitat: Tropical and subtropical forests, sometimes open woodland, mangroves, swamps and scrub thicket
Range: Formerly southern United States through Central America to South America into northern Argentina

A Variety of Colors

The jaguar varies in color from a pale yellow to reddish brown with black spots, which form rosettes. Some spots may merge to form lines. Black or melanistic individuals are not uncommon, but the spots can usually be seen even on these darker cats. The jaguar appears to prefer forests and savannah, but is also found in drier regions, sometimes even in deserts, though seldom far from fresh water. It is rarely found at altitudes above 1,000 meters.

There are eight recognized subspecies of the jaguar. They tend to be solitary animals who mark their territories with urine, much like other members of the cat family. They are good swimmers and climbers. These cats usually hunt at dawn, dusk, or during moonlit nights, and their food sometimes consists largely of aquatic animals, including capybaras, turtles, caiman and fish. Jaguars will also feed on a number of animals up to the size of deer.

The jaguar was once fairly common from Mexico to northern Argentina, and occurred as far north as the southern United States at the turn of the century. Today, it is extinct in Uruguay and virtually extinct in the United States, most of Mexico, and in many areas of Central America. Unfortunately, this cat has been killed throughout much of its former range. However, it is still widely distributed over most of South America.

Persecuted as Predators

The number of jaguars has declined almost everywhere as a result of persecution as predators of domestic cattle. Predation on livestock by big cats is a widespread problem in ranching areas throughout the world, which

Jaguars are beautiful, sleek animals that have long been admired for their attractive appearance. Unfortunately, this admiration has played a role in the animal's decline, as the jaguar's fur was once a very popular commodity.

leads to attempts to destroy the cats, regardless of whether they have actually killed livestock or not. Even today, the jaguar is treated as a pest near cattle ranches, and ranch owners may still pay bounties equivalent to the price of two cattle for an exterminated jaguar. Four jaguars were shot in a single month in 1990. One casualty was a female that was tracked by dogs and shot. She was not a cattle killer and was near giving birth to a male cub. Another was a young male that had been blinded in the left eye by a

past wound and displayed scars from additional wounds to the loins and vertebrae. However, ranchers maintained that this single animal had been responsible for the deaths of some 25 cattle. Unfortunately, past wounds lead to further predation of cattle, simply because the animal becomes too weak to hunt wild animals and must supplement its diet with the more easily captured domestic prey.

Poaching

Often jaguars are shot by poachers who are looking for other animals that reside in the jaguar's habitat. One scientist who works in Venezuela reports that of all the exterminated jaguars examined from that country, 75 percent of the suspected cattle killers had

previous wounds to head or body. A specialist in Belize found that 40 percent of the problem cats there had shot wounds that damaged sight and/or teeth.

Fortunately, there are ranchers who want to preserve the wild cats while bringing predation to acceptable levels. One Venezuelan rancher who raises about 15,000 cattle notes that his losses amount to some 200 head a year, mainly calves and juveniles. Nonetheless, he sees the jaguar as a major attraction to tourists and an important part of the country's natural history, and has banned all jaguar shooting on his 270-square-mile (700-kilometer) ranch—even if predation occurs. A group of cat specialists is hoping to sponsor a study of jaguar and puma predation

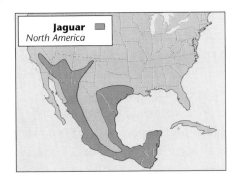

Jaguar
North America

Jaguar
South America

on livestock at this ranch to develop management recommendations that may be enlisted on other ranches as well.

In addition to this problem, jaguars have also been widely hunted for sport, and the skins of these beautiful cats once commanded high prices in the fur trade. The jaguar was hunted with both guns and traps, the latter often baited with monkeys that were also a threatened species. The demand for the fur of Latin American spotted cats was high in the 1960s, when an estimated 15,000 jaguars were killed annually in the Brazilian Amazon alone. Known exports of the skins dropped substantially by 1969, however, when new conservation restrictions were enacted. In 1968 the United States imported 13,516 jaguar skins; in 1969 the number dropped to 9,831.

Unfortunately, hunting and export is still allowed in some Central American countries, and restriction in others is poorly enforced. Even where hunting is prohibited, the import of skins originating from elsewhere is often allowed. Habitat loss is also greatly responsible for the decline of the jaguar. Building of highways throughout the Amazon basin, such as the Trans-Amazonian Highway, is a continuing threat to cats as well as all other wildlife in the area. Conversion of forest into cattle pasture, and clearing for timber, firewood, crop land, and pine or eucalyptus plantations have greatly reduced the jaguar's habitat, as have construction of airstrips for mining and oil exploration. The development of these once-remote areas has also made the habitats more accessible to hunters. Vast areas of savannah are also burned during the dry season, further reducing the wood cover and prey needed by the jaguar.

Restrictions have been placed on commercial trading of the jaguar, and though enforcement can be difficult, improvement has been noted. A few large national parks in South America protect limited populations of the cat, and several reserves protect isolated pairs or families.

Studies of population densities and ecology of the jaguar need to be conducted to further protect the species, and illegal hunting and trade in skins must be stopped in order to save the jaguar. Its survival depends largely on preservation of habitat, and a few suitable reserves have been proposed. Unfortunately, these proposals have met with opposition because the areas are valuable as potential pasture.

—*Elizabeth Sirimarco*

JAGUARUNDI
(Felis yagouaroundi)

Status: Threatened

Class: Mammalia
Order: Carnivora
Family: Felidae

Description:
Size: 21.7-30.3 in (55-77 cm)
Tail length: 13-26 in (33-60 cm)
Shoulder height: 14 in (35 cm)
Weight: 9.9-19.8 lb (4.5-9 kg)
Gestation period: 63-70 days
Litter size: 4 kittens
Diet: Various animals from frogs to birds, to small mammals
Habitat: Brushlands, forests, and grasslands, avoiding very dry regions
Range: Widely distributed from extreme southern United States through Central and South America

An Unusual Form

The jaguarundi differs from all other types of cats by the form of some of its chromosomes, and by the number of chromosomes—there are 36 instead of the 38 found in other cats. While it is often considered part of the genus *Felis*, some scientists consider it the single member of the genus *Herpailurus*.

An unusual, small cat found from the southern United States to northern Argentina, this cat is quite different from Old World cats, particularly in the structure of its skull. The most conspicuous features. are the processes on the

595

Individuals with red coats were once though to be a separate species, but it is now clear that red, gray, and black animals can occur in one litter.

The habitat requirements of the jaguarundi are not well known, but it is normally considered a lowland species. It appears to inhabit areas of thick undergrowth, preferably near water, and is reputedly a good swimmer. In any case, frogs and possibly fish make up a portion of its diet, together with birds and small mammals. In areas inhabited by humans, it is also known to prey upon domestic poultry, which has in turn made the jaguarundi prey to angry ranchers. Most scientists refer to the animal as a lowland forest dweller, and it seems to favor clearings and forest edges. Its body seems to be highly adapted to living in areas of thick undergrowth, as the shape of its body allows it to maneuver swiftly through thick vegetation. The jaguarundi appears to be more cursorial, or adapted to running, than arboreal, which is different than most other New World small cats. Scientists believe it may hunt its prey in much the same way as the cheetah. That is, it will use a quick burst of speed to capture its prey, rather than chase it for a long period of time.

Reproduction

Little is known about the reproduction process of the jaguarundi, but mating in Paraguay was recorded in September-November and in Mexico in November-December. It is possible that there are two litters per year. In captivity the gestation period is between 63 and 70 days. Although the cat appears to be predominantly

A uniformity in color has led scientists to believe that the jaguarundi may be closely related to the panther, although the skull structure and chromosomes do not support this view.

frontal bones of the head that support and protect the eye sockets. These are directed toward the back of the head instead of to the side, which gives the jaguarundi a streamlined shape.

This cat is characterized by a slender, elongated body and a small, slim head; small, round ears; and a long tail. The forearms are slightly shorter than the hind limbs, and it is slightly larger than the domestic cat. It is almost uniform in color, being black, gray, or reddish-brown, with no spots or bands, although the kittens are said to have spots for a short time. This uniformity in color has led scientists to believe that the jaguarundi may be closely related to the panther, although the skull structure and chromosomes do not support this view.

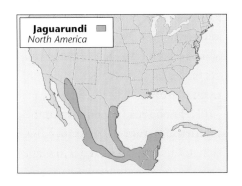

Jaguarundi
North America

Jaguarundi
South America

solitary, pairs have been seen sharing their territory—an unusual habit for cats. They also have very complex vocalization, which scientists believe may indicate a high level of social activity. The fur of the jaguarundi apparently has little commercial value, and the species does not appear to have been subjected to the intense hunting that has affected other American small cats like the ocelot and margay. However, because the pelt is not immediately recognizable, it would be listed under "any other skins" in import statistics, so the extent of trade is unknown.

In addition, when traps are used, animals that are not necessarily desired by hunters are often captured. So even though the jaguarundi may not be particularly desirable to the fur industry, it may still face being the victim of

indiscriminate hunting. There is very limited trade of live animals, primarily for zoos, though there has been some demand for the cat from the pet trade. Its biggest threat comes from uncontrolled hunting and habitat destruction, although it has been suggested that it is less affected by loss of vegetative cover than other New World cats.

Eight Subspecies

While the jaguarundi has certainly declined in numbers, it is difficult to know exactly how significantly it has been affected. There are eight subspecies of the cat, and the distribution of these varying types is patchy. While it occurs in the majority of Central and South American countries, it is not recorded in Chile; and if it occurred in Uruguay, it is now extinct in that country. There is a lack of data describing past population numbers, and no substantial information about current numbers. Trade of the

jaguarundi is now subject to strict regulation and monitoring, and trade for any commercial purpose is virtually banned. It is known to exist in a number of national parks and reserves, including two in Texas and others in Central and South America. There are a number of jaguarundi in captivity, and it appears to breed relatively well in these circumstances. Captive individuals may be a significant factor in improving the status of the species.

There have been virtually no studies conducted on the animal in the wild. Such research is necessary throughout the animal's extensive range to provide accurate information on distribution, population sizes and trends, habitat requirements, and the effects of hunting and environmental disturbance. Until such studies have been conducted, the status of the jaguarundi will remain somewhat controversial.
—*Elizabeth Sirimarco*
See also Cats.

JAYS

Class: Aves
Order: Passeriformes
Family: Corvidae

Jays make interesting animals for study. They live active, busy lives filled with unusual behaviors. Bold and curious birds, jays put these instincts to work. They store food during plentiful seasons, then retrieve it when supplies are harder to find. These food caches may also help parent birds keep themselves fed while they raise their young. Their searches often bring them across objects for which they have no particular use but which they stockpile anyway. Jays are the bird world's equivalent of the pack rat. Perhaps their most fascinating behavior is one they share with their cousins the crows: offspring help their parents at the nest.

Nest helpers are either adult or immature birds that remain in their parents' territories. They help build nests, defend against predators and intruders, and feed their younger siblings from later nestings. Not all 105 species in this family exhibit nest-helping behavior. Of those that do, not all pairs have nest helpers all the time. However, those birds that do use helpers enjoy greater nesting success, measured by the number of nestlings that survive to adulthood.

The jay and crow family also includes magpies, treepies, and nutcrackers. Around 45 species in 13 genera carry the English name "jay." At least a half-dozen jays are considered jeopardized by habitat loss. Two of them are now listed as threatened.

FLORIDA SCRUB JAY

(Aphelocoma coerulescens coerulescens)

Status: Threatened

Description:

Length: 12 in (30.5 cm)
Weight: 2.9 oz (80.2 g)
Clutch size: 3-6 eggs
Incubation: 15-17 days
Diet: Acorns, insects and other invertebrates, small lizards
Habitat: Shrub lands
Range: Scattered localities in peninsular Florida

Cape Canaveral Population

People know the mid-Atlantic Coast of Florida as the launching

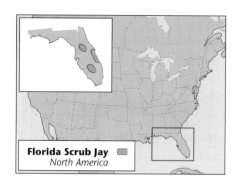

Florida Scrub Jay
North America

pad of America's space program. The famous Cape Canaveral and adjoining Merritt Island also shelter the largest surviving population of the rapidly dwindling Florida scrub jay.

A round head with no crest and a dark blue wing and tail with no white, immediately distinguish the Florida scrub jay from the more abundant and commonly seen blue jay (Cyanocitta cristata). The Florida scrub jay appears hooded. A sky-blue rear crown, nape, and cheek are offset by a pale bluish gray forehead and a grayish white chin and throat. A sooty smudge extends from the base of the beak, through the lore, and past the eye. Another smudgy line, slung across the breast like a necklace, separates the bib-like whitish chin and throat from the dingy gray breast and side. The upper back is also dingy gray but fades to a blue rump. The stout, blackish beak ends with a tiny hooked tip. Feathers at the base of the beak project forward, covering the nostrils, typical of birds in the jay and crow family.

Scrub Is Good Enough

Florida scrub jays also possess the saucy curiosity often seen in jays. They can be quite tame around people. Tolerance and curiosity have probably cost the

jays less than has their dependence on a habitat that people view as worthless. In fact, the bird derives its name from that habitat. The term "scrub" refers to plants that grow somewhat large but never attain the stature of trees. In general usage, "shrub land" and "scrub" refer to the same habitat. Shrub lands of oaks (Quercus sp.), pines (Pinus sp.), wax myrtle (Myrica pumila), and saw palmetto (Serenoa serrulata) harbor the last of the Florida scrub jays. All woody plants, including some of these species, can produce dense thickets covering many acres. The jays prefer the edges of the thickets, especially openings within the shrub cover. Roadways that cut through shrubby thickets seem to appeal to them.

Shrub Habitat

The jays nest in the shrubs and find much of their food there. The jays also eat many larger insects, spiders, millipedes, snails, and even the eggs and nestlings of other birds. They like seasonal food such as acorns and fruits of the saw palmetto, plus other fruits and seeds. They bury excess acorns in loose soil and sand among the shrubs, then later recover and eat at least some of them.

Important as the shrub lands are to the Florida scrub jay, people have disregarded the bird's needs. They have cut and burned the inland shrub lands to open the land for cattle grazing and citrus orchards. Coastal shrub lands have been cleared for ocean-front development. Probably more than half of the Florida scrub jay's habitat has been lost. The jay's population has declined from probably close to 50,000 in the

1880s to less than 22,000 in 1984. The rate at which habitat was being lost in the 1980s indicated a rapid population decline for the Florida scrub jay. Many ornithologists expect few jays will survive through the 1990s.

Many People

The human population in Florida grew tremendously in the last decades of the 1900s, from fewer than one million people in 1930 to more than 13 million people in 1990. Many people found the climate agreeable for retirement. Others found it suitable for growing vegetable and fruit crops, or for grazing beef cattle and dairy cows. Carefully tended, the land also yields a fair crop of pine wood from plantations. Inevitably, human ambitions for the Florida landscape require vast alterations that leave little native plant growth. The human presence grew so quickly that little attention was paid to the consequences. Human intrusion upon the land has left few places for the Florida scrub jay to exist.

Wide Range

There are many subspecies of scrub jay that range from Washington state south into Baja and eastward into Wyoming, then south to Texas and mainland Mexico. There are two species that are closely related to the scrub jay, and these also live in the southwestern United States and Mexico. These are the Mexican jay (*Aphelocoma ultramarina*) and the unicolored jay (*Aphelocoma unicolor*).

Scrub jays do not migrate, and they are not known to wander; therefore, the Florida scrub jay

The Florida scrub jay depends on shrubs to make its home and to forage for food. Unfortunately, people have cut and burned scrub lands for cattle grazing and citrus orchards.

constitutes an isolated subspecies. This means that the Florida population cannot be bolstered by individuals that wander in from other parts of the species' range. Even if they did appear, the consequences would not be ideal. If these subspecies interbred with the Florida scrub jays, the genetic character that makes the Florida birds distinct would be lost.

Some ornithologists expect the Florida scrub jay to disappear entirely because so much of the

species' habitat occurs on private land. Good jay habitat does remain in Ocala National Forest between Gainesville and Orlando and on Merritt Island National Wildlife Refuge. It is quite likely that at least small populations will persist in these areas as other populations on private land continue to dwindle.

SICHUAN JAY
(Perisoreus internigrans)

Status: Threatened

Description:
Length: Unknown
Weight: Unknown
Clutch size: Unknown
Incubation: Unknown
Diet: Unknown
Habitat: Dense coniferous woodlands
Range: Southeastern Qinghai, western Gansu, northern Sichuan, and eastern Xizang provinces of China

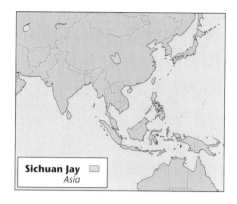

Sichuan Jay
Asia

Little Information

People cannot save what they do not know they have lost. The Sichuan jay has become increasingly rare in recent years, yet virtually nothing is known about this bird. It could slip into extinction before anyone even bothers to write down how long it is or how much it weighs.

The Communist rulers of the People's Republic of China have not favored research on a wildlife species that does not provide immediate value to the people. Nearly all wildlife research has been conducted from an economic perspective. Wildlife species that possess value or cause problems have captured all the attention. Many American travelers to China have returned with stories of never having seen a rabbit or a squirrel, even in the rural areas. One traveler remarked that he had been in China for a week before he realized he had not heard a single

bird singing since he had arrived.

Roughly two-thirds of China consists of mountains and deserts, and only one-tenth of the land supports crops. More than one billion people now live there. Most of these people live along the coast, while the Sichuan jay lives in China's mountainous interior. It inhabits pine (*Pinus* sp.) and spruce (*Picea* sp.) woodlands at fairly high elevations, probably to the timberline. It has been described as slightly larger than a gray jay (*Perisoreus canadensis*), which measures 11.5 inches (29.2 centimeters) and weighs 2.5 ounces (70 grams). It wears plain gray plumage overall, highlighted only by a black head and throat. Some observers report that it mimics other birds' calls. No other information is available on this species; but if the Sichuan jay behaves anything at all like its close relative the Siberian jay (*Perisoreus infaustus*), then ornithologists can assume a little more.

If it is like the Siberian jay, then the Sichuan jay probably eats insects, carrion, various small fruits, and conifer seeds. After building a nest up to 20 feet (6 meters) above ground, it probably lays three to five eggs that require around 19 days of incubation. Lacking specific information about its habitat needs, no definite

reasons or events can be cited as the cause for the species' decline. Presumably, habitat loss plays some role. Possibly, the cutting of forests for lumber products is important. Unless someone within the mainland of China takes a specific interest in the jay and investigates its life needs, no meaningful actions can be recommended to preserve it.
—*Kevin Cook*

JUIL CIEGO
(Rhamdia reddelli)

Status: Threatened

Class: Osteichthyes
Order: Siluriformes
Family: Pimelodidae

Description:
Length: 4.3 in (11 cm)
Reproduction: Egg layer
Habitat: Cave streams and stream pools
Range: Cave at Cañada San Antonio, Mexico

A Whiskered Wonder

When we think of caves, we think of creatures likes bats, large insects, or other less-than-admired creatures that shun bright light. In the dark, cool recesses they can prey on unsuspecting victims as they grope through the darkness. However, we seldom consider that many caves hold water or are completely filled with water, and that fish might live in these underground recesses, pools, and

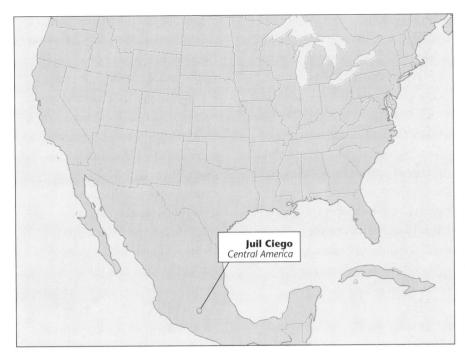

Juil Ciego
Central America

streams. Indeed, many fishes have evolved exclusively underground in the absence of light. Caves offer conditions that are very different from those at the surface. Cave-dwelling animals live in total darkness in an "energy-poor" environment. Caves cannot sustain green plants that capture sunlight and turn it into food for other plants and animals. Because of their isolation from the surface, subterranean fishes depend on the movement of food items from the surface to their underground domain. In addition to the absence of light, caves are very stable temp-erature-wise. Cave temperatures vary little, if at all, and usually correspond with the average yearly temperature at the surface.

In response to their unusual environment, cave-dwelling fishes have adapted by developing unique physical characteristics. These fishes lack eyes and are totally blind. Eyes would not only be useless in the dark cave recesses, but could also be damaged by the darkness and would require energy to develop and maintain. As a

replacement for eyes, the exterior of these fishes is packed with other sensory organs—touch, taste, and smell are extremely important. A less obvious expectation in cave-dwelling fishes is their lack of skin pigmentation; all of these fishes are white and pink, called albino. Camouflage as a means to avoid predators and as protection from the damaging rays of the sun are not requirements of their cavernous environment. To cope with the reduced availability of food, these fishes have a slower metabolism than many others and have larger fins for more efficient swimming. Additionally, cave-dwelling fishes are able to store fat more efficiently during times of plenty. All blind catfishes, like the juil ciego, lack a swim bladder, an organ used by most fish to regulate their buoyancy. Instead, these fish rely on their stores of fat to provide buoyancy, as well to provide an energy supply when food is hard to find.

Creatures of both the outside and subterranean world, bats play an important role in the lives of some of these fishes. In caves that

are not completely filled with water, bats are one of the transport mechanisms that support fish populations. Solid wastes such as bat guano and dead bats are key sources of food for cave fishes and other inhabitants of the cave ecosystem. Aquatic plankton, fungus, decaying organic material, small amphibians, and other fish also are important food.

The juil ciego can be found at the cave at Cañada San Antonio, southeast of Mexico's capital of Mexico City. The primary threat to the juil ciego is the very limited extent of its range. The cave is only about three miles in length, and the water supply is a single groundwater source. If the water supply is severely polluted by human activities, the entire population of juil ciego could be lost.

This small blind fish is ideally built for life in a cave. From the side, the head of the juil ciego appears somewhat flattened, so that it can more easily fit into tight spaces. The dorsal fins on the back, while average in their length, extend from just behind the head to the base of the tail. Most likely, this adaptation makes swimming more efficient. The tail fin is deeply forked, and the sensory barbels on the face ("whiskers") are unusually long (a trait of all catfishes in the family *Pimelodidae*).

Given the thin margin between death and survival for the juil ciego, it is not surprising that little energy remains available for reproduction. It does not breed on a regular schedule and, depending on the food supply, may not breed even once per year. When breeding does occur, relatively few eggs are produced. An important adaptation of the blind catfishes is their ability to protect newly hatched fish by holding them in their mouths, thereby dramatically decreasing the likelihood that a predator will feast on precious offspring.

—*William E. Manci*

GUADALUPE JUNCO
(Junco insularis)

Status: Threatened

Class: Aves
Order: Passeriformes
Family: Emberizidae
Subfamily: Emberizinae

Description:
Length: 6.25 in (15.9 cm)
Weight: .7-.8 oz (20-22 g)
Clutch size: Probably 4-5 eggs
Incubation: 12-13 days
Diet: Seeds, insects
Habitat: Forests, woodlands
Range: Guadalupe Island, west of Baja, Mexico

Troubled Island

No island in the eastern Pacific Ocean has been more brutalized than has Guadalupe. The natural plant and animal communities of the island have been destroyed, and one species after another has vanished. Now, the Guadalupe junco may be the next victim of premature extinction.

A small bird on a medium-sized island, the Guadalupe junco closely resembles the juncos of the North American mainland. A light belly and pinkish tan side highlight an overall gray plumage. It sports the white outer feathers on an otherwise gray tail as do all juncos. It also bears the ivory-colored beak and black lore characteristic of this group. Originally considered a distinct species from the mainland dark-eyed junco (*Junco hyemalis*), the bird was regarded for many years as just a subspecies. Opinion has swung back to treating it as a species unique to Guadalupe Island.

Guadalupe itself resembles many other islands along the Pacific coast of the continent. But Guadalupe sits 157 miles (251 kilometers) off the Baja Peninsula, roughly 250 miles (400 kilometers) southwest of San Diego, California. That expanse of open ocean gave Guadalupe enough isolation so that, over time, a few species developed unique characteristics that set them apart from their mainland ancestors. Among them were about 30 plants found only on Guadalupe, and another two dozen scattered across a few other islands. Roughly 60 birds have been recorded on Guadalupe, and three of them are (or were) unique species, with six others classified as unique subspecies. Two of the three unique species are now extinct, and several of the subspecies have also disappeared or are drastically reduced.

Old Problems

Spanish sailors found Guadalupe in 1565 and again in 1602. A string of sea travelers stopped at Guadalupe throughout the 1700s. Their visits are largely secrets of the past, for Guadalupe was uninhabited by people and difficult to negotiate for ships. Many ships passed it by; few stayed for long. Russian sealers found the island as they explored the Pacific Coast in quest of sea otters and fur seals in the early 1800s. By 1895 the Guadalupe fur seal (*Arctocephalus townsendi*) was believed extinct. The northern elephant seal (*Mirounga angustirostris*), once believed extinct, managed to survive the ravages of hunting and was rediscovered on Guadalupe in 1954.

As the seals and fur seals declined on Guadalupe, the plants and the birds did also. They were each lost for different reasons, however. For example, several unique plants were grazed into extinction by feral goats, and those native plants which did survive were badly depleted. Goats were introduced to Guadalupe by sailors who planned future trips at sea. When the old sailing ships stopped at islands to take on firewood and water, goats were shot as a source of fresh meat—relief from the salt pork diet on board ship. To the sailors the stocking of goats made good sense. The goats, however, proved disastrous on Guadalupe.

Unchecked by natural population controls, the goats multiplied tremendously. They ate everything possible, including the lowest branches of native trees, seedlings, saplings, and the bark off tree trunks. The only trees that survived the goats were the old trees with branches growing well above reach. The Guadalupe cypress (*Cupressus guadalupensis*) and Guadalupe palms (*Erythea edulis*) are native to the island and were severely depleted by the hungry goats. As these trees dwindled, habitat for unique birds such as the Guadalupe ruby-crowned kinglet (*Regulus calendula obscurus*) and the Guadalupe flicker (*Colaptes cafer rufipileus*) disappeared. The flicker is now extinct and the kinglet is drastically reduced.

Cats and the Junco

Sailors also released cats on the island. Cats were routinely kept aboard sailing ships to catch rats and mice. It is likely that these cats had litters, and the sailors put the excess cats ashore when possible. The cats acted like the goats, only they killed birds for food rather than eating plants. They undoubtedly caused the extinction of the Guadalupe storm-petrel (*Oceanodroma macrodactyla*), a small seabird that nested in island burrows. This bird was only discovered and described in 1887, but was extinct by 1912. The Guadalupe caracara (*Polyborus lutosus*) suffered the same fate, becoming extinct within 25 years after people discovered it. The northern elephant seals and Guadalupe fur seals fared much better than did the birds; they were hunted commercially for profit so that when the profit in hunting them failed, the hunting stopped. Goats and cats had no such restrictions.

In 1922 the Mexican government declared that the wildlife and other resources of Guadalupe Island should be protected. Soldiers were garrisoned there, but the move was half a century or more too late. Undaunted, the Mexican government decided to commercially process goat meat. A meat cannery was established, and it actually produced for several years before failing after World War II. Canned goat meat did not

Guadalupe Junco
North America

find a large market, but the goat population has declined somewhat, largely because they ate themselves into starvation. Cats still prowl the island as well, but they too suffer starvation. Exotic plants have replaced much of the native vegetation, which degrades habitat for the island's surviving small birds.

Unlike islands such as New Zealand, Hawaii, and Mauritius that have also been ravaged by the presence of humans, Guadalupe does not have a resident culture. The only people are peasant fishers. Ornithologists are aware of the plight facing the Guadalupe junco, but they may be powerless to protect it. Probably nothing short of ridding Guadalupe of exotic plants and animals will save the Guadalupe junco.
—*Kevin Cook*

KAGU
(Rhynochetos jubatus)

Status: Endangered

Class: Aves
Order: Gruiformes
Family: Rhynochetidae

Description:
Length: 20-22 in (50.8-56 cm)
Weight: 1.9 lb (860 g)
Clutch size: 1 egg
Incubation: 36 days
Diet: Snails, worms, insects
Habitat: Montane forests
Range: New Caledonia, South Pacific

Special Land

Great treasures lie hidden in the islands of the Pacific Ocean, but not everyone views treasure the same way. Some people regard ore

The kagu makes its home on the exotic island of New Caledonia in the South Pacific, a region rich in natural wonders.

in the ground or wood in a tree trunk as treasures. These resources can be cut or mined, then exchanged for money. But in these same forests live unique plants and animals found nowhere else on the Earth. Some people believe these unique species endow the planet with a richness beyond money. The wealth lies in their very existence, not in buying and selling them or parts of their habitat. The kagu is such a species.

Above, the kagu is the pale gray-brown color of old barn wood. Below, it is the dingy color of a whitewashed picket fence. A shaggy crest adorns its crown. Its beak, foot, and toe are the color of seasoned straw. A bold pattern of black and white bars streaks across the flight feathers in the wing, but the pattern is hidden when the wing is folded.

The only member of its family, the kagu leads a secretive life. It prowls the forest floor, where it finds various worms and insects, but snails (*Placostylus bavayi*) are its favorite food. Whacking the mollusk with its pointed beak, the kagu smashes the shell, then shakes off the loose fragments before swallowing the snail. Ornithologists long suspected that the kagu is both nocturnal and terrestrial. However, those few birds in captivity busy themselves by day and, occasionally, people report seeing a wild kagu perched in a tree. This complicates an already disputed notion that the kagu either cannot or does not fly. If it cannot fly, how does it perch in the trees?

Wild kagus call noisily by night, making a loud sound likened to both yelping and barking. The nights on New Caledonia have

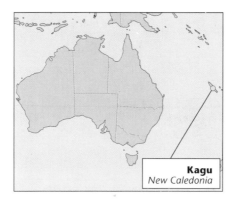

Kagu
New Caledonia

grown quieter over the years as the kagu has slowly dwindled away. A narrow island 248 miles (397 kilometers) long and 31 miles (49.6 kilometers) wide, New Caledonia is about 930 miles (1,488 kilometers) east of Queensland, Australia. The island was already inhabited by people when Captain James Cook discovered it in 1774. By 1800 the island was well known to sandalwood cutters and those who trapped seals for hides. The hides and oil of seals kept many sailors employed. France and Britain both claimed the island, a quarrel that spread across many islands of the South Pacific. France eventually took control.

By 1989 just under 200,000 people lived in New Caledonia's 6,530 square miles (16,978 square kilometers). They raise cattle and grow many different crops including taro, maize, yams, sweet potatoes, and coconuts. Coffee, tobacco, bananas, and pineapples are the most important crops for export. Most farming occurs on the plains that lie between the sea coast and the mountainous interior. Once heavily forested, New Caledonia's mountains have been stripped to develop grazing land, later to be mined for iron, gold, silver, antimony, lead, cobalt, and mercury. Nickel, however, is the source of economic wealth for the

island. New Caledonia ranks among the world's leading producers of nickel ore.

Mining leaves the land uninhabitable for the kagu. Once distributed throughout New Caledonia, the kagu now survives only in the southern third of the island. There, a few valleys have escaped the axe and retain their primary forests. The kagu easily eludes those who want to study it, so population figures are difficult to estimate. Considering the extent of habitat loss and the remaining habitat available, ornithologists suspect that only 500 to 1,000 kagus survive in the wild. As the bird's population declines, other factors besides habitat loss aggravate its potential for survival. Exotic mammals may finish what deforestation started.

Exotic Species

People brought more than coffee and tobacco to New Caledonia. Dogs and pigs came along as pets and livestock. Rats (*Rattus* sp.) probably arrived as uninvited hitchhikers. No terrestrial mammals were native to New Caledonia. Consequently, the kagu developed in a landscape free of significant predators. Exotic mammals posed an immediate threat. Dogs, of course, can find adult birds and their chicks. The domestic pig (*Sus scrofa*) eats not only table scraps and feed designed for their nourishment, but also vegetation and small animals. As pigs root around searching for tubers, fruits, and fungi, they readily eat whatever rodents, lizards, frogs, snakes, insects, worms, birds and birds' eggs they come across. Ground-nesting birds are particularly vulnerable to pigs. When terrestrial birds such as the kagu are confronted with unfamiliar predators, they typically suffer enormous population declines.

As habitat destruction reduces the kagu population, the effects of predation by exotic mammals become more critical. Small populations are more vulnerable. After New Caledonia's forests are cut and its ores are mined, the island will be a very different place. If protective measures are not taken now, the day will arrive when New Caledonians have no forests, no precious metals, and no kagus.

Some forest will always grow back, but the secondary forest will probably not bear the same character as the primary forest. There is no evidence that kagus will accept and thrive in secondary forests. People must review their idea of just what constitutes a "treasure." An island can be as impoverished by the loss of its wildlife as by the failure of its economy.

—*Kevin Cook*

KAKAPO
(Strigops habroptilus)

Status: Endangered

Class: Aves
Order: Psittaciformes
Family: Psittacidae
Subfamily: Strigopinae

Description:
Length: 22-26 in (55.9-66 cm)
Weight: Males, up to 7.8 lb (3.5 kg); females, up to 3.3 lb (1.5 kg)
Clutch size: 1-2 eggs, rarely 3
Incubation: Unknown
Diet: Mostly plant materials; also fungi and adult and larval insects
Habitat: Beech (Nothofagus) forests along rivers
Range: South and Stewart Islands of New Zealand

Strange Sound
A strange booming sound drifts

down from the ridge tops and disturbs the night. Again and again the booming can be heard. This eerie sound once filled the New Zealand mountains. The sounds came from the kakapo—a giant parrot—seeking a mate. The kakapo was strange almost beyond imagination compared to other birds. But the coming of people to New Zealand nearly exterminated this bird and its "music."

Polynesians first arrived in New Zealand around 950 to 1000 A.D. Some historians believe Polynesian immigrants even settled the islands more than once. In any case, the human presence on New Zealand disrupted an ancient plant and animal system. Many birds became extinct even before European explorers found the region. Britain eventually claimed the islands and began settling them in 1840.

The native Maori, descendants of the Polynesian immigrants, resisted British colonization and fought bitterly against them. The presence of the Maori drastically affected New Zealand birds, and the travesty continued with the British. Colonists started "acclimatization societies" to rebuild the plant and animal communities of New Zealand. Their goals were to diversify the species but, more importantly, to recreate the character of their homeland. These societies operated by importing plant and animal species and releasing them to establish wild populations. Many native plants and animals were overwhelmed by these exotic species and suffered as a result. Birds were particularly vulnerable to predatory mammals such as rats (*Rattus* sp.), house cats (*Felis sylvestris*), and weasels (*Mustela*

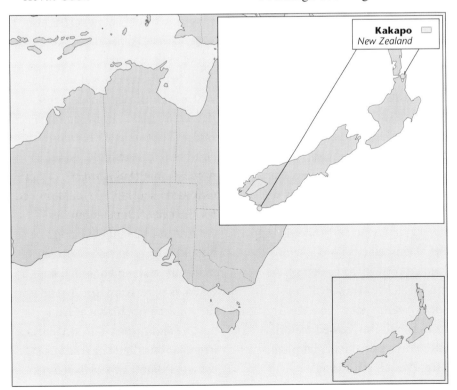

Kakapo
New Zealand

A large bird, the kakapo was hunted as food by both Maori and British colonists.

erminea). The combined predation by these mammals nearly drove the kakapo into premature extinction. But other factors also contributed.

Early naturalists, driven to possess the peculiar and the bizarre in animal species, found the kakapo irresistible. They compulsively collected specimens for stuffing and mounting. Specimen collecting certainly would not have driven the kakapo into extinction, but combined with other problems, it played a part.

A Flightless Bird

One of seven parrots unique to New Zealand, the kakapo long ago lost its powers of flight. Living on an island with no terrestrial mammalian predators caused flying to be unimportant. Once the predators arrived, the kakapo was powerless to protect itself; it could run, but not swiftly enough. Adults, immatures, nestlings, and eggs were equally vulnerable. With such aggressive predation, the

kakapo failed to reproduce, and its population plummeted. By about 1970 the kakapo was believed doomed to extinction because the only known surviving birds were all males. Fortunately, a small kakapo population with females was discovered on Stewart Island in 1976. Aggressive protection by New Zealand wildlife specialists has saved the kakapo from oblivion. Its population has slowly recovered, so extinction is not as imminent. Still, only 50 live birds were known in 1985.

Appearance

Olive green upperparts and golden green underparts, all finely barred and patterned for camouflage, highlight the kakapo. Its wings and tail are banded with dull green and khaki. A facial disc gives it a unique owlish look, but the resemblance is superficial—the kakapo is mostly vegetarian. As it crushes leaves and small fruits, it sucks out the juices and leaves fibrous balls of chewed material still clinging to the parent plant. These peculiar wads tell researchers where kakapos are

feeding and what they eat.

Another clear sign of kakapos is the trail they make. Males trample vegetation to form interconnecting pathways. Individual males then defend portions of the trails against other males. Many males build their hollows in the same general area. Those areas where many males gather to attract females are called leks. Each male finds a suitable spot in which he scoops out a bowl-shaped hollow. The leks, complete with trail systems and hollows, are invariably on or near ridge tops. As night falls, males move into their hollows. There, they puff themselves up with enormous volumes of air and release it with a booming sound. The hollow amplifies the sound, so it carries great distances. Females, attracted to the booming, move toward the sounds. After mating, females leave to nest on their own. The males remain at the lek and continue booming. At the rate of 16 booms per minute, the males call about 1,000 times every hour for as long as six hours a night. But the time when kakapos decide to boom is not yet predictable.

When the kakapos boom, the males do little else but call and defend their area from intruding males. They must be in healthy condition to sustain the booming for any appreciable time. Ornithologists believe that the abundance of food largely determines when the kakapos boom. Several successive years may pass with no booming at all. Females may, likewise, depend on the food supply for successful nesting and laying. This eccentric, irregular breeding complicates preservation work for this parrot.
—*Kevin Cook*

KANGAROO RATS

Class: Mammalia
Order: Rodentia
Family: Heteromyidae

Kangaroo rats (genus Dipodomys*) are members of the family* Heteromyidae, *a category they share with kangaroo mice and pocket mice. The genus* Dipodomys *contains 21 species, and its members are found in semi-arid habitats from the southern plains of Canada south to central Mexico. Although many species of kangaroo rats seem to have experienced population decline, it is in the California region that the situation is most alarming.*

Kangaroo rats are distinguished from other rodents by their hairy tail; the tail is longer than the entire body (with a tuft of hair at the end). They also have skulls formed by thin bone. Kangaroo rats and kangaroo mice are distinguished from pocket mice by their means of locomotion. Rather than running around on four legs as most rodents do, they make good on their kangaroo name by hopping about on their highly developed hind legs. They use their tails for balance when moving, and as a prop when standing (just like their namesakes, the kangaroos, from Australia). The small forelegs are used primarily for manipulating food and for cleaning their external, fur-lined cheek pouches. Both species of kangaroo mice are much smaller than the smallest kangaroo rat. High-speed, long distance travel by kangaroo rats involves jumps that can be over six feet (two meters) in length.

Because they can move rapidly, kangaroo rats prefer open areas with sparse brush or grass that allows both a clear view and room to jump. Kangaroo rats have excellent hearing that also helps them avoid predators. Studies have shown that these little rodents are able to detect the low frequency sounds made by flying owls and by rattlesnakes just before they strike. This means they can leap out of harm's way a split second before being struck by these nocturnal predators.

Kangaroo rats have a curious way of drumming their large hind feet on the ground. No one knows exactly why. One theory purports that male kangaroo rats drum to advertise for mates. Another theory is that drumming by males is used to announce their territorial claim, and to warn intruders. Perhaps drumming by both sexes is an alarm to other kangaroo rats that danger is near.

Kangaroo rats are mostly nocturnal. They prefer areas with loose, well-drained soil in which to dig burrows. Burrow length and the number of exit holes varies with the species. Individuals make food caches by collecting seeds and other materials in their cheek pouches and burying this food in or near their burrows. These underground storerooms can be 10 inches (25 centimeters) in diameter and contain up to 12.5 pounds (5.75 kilograms) of food! Kangaroo rats seldom drink water due to its scarcity, relying instead on water derived from digestion of their food.

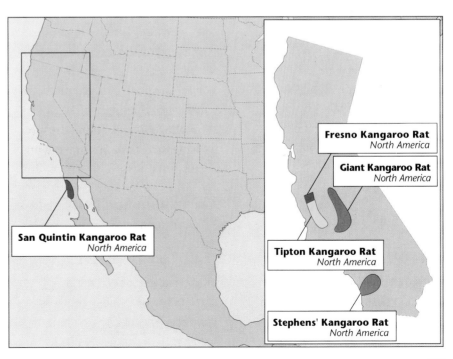

Fresno Kangaroo Rat
North America

Giant Kangaroo Rat
North America

San Quintin Kangaroo Rat
North America

Tipton Kangaroo Rat
North America

Stephens' Kangaroo Rat
North America

Why the Decline?

Habitat loss is the major factor affecting all endangered species of kangaroo rats. Recent years of drought in their range complicate their survival. Another concern in recent years is rodent control that is primarily directed at ground squirrels in agricultural areas surrounding prime kangaroo rat habitat. Many of the methods used to kill the squirrels take kangaroo rats as well.

FRESNO KANGAROO RAT
(Dipodomys nitratoides exilis)

TIPTON KANGAROO RAT
(Dipodomys nitratoides nitratoides)

Status: Endangered

Description:

Weight: 1.2-1.4 oz (35-40 g)
Body length: 3.9-4.3 in (9.9-10.9 cm)
Diet: Seeds, plant material, some insects
Gestation period: 32 days
Longevity: Unknown
Habitat: Sparsely vegetated scrub, especially saltbush scrub and arid grassland with alkali sinks
Range: San Joaquin Valley, California

California Rodent

When first discovered in 1891, the Fresno kangaroo rat probably ranged over 250,000 acres (101,000 hectares). It lived east of Fresno, California, between the San Joaquin River and the Kings River in open grasslands containing alkali sinks.

The Fresno kangaroo rat is a dull, yellow color above and is white below. The gestation period is around a month, and because they breed year-round, females are able to bear three litters yearly, each with up to five offspring. Little else is known of the life history of the Fresno kangaroo rat, but it is probably similar in many ways to those of its relative, the Tipton kangaroo rat.

The Tipton kangaroo rat was historically indigenous to over 1.7 million acres (695,000 hectares) in parts of four California counties. Its habitat occurred in the Tulare Lake Basin, where the soft basin floor did not experience the seasonal flooding common to the region. The Tipton kangaroo rat is a dark tannish brown color above with a white underside. It also has a white stripe across each flank, extending down both sides of the tail. Its main breeding season occurs from December to August, and, when conditions are good, as many as three litters a year—each with up to five offspring—may result. The young, which are born blind, open their eyes at 10 to 11 days, begin to leave the burrow at 18 to 21 days, and are weaned after 21 to 24 days.

Civilization Spells Trouble

Unfortunately for both of these subspecies, population decline began soon after their discovery due to habitat loss from agricultural activities. This loss continued during the first half of the twentieth century, with residential development being added to the agricultural pressure. It was thought that the Fresno kangaroo rat had become extinct until a population was discovered in 1933. By that time the area of suitable habitat was down to about 100,000 acres (41,000 hectares). Its habitat today is down to slightly over 6,000 acres (2,400 hectares), and this is degraded due to heavy grazing by livestock.

By the summer of 1985, the Tipton kangaroo rat's range was only 63,400 acres (25,700 hectares), a reduction of over 96 percent from its estimated range early in this century. Habitat conversion still threatens this subspecies, as most of its remaining habitat occurs on small fragments of private property surrounded by agricultural land. About ten percent of the remaining Tipton kangaroo rat habitat is administered by local, state, and federal agencies, and appears secure from habitat modification. As of 1988, these protected areas contained low-to-moderate populations of Tipton kangaroo rats, but there is concern that these areas are too small to ensure long-term population survival.

Their Importance

Tipton kangaroo rats dig shallow burrows near shrubs where winds deposit fine soil. The burrows aerate the soil and serve as refuges for other species in the region, including the blunt-nosed lizard (*Gambelia silus*). Like many other small rodents in the region, this kangaroo rat is prey for the endangered San Joaquin kit fox (*Vulpes macrotis mutica*). If both subspecies of this kangaroo rat are wiped out, the kit fox will have one less species to prey on, and another species may become a victim. It is vital that habitat areas of adequate size be preserved. Experts say this means at least 800 and as much as 3,000 acres (325 to 1214 hectares) for the Tipton kangaroo rat. Today, few of the secure areas in California's San Joaquin Valley are of this size, and continued pressure from farming, as well as commercial and residential building, threatens to wipe out what is left of both subspecies.

GIANT KANGAROO RAT
(Dipodomys ingens)

Status: Threatened

Description:
Weight: 6.0-6.3 oz (170-180 g)
Body length: 5-6 in (12.7-15.2 cm)
Diet: Seeds, fresh vegetation
Gestation period: About one month
Longevity: Unknown
Habitat: Arid, open native grassland
Range: South-central California

A Large Species
As its name suggests, this is the largest of the kangaroo rats. Its large size, however, has not protected it from the activities that threaten other species of kangaroo rat. Like its other relatives found in central and south-central California, this species has suffered greatly under intense agricultural development.

Accounts from the early twentieth century estimated the range of the giant kangaroo rat at anywhere from 1 to 2.5 million acres (.5 to 1 million hectares). This range was spread out over six counties in southern California: Fresno, Kings, Merced, San Benito, San Luis Obispo, and Santa Barbara. By 1980 the species was found in scattered colonies in areas totaling less than 77,000 acres (32,000 hectares). Its range has continued to decrease, and has been reduced over 50 percent since 1980. As of 1990 this species has been eliminated from one county, has a few isolated colonies in three other counties, and finds large areas of suitable habitat in parts of four other counties.

The giant kangaroo rat is about 14 inches long (35.5 centimeters) including its 8-inch (20-centimeter) tail. It is medium brown in color on the back and sides, and is white below. Females bear two to four young after a gestation of about one month, and the young are weaned when about one month old. Like many of the other kangaroo rats, giant kangaroo rats store food

in their burrows during times of plenty. They do this in order to make it through the times of sparse rainfall. Burrows are shallow, but deep enough to prevent spoilage due to seepage from the infrequent rains.

These rodents forage above ground for around 20 minutes each night, searching for food items that they can stuff in their cheek pouches and take to their storage places. Forage areas are less than an acre (.4 hectare), and occur in annual grasslands with well-drained, sandy loam soils having sparse vegetation. Unfortunately, this type of habitat has been in great demand for agriculture.

Human Use of the Habitat
Although some populations are found within protected areas, many others continue to be threatened by human activities. Besides loss of habitat to agriculture, oil-related activities have taken their toll. An

Since all kangaroo rats are primarily granivorous, or seed eating, they tend to reduce breeding when drought causes a drop in seed production.

oil spill in 1986 resulted in the death of 14 individuals—seemingly a small number, but for an endangered species, every loss can be critical. Other populations could be at risk from seismic exploration for oil reserves, because the explosion of dynamite charges could cause collapse of burrows. As with so many other species that occur in the rapidly developing regions of California, it is difficult to tell what the future holds in store for the giant kangaroo rat.

SAN QUINTIN KANGAROO RAT
(Dipodomys gravipes)

Status: Endangered

Description:
Weight: 2.8-3.2 oz (79-91 g)
Body length: 5.0-5.2 in (12.6-13.2 cm)
Diet: Seeds
Gestation period: Unknown
Longevity: Unknown
Habitat: Flat, arid coastal plain with short, sparse vegetation
Range: A 12.5-mile-wide (20-kilometer) coastal strip from San Telmo to El Rosario, Baja California

Crop Cultivation

One of the bigger kangaroo rats, the San Quintin species has large-boned hind feet. First described in 1925, this species has suffered greatly from crop cultivation in its Mexican habitat. There appears to be a separate southern population occupying a different geographic area with somewhat different habitat traits. This population, near El Rosario, apparently has no contact with the northern populations and, therefore, is reproductively isolated. This El Rosario population is composed of individuals which are, on average, larger than the northern individuals.

Throughout its range, the San Quintin kangaroo rat is found in flat and sparsely vegetated habitats at low elevations. The upper body of the San Quintin kangaroo rat is a pale, pinkish buff with occasional black hairs. The underside of the body, including the forelegs and the upper surface of the hind legs, is white. There is a white spot above each eye and a white stripe down both sides of the tail. The soles of the hind feet are black.

There have been few studies on the natural history of this species, and there is little data concerning its reproductive biology. One study indicates that while young are born during several months of the year, there appears to be distinct peak birth periods in winter and spring. While kangaroo rats eat seeds, they do not eat enough to cause much in the way of economic hardship to farmers. Still, any rodent this size is automatically considered a pest by farmers and is often dealt with accordingly. The changes in their habitat expose them to other predators. Nevertheless, it is cultivation that is the primary culprit in the decline of this species. Since this species lives in an area where human populations are placing increasing demands on land use, if nothing is done to ensure some protected habitat, this species may soon be known only by museum specimens.

STEPHENS' KANGAROO RAT
(Dipodomys stephensi)

Status: Endangered

Description:
Weight: 2.3-2.4 oz (66-69 g)
Body length: 4.4-4.7 in (11.3-12.0 cm)
Diet: Seeds and other plant material
Gestation period: About one month
Longevity: Unknown
Habitat: Coastal sage scrub and annual grassland
Range: Southwestern California

Highly Pressured

It is possible that no other species of kangaroo rat has been as consistently pressured as has Stephens' kangaroo rat. It is thought to have been widespread throughout several California counties (western Riverside, southwestern San Bernardino, and northwestern San Diego) early in the twentieth century. But this species' range—and its future—is of serious concern today. It has experienced a decrease in suitable habitat from an estimated 308,000 acres (125,000 hectares) in the early 1900s to approximately half that area in 1984. Most of the remaining habitat occurs in isolated fragments. Once habitat loss was attributable to agriculture; however, in recent years residential development and off-road vehicle use have posed the greatest risk.

A medium-sized kangaroo rat,

this species can be distinguished from other kangaroo rats by its pale tannish brown fur above and white fur below. The Stephens' kangaroo rat has dusky, rather than dark soles on the hind feet. Its fur appears grizzled due to the presence of shafts of dual-colored hair. It also has a narrower white tail band and a smaller number of white hairs in the tuft at the end of the tail than other kangaroo rats.

The breeding season appears to be in late spring and early summer. Females give birth to litters of hairless, blind young. The average litter size is between two and three, but up to five have been reported. The young grow a dark olive-brown coat at about nine days and molt at about three months. Their eyes open at two weeks of age, and two months after birth they are nearly adult in size.

Population densities vary from 3.0 to 23.3 per acre (7.5 to 57.5 per hectare), and home range varies from 500 to 1,915 square yards (420 to 1,699 square meters). It has been noted that when population levels go up, home range sizes go down. This decrease in home range size probably means that individuals are reluctant to disperse into surrounding areas during population increases, and this may be a sign of the strict habitat needs of this species. For example, trapping programs have generated high catches in open areas, while immediately adjacent areas of light chaparral yield few kangaroo rats.

Evicted by agricultural development from low-lying areas to the edges of fields, this species is currently found in sparsely vegetated, gently rolling habitat with graveled soils—the kind of lands residential developers look

for in southern California. These areas, previously disturbed by the growth of off-road vehicle recreation, have been further fragmented by housing and commercial development.

It is currently believed that only about six percent of the land within the remaining range of this species will remain safe. Much of this "safe" area occurs in fragments which may be too small for long-term population support. Furthermore, there are reports of developers and private landowners grading areas suspected to contain kangaroo rat habitat. Conservative estimates put the total habitat destroyed in this manner at over 1,000 acres (400 hectares). It is even alleged that strychnine or other rodent poisons have been set out to destroy the kangaroo rat. People do this to avoid restrictions on the land use that might be imposed under the Endangered Species Act.

Such practices involving the loss of habitat of endangered species illustrate the need for increased scrutiny of areas set aside for rapid development, where species like the Stephens' kangaroo rat are being squeezed out of existence.
—*Terry Tompkins*

Mauritius Kestrel
Mauritius Island

MAURITIUS KESTREL
(Falco punctatus)

Status: Endangered

Class: Aves
Order: Falconiformes
Family: Falconidae

Description:
Length: 11.5 in (29.2 cm)
Weight: Males, 4.4-5 oz (123-142 g); females, 6.2-7.3 oz (173-204 g)
Clutch size: 3 eggs
Incubation: 30-32 days
Diet: Predominantly geckos and large insects, but also small birds and mammals
Habitat: Primary evergreen forests
Range: Mauritius Island west of Madagascar in the Indian Ocean

Famous Kestrels
Two little falcons have earned fame for vastly different reasons. The American kestrel achieved general recognition because it is the most abundant and widespread bird of prey in North America. The Mauritius kestrel became a celebrity because, for many years, it was the rarest bird on Earth. In 1974 only four birds were known to exist.

The circumstances that brought the Mauritius kestrel to near extinction are not unique to the kestrel nor to Mauritius Island. The same events similarly affected the birds of Hawaii and New Zealand.

In 1974 the Mauritius kestrel had the dubious honor of being the rarest bird in the world—only four of them were known to exist.

The people of Mauritius did no more to promote the extinction of a species than other people have done. Americans doomed passenger pigeons (*Ectopistes migratorius*) and Carolina parakeets (*Conuropsis carolinensis*), and have yet to fully understand the impact of these losses. But Mauritius is where three centuries of modern-day extinctions began when the last dodo (*Raphus cucullatus*) was seen there in 1680.

Mauritius lies about as far south of the equator as the big island of Hawaii lies north. Situated 500 miles (800 kilometers) east of Madagascar, Mauritius frequently experiences violent cyclones born at sea. Portuguese sailors probably found Mauritius in 1507, but no one claimed the uninhabited island until the Dutch laid claim in 1598. Then the French and British took turns colonizing it. Mauritius finally became independent in 1968.

Over the centuries, people cut the island's forests partly for the ebony wood (*Diospyros tesselaria*) and partly to open the land for agriculture. People also brought their pets, livestock, and vermin to Mauritius, including crab-eating macaques (*Macaca fascicularis*) from Java. Much later, people introduced eucalyptus trees (*Eucalyptus* sp.) and pines (*Pinus* sp.) as plantation crops. All of the forest cutting and imported species changed the island's habitat. At least two dozen bird species have become extinct there in historic times, beginning with the dodo.

Heavy Deforestation

Most of the island's 787 square miles (2,046 square kilometers) were originally forest—as much as 80 percent in the 1750s. About one percent of primary forest remained intact in 1984. The Mauritius kestrel inhabits primary forests, so only one percent of the bird's habitat remains today.

Unlike its kestrel relatives, the Mauritius kestrel inhabits forests rather than open country. Instead of the long, pointed wings of most falcons, the Mauritius kestrel has shorter, rounder wings typical of forest birds. Its tail is also proportionately longer. The bird's upperparts are uniformly a warm, cinnamon brown with darker brown or black barring. The crown is finely streaked with brown, and the wing is nearly black. Its underparts are white with distinct black spots. All in all, this is a rather plain-looking falcon.

The Mauritius kestrel does hunt somewhat differently than other kestrels, however. It occasionally hovers while searching for food, and it will sit on an exposed perch so it can scan the area. However, it uses these techniques far less often than do other kestrels. Most often, it directly pursues its prey. The Mauritius kestrel's favorite food is a small gecko (*Phelsuma* sp.) that suns itself on tree branches. The kestrel will snatch the geckos off of limbs, or will hop from branch to branch to find geckos hidden in loose bark.

Competition Everywhere

Most kestrel species nest in tree cavities, but the Mauritius kestrel uses large recesses in cliffs for nesting. This behavior may be an important adaptation in an area where cyclones can demolish trees. Nesting in cliffs cannot protect the kestrels from hungry macaques, however. Macaques readily eat any eggs and nestlings they can find, including many species other than kestrels. Other exotic species also cause problems. Common mynas (*Acridotheres tristis*) and red-whiskered bulbuls (*Pycnonotus jocosus*) eat the same geckos that kestrels like to eat. Feral rock doves (*Columba livia*)—pigeons —compete for nesting spaces in the cliffs. The native white-tailed

The human presence on islands such as Mauritius has doomed many native species by failing to preserve the original habitat.

tropicbird (*Phaethon lepturus*) also uses cliff recesses for nesting. Some ornithologists believe that the cliffs have so many holes that competition for a nesting site is not a significant problem. Other ornithologists believe that every setback is a problem for a species with a critically low population.

Exotic plants lessen the kestrel's habitat. Many exotics are cultivated as crops, but with regard to native bird species, sugar cane and tea are no substitute for primary forest. Plantations of pine and eucalyptus provide some limited forest or woodland character, but the kestrels have shown no willingness to use these plantations.

Grazing animals such as Timor deer (*Cervus timorensis*), cattle (*Bos* sp.), and goats (*Capra* sp.) eat young native plants before they mature enough to produce seeds. This causes entire generations of forest trees to be lost. Indirect damage comes from animals

spreading exotic plants even more as they distribute seeds in their feces. Both events, grazing and spreading seeds, alter the composition of plant species in any given area. As the plant community changes, the geckos decline because they have specific habitat requirements, too. A depressed prey population, with exotic as well as native species competing for it, means less food is available to the Mauritius kestrel.

So the kestrel's habitat has shrunk. At the time when the human population on Mauritius numbered only a few dozen Dutch colonists, people still managed to damage the land so severely that they exterminated the dodo. The human population on Mauritius now surpasses one million. So many people on such a small island creates an enormous demand for basic resources such as food, water, and shelter. The Mauritius kestrel needs the same basics.

The Mauritius kestrel is protected by law; the last remnants of primary forest have been designated a reserve; and captive breeding has helped boost the population to about 50 birds by 1990. Estimates from the early 1970s probably failed to locate some nonbreeding birds. Even so, the population had to have been critically small.

The Mauritius kestrel will never be as familiar to people as are kestrels in other places. It will never become a common sight on telephone wires, as some kestrels are. Probably no more than 328 pairs—possibly 800 or so birds— ever lived on Mauritius. Sadly, not enough habitat exists to accommodate that many kestrels today.
—*Kevin Cook*

KILLIFISHES

Class: Osteichthyes
Order: Atheriniformes

In terms of their distribution around the world, killifishes have been very successful and can be found across the tropical and temperate latitudes of the world. As a group the killifishes are capable of tolerating a wide range of environmental conditions, particularly in terms of salinity. They can be found in fresh water as well as in water that is more saline than sea water. They can survive cool conditions, and they also occur in warm thermal springs. Most killifishes prefer shallow water that is rich in aquatic vegetation; they use vegetation for cover and as a likely source of aquatic insects, their favorite food.

Killifishes are well known around the world to aquarium hobbyists and are prized for their diverse color patterning, relative tolerance of aquarium conditions, and ease of spawning in captivity. In some cases this demand has been partially responsible for the status of some killifishes as threatened or endangered, as a legal or black market has developed for individual species. Additionally, because of their small size, many species are captured and used as bait fish. These types of over-exploitation are difficult to combat because of the profit motive. However, educating the general public and those directly engaged in over-exploitation of sensitive species may begin to curb their demand.

All killifishes display a fairly uniform pattern of physical characteristics. Almost without exception, they are less than four inches in length, with an elongated, robust body, a plump belly, and flattened tail section. The rounded and fan-shaped fins are never large and lack spines for protection against predators. An upturned mouth, jutting lower jaw, and eyes set high on the head aid in the capture of insects at the surface.

Killifishes depart from uniformity when it comes to color. Without a doubt, killifishes are some of the most spectacularly colored fishes in the world; the wide variety of patterns and hues within individual fish and across species makes them a joy to watch.

CAPRIVI KILLIFISH
(Nothobranchius sp.)

Status: Endangered

Description:

Length: 1.6 in (4 cm)
Reproduction: Egg layer
Habitat: Shallow vegetated lakes or stream pools
Range: Caprivi Strip, Namibia

A Fish Out of Water

Just north of the great Okovango Swamp of northern Botswana in Africa is a narrow strip of land claimed by Namibia called Caprivi. This land is the home of the Caprivi killifish, a beautiful fish of the *Aplocheilidae* family that must endure both natural and man-made hardships to survive in one of the most hostile environments in the world. These hardships include, on a seasonal basis, a complete lack of water in which to live. This species, and others of the genus *Nothobranchius*, are remarkable in their ability to survive in an environment that is intolerable to other fishes. During the wet season, the Caprivi killifish spawns, depositing eggs in the bottom sediments. As the wet season passes and the dry season arrives, many of the areas that this fish occupies completely dry up. The adult fish are not able to survive during this period, but the developing young within the eggs sense this lack of water and enter a phase of arrested development called diapause. Not until the rains return do the eggs continue to develop and hatch. As if this kind of hardship were not enough to endure, the Caprivi killifish, like other killifishes, is sought as an aquarium fish. This drain on the population, predation by birds and other animals, and the ongoing destruction by people living in the Caprivi killifish habitat on the Caprivi Strip have brought this species to the brink of extinction. Given the growing demand for land by people for agricultural purposes and the potential for income to this Third World country, the future of this amazing survivor is not bright.

The Caprivi killifish is like other killifish in body shape and size. With a total length of only 1.6 inches (4 centimeters), bright coloration, and a propensity to breed in captivity, this warmwater species is an aquarist's dream. It has an upturned mouth and concave forehead for greater ease of feeding at the surface, and an overall shape that is fairly plump. The dorsal fin on the back, the anal fin just behind the anus and genitals, and the tail fin are quite large and rounded; the dorsal fin is set far back on the body. In contrast, the paired pectoral fins just behind the gill covers and the pelvic fins on the belly are unusually small. The entire body, including the head and cheeks, are generously scaled. The skin is quite uniform in coloration but the scales are edged with a bold contrasting shade, creating a cross-hatch pattern; these colors continue into the fins; the dorsal fin is spotty and blotchy. The anal fin is striped at the base, and the tail fin is solidly pigmented.

This killifish is primarily an insect eater and has a voracious appetite for mosquitoes. It will consume other small aquatic animals when available.

Killifishes are some of the most spectacularly colored fishes in the world. They display a wide variety of patterns and hues within individual fish and across species.

SCALELESS KILLIFISH
(Kosswigichthys asquamatus)

Status: Threatened

Description:
Length: 2.8 in (7 cm)
Reproduction: Egg layer
Habitat: Shallow shoreline areas
Range: Lake Hazar, Turkey

A Shrinking Home

Like many other fishes that are threatened with extinction, the scaleless killifish takes a back seat to people when it comes to water and its use. A resident of Lake Hazar near the city of Malatya, Turkey, the scaleless killifish has had many square miles of its preferred shoreline habitat destroyed by lowering of the lake level for the irrigation of crops and as a domestic water source. People in this arid region of Turkey are desperate for any source of water that they can tap. Lake Hazar is somewhat saline and alkaline; these qualities limit its value to people but they provide ideal environmental conditions for this species. However, unless other sources of water can be utilized by local residents as an alternative or supplemental source, the demand on Lake Hazar will continue to grow, and the scaleless killifish population will most likely fall to dangerously low levels.

As the common name suggests, this small species has no scales covering the skin; the species name asquamatus means "without scales." The scaleless killifish was named after fisheries biologist C. Kosswig and was first described in 1942. It is a member of the

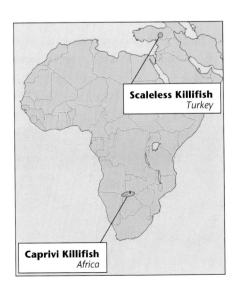

Scaleless Killifish
Turkey

Caprivi Killifish
Africa

Cyprinodontidae family, and it has many of the physical behavioral features of other killifishes, such as a sturdy body, broad head, and a preference for shallow water. But it is the only species within the genus Kosswigichthys. Other information about this fish's life history and habits are unavailable.

WACCAMAW KILLIFISH
(Fundulus waccamensis)

Status: Threatened

Description:

Length: 3.5 in (9 cm)
Reproduction: Egg layer
Habitat: Shoal and in-shore areas over clean sand
Range: Lakes Waccamaw and Phelps, North Carolina

The Cornerstone of an Ecosystem

The coastal region of the United States from Virginia to Georgia has long been an area of interest for both geologists and biologists. Within this region is a series of lakes called the Carolina Bays; most are concentrated in the southeastern region of North Carolina. Some scientists speculate that they were formed during one event many thousands of years ago: a meteorite shower caused craters in the earth's surface along the mid-Atlantic coast and, over time, the depressions filled with water. Other experts theorize that underground artesian wells and the forces of wind and water eroded

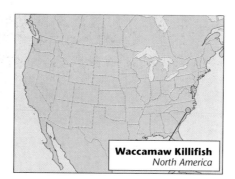

Waccamaw Killifish
North America

the basins over many years.

Whatever the answer, the shallow Carolina Bays (Lake Waccamaw in particular) have played a key role in our understanding of the process of evolution. Studying the unique processes in Lake Waccamaw provides important clues to help us understand more about the species that inhabit it.

Predatory fishes in Lake Waccamaw depend on the Waccamaw killifish as a source of food. Likewise, local fishermen utilize this species, which has a tendency to school in shallow shoreline areas, as a reliable source of bait. Nonetheless, neither this fish's natural predators nor fishermen seeking bait (longtime traditional consumers of this fish) are responsible for the decline in the Waccamaw population. However, the presence of people does play a role in this situation. As human development and agriculture encroach on areas surrounding the lake, the amount of sediment and nutrients that flow

into Lake Waccamaw have dramatically increased. These materials smother eggs and food items and generally degrade the water quality for all Waccamaw fishes. Without the Waccamaw killifish, a vital member of the Waccamaw food web, as well as a valuable biological specimen, would be lost. As a result of federal listing of the Waccamaw killifish and other Waccamaw fishes as threatened and endangered, the lake finally is being afforded some protection. Additionally, some protection against further development of the surrounding areas is provided by nearby Lake Waccamaw State Park.

Waccamaw killifish spawn from April to August over clean sand. After an elaborate courtship, about 100 eggs are deposited in the sand for incubation. During winter months few Waccamaw killifish remain within the lake. Instead, they move to adjoining feeder canals and streams and to the headwaters of the Waccamaw River. At all times of the year, the favorite foods of this fish are insects and other aquatic invertebrates.

—*William E. Manci*

Neglect of America's lakes not only jeopardizes specific species, but impacts other species who depend on each other for food.

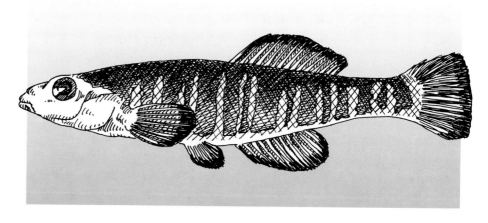

KINGFISHERS

Class: Aves
Order: Coraciiformes
Family: Alcedinidae
Subfamily: Daceloninae

Kingfishers are interesting because of their bright colors, curious behaviors, and peculiar anatomy that suits their lifestyles. Their heads usually appear too large for their bodies, and their feet look too small. A few kingfishers have shaggy crests. They all grow heavy, stout beaks, but not all kingfishers eat fish. Some species prey on large and small invertebrates. Belted kingfishers of North America have been known to stake out bird feeders when winters turn especially harsh. They do not feed on the grains, however. They simply wait for an opportunity to capture smaller birds that visit the feeders. Many kingfishers are forest birds that eat large insects. Others are large enough to catch small lizards and birds. Australia's laughing kookaburra (Dacelo gigas) may be the most famous of all the kingfishers. Although many people besides bird enthusiasts have heard of it, few people realize that the kookaburra is a kingfisher.

Traditionally, ornithologists recognized one family and three subfamilies of kingfishers. In 1990 a revised taxonomy was published, elevating each subfamily to family status, but this system has not been widely accepted as yet. The single kingfisher family treatment recognizes 90 species.

Generally speaking, kingfishers as a species appear to be doing well. However, many kingfishers isolated on small islands appear to be in trouble. Islands often limit the population sizes of unique species. When human activities disturb the islands, those species can suffer quickly and dramatically. Below are five kingfishers that are in the most jeopardy.

BIAK PARADISE KINGFISHER
(Tanysiptera riedelii)

Status: Threatened

Description:

Length: 14 in (35.6 cm)
Weight: Unknown
Clutch size: Probably 5 eggs
Incubation: Unknown
Diet: Probably insects and earthworms
Habitat: Gallery forests
Range: Biak Island off the northern coast of New Guinea

Island Bird

The common paradise kingfisher (*Tanysiptera galatea*) inhabits humid lowland island forests scattered about eastern Indonesia. These islands include the Moluccas and New Guinea. On one island the paradise kingfisher differs enough from paradise kingfishers elsewhere that some ornithologists recognize that group as a distinct species. It is called the Biak kingfisher.

Biak lies off the coast of Irian Jaya, the western half of New Guinea. The island sprawls across the mouth of Geelvink Bay like a plug or barrier. Lying just a degree or two south of the equator, Biak can be very hot and humid. The Biak kingfisher likes such conditions.

Simple beauty distinguishes the Biak kingfisher. A rich, shiny blue colors its upperparts, except for a white rump. Its underparts are uniformly white. A bright red beak punctuates the bird's appearance. Its two central tail feathers grow substantially longer than the other feathers. From the tip of the tail outwards the two feathers are just veinless shafts, but at their ends they flare out, giving the tail a racquet-like appearance.

The common paradise kingfisher nests in hollow branches, tree cavities, and chambers within termite nests. It often sits on a branch low to the ground, where it can watch for insects scuttling about the forest floor. The Biak kingfisher probably behaves much the same way.

Many specific aspects of the Biak kingfisher's natural history remain unknown. Ornithologists have not determined whether the bird can adapt well enough to survive in secondary forest. At the rate primary forests are being cut

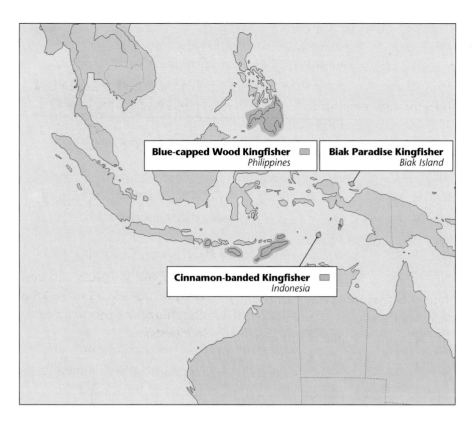

| Blue-capped Wood Kingfisher | Biak Paradise Kingfisher |
| Philippines | Biak Island |

| Cinnamon-banded Kingfisher |
| Indonesia |

on Biak, the island's namesake kingfisher may disappear before anyone learns much about it.

BLUE-CAPPED WOOD KINGFISHER
(Actenoides hombroni)

Status: Threatened

Description:

Length: Unknown
Weight: Unknown
Clutch size: Unknown
Incubation: Unknown
Diet: Unknown
Habitat: Forest
Range: Mindanao, the Philippines

Many Islands

More than 7,000 loosely clustered islands stretch more than a thousand miles (1,600 kilometers) north to south, separating the western Pacific Ocean from the South China Sea. These are the Philippines. And of those 7,000 islands, the blue-capped wood kingfisher lives on only one.

This kingfisher inhabits the forests of Mindanao. A handsome bird, the male sports a blue crown and nape. A blue stripe separates the white chin and throat from the chestnut cheek. The upper back is also chestnut, but the lower back and rump are light blue. Its tail is dark blue, the wing a deep blue-green with rufous spots. The breast and belly are a pale rufous, with some scattered black spots. The female differs in having a greener crown and tail. Both have a bright red beak. Ornithologists know little else about the blue-capped wood kingfisher.

This species was never documented by any ornithologist or skilled bird observer between 1939 and 1980. A specimen was collected one year at about 3,608 feet (1,100 meters) upon Mount Apo. Another bird was seen two years later on a different mountain. Any other sightings have not been recorded. Several explanations may account for such scant information about this kingfisher.

First, it is naturally rare. Not all birds are as common as, say, robins. Second, it lives in an area of the Philippines that is not well traveled by tourists. Many tourists are also bird watchers, and they often report rare or unusual birds they encounter. But tourists are just not likely to see the blue-capped wood kingfisher. Third, violent rebel groups fighting against the Philippine government have sometimes made traveling around the Philippines a dangerous prospect. Few people care to risk their lives just to measure and count rare birds. And fourth, the kingfisher may be actually declining owing to some set of factors related to habitat loss.

At 36,775 square miles (95,615 square kilometers), Mindanao is the second largest island in the Philippines. Being so large, Mindanao holds many of the Philippines' 55 to 60 million people. Its forests have been cut both for lumber and firewood. Lumber can be exported at a profit, and poor people need the firewood for cooking and heating. Whatever the motivation for cutting the forests, the consequence is the same for the blue-capped wood kingfisher.

No estimates of the kingfisher's population have been offered. Without knowing how many blue-capped wood kingfishers exist, and because so little is known about them, little can be done on their behalf. Until research produces more information about the bird, probably only one action can help it. The Philippine government must regulate how much primary forest can be cut, at what rate, and how much must be preserved.

CINNAMON-BANDED KINGFISHER
(Halcyon australasia)

Description:

Length: Unknown
Weight: Unknown
Clutch size: Unknown, but 2 eggs common for genus
Incubation: Unknown
Diet: Probably insects and other invertebrates
Habitat: Wooded lowlands near water
Range: Lesser Sunda Islands of Indonesia

Indonesian Species

The cinnamon-banded kingfisher inhabits one of two main island groups in Indonesia. The Greater Sunda Islands include Borneo, Sumatra, and Java. All three rank among the world's largest islands. The Lesser Sunda Islands trail off into the ocean east of Java. They include Bali, Lombok, Sumbawa, Wetar, Flores, Timor, and Tanimbar, plus many other smaller islands—some still without names. A few of them are home to the cinnamon-banded kingfisher.

This little-known kingfisher lives life its own way. Most of its relatives in the genus *Halcyon* spend their lives in forests. So does the cinnamon-banded kingfisher. If this species eats like its many relatives, it preys largely on insects and other invertebrates. These other species capture their food by sitting on a perch and dropping to pluck prey from the forest floor. Not the cinnamon-banded kingfisher, however. It captures its food up in the treetops. It lives in the forest canopy and snatches its food from the twigs and foliage of the trees. Little else is known of this bird's habits.

Ornithologists suspect this species is declining in some areas. Census work has not been conducted to provide any population estimates, but some insight into the bird's future can be gained from looking at other factors. Specifically, forests of the Lesser Sundas are being cut, partly for their own value and partly to make way for more desirable crops. Primary forests are being cut faster than secondary forests can regenerate the cut-over sites. With less habitat to occupy, the cinnamon-banded kingfisher has already become scarce on Lombok, Sumba, and Timor.

Today, Indonesia's human population exceeds 160 million people. Some areas are desperately crowded. These people need space to live and farmland to produce food. However, it is important that the Indonesian people allow some tracts of primary forest to survive. In time, research may show how to manipulate secondary plant communities to support various wildlife species such as the cinnamon-banded kingfisher.

GUAM MICRONESIAN KINGFISHER
(Halcyon cinnamomina cinnamomina)

Description:

Length: 8-9.5 in (20.3-24.1 cm)
Weight: 1.8-2.3 oz (50.5-63.8 g)
Clutch size: 2 eggs (based on four nests)
Incubation: Unknown
Diet: Mostly insects, but also worms, skinks, small crabs
Habitat: Primary forest; does use coconut groves
Range: Guam, Marianas Islands

Silent Spring

Dawn creeps silently into the forest. In any other forest, bird songs would flood the morning hours. But a "silent spring" has befallen this forest. It is not the silent spring caused by pesticides and described by environmental writer Rachel Carson. A snake is loose on Guam, and it is killing the birds.

The Guam Micronesian kingfisher has become one of the victims. As a full species, the Micronesian kingfisher occurs in the Ryukyu Islands between Japan and Taiwan, southward through the Marianas Islands and into the Caroline Islands. Three unique subspecies live on each of the islands of Pohnpei, Palau, and Guam. Whereas the Pohnpei and Palau subspecies are thriving, the Guam Micronesian kingfisher now

619

The combination of human activity and the introduction of the brown tree snake on the island of Guam has severely depleted the population of the Guam Micronesian kingfisher.

struggles to survive.

The male has a deep golden cinnamon head and underparts contrasted by a deep greenish blue wing, back, and tail. A narrow, dark greenish blue band extends from eye to eye around the nape. The black beak is thick, long, and heavy-looking. The female resembles the male, except for a lighter chin and throat and an all-white breast and belly. A noisy, forest bird, the Guam Micronesian kingfisher perches on exposed branches, where it can watch the ground below. Spying a large insect, it drops to the ground to seize it. The Guam Micronesian

kingfisher also eats worms, small lizards, and small crabs. It does not eat fish, although its name would imply otherwise.

Human activity on Guam has eliminated much of the forest habitat that the kingfisher inhabited. More than 100,000 people live in Guam's 209 square miles (543 square kilometers). The island's native plant communities have been largely cleared for live-stock grazing, farming, and growing cities and towns. A crescent of primary forest survives along the limestone cliffs of the northern coast. Whether habitat endures is moot, because the quality of the habitat has been so drastically compromised. Sometime after World War II, the brown tree snake (*Boiga irregularis*) was transported to Guam, and the island's bird life has never been the same.

The Fatal Introduction

The brown tree snake is native to Southeast Asia. Venomous and a good tree-climber, the snake specializes in eating birds. It can catch adults as well as raid nests. Its skills and appetite make it extremely deadly to an island bird species that never had a chance to adapt to this predator.

When two animals, a predator and its prey, develop together over time, they each acquire essential characteristics that help them survive. The prey develops a way to hide, and the predator develops a way to seek. The prey develops a way to flee, and the predator develops a way to chase. In natural circumstances, the predator never catches all of the prey, and the prey does not escape all the time. When a predator becomes established on an island full of birds that have no experience with surviving that predator, disaster follows. Because Guam had no native snakes, Guam's birds developed no protection against hungry, tree-climbing reptiles. Proper adaptation would take time that Guam's birds do not have.

Nesting

The Guam Micronesian kingfisher nests in tree cavities that it painstakingly excavates itself. Lacking the specialized feet of the woodpecker, the kingfisher must hover while chiseling these cavities. The kingfishers are diurnal, but the brown tree snake is nocturnal. While the birds sleep in their cavities, the snake winds up the tree, finds the hole, and goes to work. What adults, nestlings, or eggs it does not consume one night, it can return for on subsequent nights. Worse, brown tree snakes have had excellent reproductive success, so their population on Guam has grown enormously. This has delivered a critical blow to the island's native birds.

First these birds lost habitat to land development. Second, the island is now so populated with an unnatural predator that the birds cannot survive in the remaining fragments of native habitat. The Guam Micronesian kingfisher is not the only forest bird on Guam to suffer this problem. The solution for preserving one species would seem to be the solution for all. The brown tree snakes must be eradicated. Unfortunately, eradication may never be achieved, but a vigorous attempt may be adequate to save the birds of Guam.

The U.S. Fish and Wildlife Service has been studying the brown tree snake for many years. Researchers have learned enough about the serpent's natural history that they can now focus on finding the "Achilles heel" of a creature that has no feet.

MARQUESAS KINGFISHER
(Halcyon godeffroyi)

Status: Threatened

Description:

Length: 6.5 in (16.5 cm)
Weight: Unknown
Clutch size: Unknown, but 2 eggs common for genus
Incubation: Unknown
Diet: Probably insects and other invertebrates
Habitat: Forest
Range: Marquesas Islands

Spanish Exploration

Eleven small humps of land in the South Pacific make up the Marquesas Islands. Melanesian explorers discovered them in about 200 A.D. Centuries later, the islands suffered a violent first encounter with modern civilization when Spanish explorers found them in 1595. The islanders were overpowered by the Spaniards' guns and swords.

France eventually won control of the islands. With imperialist zeal they intended to cultivate the islands with crops valuable in international trade—coffee, tea, pineapples, bananas, and other commodities. But Europeans imported more than their lifestyle and agriculture to the islands. They also brought disease—smallpox, tuberculosis, syphilis, and leprosy. The population of islanders dwindled from 100,000 at the beginning of the colonial era to a mere 3,000 by 1960. Similar circumstances have afflicted the islands' birds.

Found on a Single Island

The Marquesas kingfisher once lived on at least two and possibly five of the islands in the chain. If

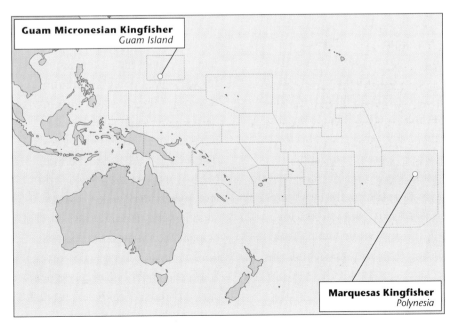

Guam Micronesian Kingfisher
Guam Island

Marquesas Kingfisher
Polynesia

it ever lived on the islands of Fatuiva, Mohotani, and Uapou, it has vanished from them completely. The kingfisher now survives only on Hivaoa, where about 100 birds were known to live in the late 1980s, and on Tahuata, where as many as 1,000 birds yet live.

A forest bird, the Marquesas kingfisher probably makes its way by catching insects, spiders, worms, and other invertebrates in much the same way as other forest-dwelling kingfishers. Ornithologists do know that a bird cannot live without habitat, and on Hivaoa and Tahuata the kingfisher's habitat is disappearing. Native forests are still being cut and the land replanted into crops. Furthermore, great horned owls (*Bubo virginianus*) and common mynas (*Acridotheres tristis*) have been released on Hivaoa. Great horned owls regularly eat birds the size of the Marquesas kingfisher. Common mynas nest in tree cavities and have the potential to displace the cavity-nesting kingfisher.

A Changed Island

Just like the island peoples, the island birds have been displaced. The Marquesas kingfisher is a tiny bird on a tiny island. Its numbers were probably never abundant, so if it were to pass into extinction, its passing would not make headline news. Such an event would be, however, unnecessary and completely avoidable. Humans can save some habitat for these forest birds, refrain from introducing wildlife species that do not belong on the islands, and encourage the replacement growth of more native forest communities.

—*Kevin Cook*

KITES

Class: Aves
Order: Falconiformes
Family: Accipitridae

Kites fly with a graceful style. They enjoy neither the soaring ability of the great hawks nor the divebombing speed of the falcons. Their buoyancy in the air suits them for capturing large insects on the wing, and for picking other insects off the outer foliage of trees and shrubs. Some species even eat smaller birds as a regular part of their diet. Many kite species nest in loose clusters. Their nests are spaced too far apart to qualify as colonies, but they are too close together to be treated merely as closely spaced mating pairs. They use the same breeding areas year after year.

Ornithologists have classified kites differently over the years. Some have classified them into one or more subfamilies to distinguish them from other hawks. The osprey (Pandion haliaetus), plus fish-eagles and sea-eagles, appear more closely related to the kites than other hawks and eagles, but most ornithologists still do not place kites in a separate subfamily.

Decline

Because so many kite species associate with one kind of wetland or another, many species have experienced decline. This is because wetland destruction is occurring on a worldwide scale. Wetland destruction inevitably results when vast tracts of land are needed for agriculture. Historically, many wetlands have been destroyed for reasons of public health; fewer wetlands mean fewer disease-carrying mosquitos. Some kites have been deliberately persecuted by humans, such as the red kite (*Milvus milvus*) in Europe. Most species recover quickly if the shooting and trapping can be controlled, but they always need habitat. Once habitat is destroyed, a species—be it kite or any other—can only recover to the extent that essential habitat is available.

CUBA HOOK-BILLED KITE
(Chondrohierax uncinatus wilsonii)

Status: Endangered

Description:
Length: 15-16 in (38-41 cm)
Weight: 12-14 oz (336-392 g)
Clutch size: Probably 2-3 eggs
Incubation: Uknown
Diet: Mostly snails, but also insects, frogs, and salmanders
Habitat: Forests, swamps
Range: Cuba

Popular Bird
When hook-billed kites cross

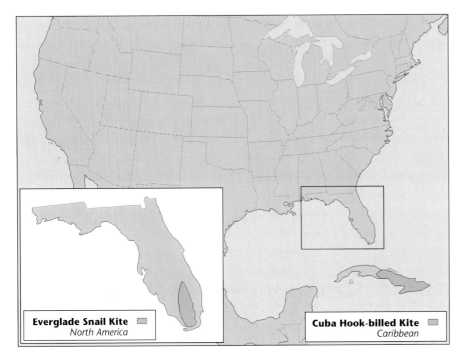

Everglade Snail Kite
North America

Cuba Hook-billed Kite
Caribbean

female is browner, not so gray. Her underparts are oranger, more rufous, with dingy buff separating the bars. Dark patterns probably help camouflage the bird in its forest haunts (even hawks have enemies).

An Island Dweller

The Cuba hook-billed kite has been steadily dwindling for years. As the Cuban people drain swamps to develop more sugar cane plantations, the kite loses vital habitat. With more than ten million people, Cuba has both the size and population of Pennsylvania. Although the Cuban people raise various crops, including coffee, tobacco, pineapples, and bananas. Sugar cane accounts for more of the island nation's farm exports than all the other crops combined. Sugar cane takes space, and the best space in Cuba is south of the

the Rio Grande into Texas, word spreads like wildfire. Birdwatchers show up from all over the country just so they can say they saw a hook-billed kite in the United States.

Hook-billed kites range over all of Central America southwards. They occupy all of northern South America and most of central South America east of the Andes. One small group of hook-billed kites still lives on the island of Cuba, and ornithologists have designated these birds as a separate subspecies. This group has declined steadily over the years, and its survivability is in doubt.

The hook-billed kite is average in size for a hawk, although it has an unusual beak. This bird is appropriately named, because its over-sized, heavy-looking beak curves down sharply at the tip. It uses its beak to open snails that it finds on tree trunks and branches. Typical of a forest bird, the hook-billed kite has a slightly shorter and broader wing than would be expected for a bird its size. This wing shape and proportion allows

the bird to maneuver among the tangled limbs and twigs of forest trees. Like other forest birds, the hook-billed kite is also dark both above and below. The male sports a dark gray plumage, washed over with a faint brown hue. Its underparts are reddish brown with white barring, from the lower throat down across breast, belly, and side. Its tail is the same dark gray-brown, but a white band sweeps across the middle. The

All species of kites appear to use the same breeding areas year after year. This arrangement leaves large areas of seemingly good habitat unused.

low mountains along the coastal plain. Swamps and drier forests once stretched across much of that area, and the Cuba hook-billed kite lived in those forests.

No one knows for certain whether the numerous chemicals used to sustain the massive agricultural development have had any direct effect on the Cuba hook-billed kite. Useful population estimates are not available. However, comparing how much kite habitat used to exist on Cuba with how much of that habitat remains makes the problem and the solution clear: the only way to preserve the Cuban subspecies of the hook-billed kite is to preserve its habitat.

EVERGLADES SNAIL KITE
(Rostrhamus sociabilis plumbeus)

Status: Endangered

Description:
Length: 17 in (43.2 cm)
Weight: 13.6 oz (380 g)
Clutch size: 2-4 eggs
Incubation: Unknown
Diet: Snails
Habitat: Marshes
Range: The Everglades, southern Florida

Bird of Prey

Gliding over the marsh, first flapping strongly then sailing lightly, then flapping again, the hawk scans for its prey. With no great drama of power and pursuit, the bird flares its wings and drops toward the water with feet and talons outstretched. Before hitting the water it flaps again, regaining flight just as its talons pluck a curious brown ball from the water. With steady wingbeats, it flies to a branch where it alights and quickly settles itself. Looking first left then right, it shows the profile of its specialized beak. The upper half curves sharply downwards. The hawk bobs its head slightly, then turns its attention to the brown ball. An Everglades snail kite is about to eat a snail.

The male Everglades snail kite appears sooty gray overall, with a two-tone tail, the base half is white and the tip half slate gray. It is a long-winged bird, well built for a life of snatching snails from marshes. The Everglades snail kite eats apple snails (*Pomacea paludosa*) almost exclusively. The snail defends itself from many would-be predators with an operculum, a tough, leathery plate that covers the shell opening like a door. The kite defeats the snail by inserting its needle-like upper beak between the operculum and shell. With a twist of its head it snaps the nerve that controls the muscles holding the operculum closed. Once the nerve is severed, the muscle goes limp, the door opens, and the kite scoops out the snail for a meal.

The snail kite species ranges over nearly all of South America east of the Andes, portions of Central America, Cuba, and Florida. The Florida birds belong to a distinct subspecies. Originally, they inhabited much of the Everglades, a unique marshland sprawling over more than 13,000 square miles (33,800 square kilometers) of southernmost Florida. The vast open expanses of sawgrass (*Cladium jamaicense*) are the most distinctive feature of the "Glades." Actually a sedge and not a grass, the sawgrass grows in the slowly moving water. Apple snails also live in that water. The apple snails must periodically surface to breathe, and they leave the water to lay their eggs on plant stems several inches above the water line.

In many places the sawgrass grows too tall and too dense for the Everglades snail kites to reach the snails. Some areas are more open than others, and in these open areas the kites do most of their hunting. The Everglades is like a great puzzle of interlocking pieces, where water, sawgrass, apple snails, and kites all fit together. If something happens to one piece, there is a definite effect on all the other pieces. Much has happened in the Everglades to jumble the pieces, and the Everglades snail kite has reacted by dwindling away.

During the early settlement years of Florida, people largely disregarded the Everglades as too inhospitable to bother with. Various schemes to drain the Everglades were occasionally devised, but no single method succeeded. However, many unrelated activities pressured the Glades. Working from the border lands, people steadily drained small portions of the Glades so they could build houses and plant crops. Agriculture meant using fertilizers and pesticides, both of which affected plant communities beyond farmers' fields. People dug peat from the Glades. They built highways across the open expanse of sawgrass. They redirected the

flow of water.

In 1934 the land that was to become Everglades National Park was set aside. Much of the park's 2,186 square miles (5,684 square kilometers) includes portions of Florida Bay and coastal mangrove swamp. These areas, strictly speaking, are not portions of the true Everglades, although they are intimately connected to it. Thus, the actual area of Everglades protected by the park is roughly six percent of the Everglades' original size. Everglades snail kites do seasonally use habitat inside the northern border of the park, but for the most part the surviving population resides outside the park. What happens to the Everglades beyond the park boundaries really determines what happens to the kite.

Historically, people have treated the Everglades as if it were expendable. Manipulation of water levels and chemical contamination from agricultural sources have combined to alter the natural landscape. Quite possibly, these changes affected the apple snail population. Ordinarily, apple snails are so prolific that fluctuations in their population would not seriously affect the kites. However, artificial changes in the plant communities of the Everglades could easily affect how accessible snails are to the kites, at least in local areas. Probably more important than snail populations, the kites have experienced the loss of suitable habitat for nesting and hunting.

Everglades snail kites have in past years frequented Loxahatchee National Wildlife Refuge and areas near Lake Okeechobee, as well as

Today, enough people use the same recreation areas within the Everglades to cause major disturbance to nesting and feeding Everglades snail kites. Important nesting areas had to be closed to public use.

the Shark Valley area of Everglades National Park and the Miccosukee Indian Reservation (and some points in between). Before 1970, the Everglades kite population numbered perhaps as low as 10 birds. By the 1990s, the species numbered several times more than that. The population survived and rebuilt its ranks largely due to wildlife specialists protecting known nesting sites from human disturbance. Preserving the Everglades snail kite ultimately depends on people's willingness to allow it to exist by protecting the amount and the quality of its habitat.
—*Kevin Cook*

625

LITTLE SPOTTED KIWI
(Apteryx owenii)

Status: Threatened

Class: Aves
Order: Apterygiformes
Family: Apterygidae

Description:
Length: 13.8-17.7 in
(35-45 cm)
Weight: 2.5-3 lb (1.14-1.35 kg)
Clutch size: Usually 1,
occasionally 2 eggs
Incubation: 63-76 days
Diet: Invertebrates, including
earthworms, millipedes, spiders,
insects, and some fruits
Habitat: Evergreen forests with
well-developed undergrowth;
also evergreen shrub land
Range: Kapiti Island, New
Zealand

Very Unusual Bird

A bird with a sense of smell is strange enough. But when that bird sports no tail, has puny wings with which it cannot fly, grows shaggy hair-like feathers, has a long beak, and seems to have overgrown feet, it is not strange—it is a kiwi.

People tend to love the kiwi. They love to smile at its peculiar appearance, love to shoot it for its skin, and love to eat it for supper. Everyone loves a kiwi, but not enough people cared about it to avoid this species' brush with extinction.

The little spotted kiwi is one of

three kiwis that lives in the forests and dense shrub lands of New Zealand. Smallest of the trio, it has a gray-brown head and neck. The rounded body is largely a dull brown, textured by dingy white, giving the bird a vague barred or spotted look. The wing is tiny and usually hidden by the shaggy, hair-like plumage. The foot and toe are powerfully built, but are not used to scratch for food. The beak is long, slender, and slightly decurved. The face has many long, hair-like bristles that probably serve as whiskers.

Kiwi fossils go back 60 million years, making them the oldest bird group on the islands. The kiwi occupied New Zealand with the moas, extinct birds in the order Dinornithiformes. The extinctions followed the first settlement of New Zealand by Polynesians around 950 to 1,000 A.D.

Divided Land

New Zealand is composed of two large islands, North Island and South Island, and a third one called Stewart Island, in addition to many

coastal isles and islets. The brown kiwi (*Apteryx australis*) formerly occurred over much of North Island, large tracts of South Island, and Stewart Island. The great spotted kiwi (*Apteryx haastii*) inhabited only portions of South Island. The little spotted kiwi, smallest of the three, occupied much of North and South Islands, plus many small coastal isles. Although it is secretive and nocturnal, the little kiwi could not escape a hungry people.

New Zealand had no large land mammals as a meat source, but it had many birds, including flightless birds. The native Maoris hunted the birds and repeatedly burned the land. The activities of relentless hunters and the pressure of habitat changes eliminated the little spotted kiwi from one major island and from several smaller islands. This loss challenges the notion that primitive aboriginal peoples were less exploitive of wildlife than modern peoples. But when the British colonized New Zealand in the mid-1800s, life became even more precarious for the little spotted kiwi.

The British colonists were eager to recreate the familiar look of home in their adopted land. To do this, they imported various plants and animals and then released them on the islands. They introduced elk (*Cervus elaphus*) and European rabbits (*Oryctolagus cuniculus*) to the islands. Without natural controls in place to suppress their populations, the rabbit population exploded. But colonists had a solution: they imported a predator called a stoat—known in the United States as an ermine or short-tailed weasel (*Mustela erminea*). They thought the stoats would eat the rabbits and all would be well. Unfortunately, the stoats, or weasels, did not cooperate. They found various flightless ground birds to prey on instead, and the little spotted kiwi was a target.

Kiwis nest in long tunnels which they dig in embankments, especially among large, exposed tree roots. These tunnels may go back as much as 12 feet (3.5 meters) to the actual nesting chamber. The weasels, being long and skinny, had no trouble entering these burrows in search of nestlings. House cats (*Felis sylvestris*) also found their way into the New Zealand wilds, as did several rat species (*Rattus* sp.). All of these mammals preyed on the little spotted kiwis, but the presence of certain plants affected them, too.

Many native forests on the islands of New Zealand were cut down and replaced by lodgepole pines (*Pinus contorta*) and Monterrey pines (*Pinus radiata*). Pines are not native to the Southern Hemisphere, so vast acres of them on plantations are not immediately recognizable or useful to native

Little Spotted Kiwi
New Zealand

birds. The lodgepole pine escaped cultivation and began growing wild in New Zealand. Along with many other exotic plant species, the pine changed much of the character of the primary forests.

As New Zealand's population grew, sheep production for meat and wool became a major agricultural activity on the islands. The space needed for all of these human pursuits left less space for the kiwis. Less habitat ultimately means fewer kiwis. Also, as populations decline, hunting by exotic predators becomes an even more serious threat.

New Zealand wildlife specialists have developed a strategy to save many of New Zealand's birds. They trap cats and other unwanted animals to remove them from the islands. Native birds are then moved to these islands and released. This idea is not new. Some records indicate that five little spotted kiwis were trapped in 1912 and moved to Kapiti Island, off the southwest coast of North Island. They persist there to this day. Kiwis have also been moved to Hen, Red Mercury, and Long Islands, although with uncertain results. Weasels and rats are known to swim channels between main islands and islets, so the populations are not without exotic predators.

By 1990 the population

estimates of little spotted kiwis ranged from 500 to 600 birds, up to a high of about 1,000. Preserving the little spotted kiwi depends on guarding Kapiti Island against unintentional invasion by rats, cats, and weasels. Further work is being done to eradicate cats on other islands. Barring disasters, this species will probably survive, but the little spotted kiwi may have to adapt to an environment far different from the one its ancestors knew.
—*Kevin Cook*

KIYI
(Coregonus kiyi)

Status: Threatened

Class: Osteichthyes
Order: Salmoniformes
Family: Salmonidae

Description:
Length: 10 in (25 cm)
Reproduction: Egg layer
Habitat: Deep open water
Range: Lake Superior, possibly Lake Huron

A Last Stand

The kiyi is a species of cisco and a member of a larger group commonly called whitefish that live, primarily, in the icy waters of northern latitudes and prefer large pristine lakes. Some whitefish like *Coregonus artedi* that live in the northern United States tolerate more fertile conditions and do well.

Centuries ago, Lake Superior, Lake Michigan, Lake Huron, Lake Ontario, and other large lakes of

North America like Great Slave and Great Bear were relatively untouched by humans. Fish populations, including the ciscoes, flourished in clean water and were not threatened by foreign, non-native fishes. With the explosion of the human population and the expansion of industry came pollution, over-fishing, and introduction of foreign predators.

Ciscoes that were marketed under names like lake herring, chub, tullibee, and bloater used to be considered delicacies in the United States before the 1950s as a smoked product; fishermen went out of their way to find new and better equipment to catch these prized fishes. By the 1940s the kiyi was eliminated from Lake Ontario, and by the late 1960s and early 1970s there simply were not enough cisco left to justify a catch in any of the Great Lakes.

Pollution in the forms of sewage and industrial waste, and predation by the invading sea lamprey on ciscoes and fishes associated with ciscoes (like lake trout, *Salvelinus namaycush*) added to the problem. Today in North America three species of cisco, including the kiyi, and three other whitefishes are either threatened or on the verge of extinction, with the kiyi restricted to Lake Superior.

For the kiyi and other ciscoes to make a comeback in the Great Lakes, commercial fishing must be tightly controlled or halted until the fish have an opportunity to recover. The decades of pollution in most of the lakes have left a legacy that will have future consequences. However, the Canadian and U. S. governments are at least beginning to curb the discharge of destructive and insidious pollutants into the kiyi's only remaining home.

Ciscoes and other whitefishes are related to salmon, trout, and grayling (*Salmonidae*), and have a long history of controversy about their classification and naming. As previously mentioned, during their "heyday" as food fishes, ciscoes were marketed as chubs or herring. The true chubs that we know today are very different from the "chubs" of yesterday and, indeed, are classified as cyprinids, not salmonids. This kind of regional naming of fishes is fairly common. However, fisheries scientists admit to some confusion and disagreement when it comes to naming these deep-water dwellers. Eighteen North American species of whitefish (including ciscoes) are included in the subfamily Coregoninae. Some argue that this group should be given family status. Others claim it is a subfamily under the family Salmonidae. There are valid arguments for both positions.

The confusion is compounded by a disturbing development in the life of the ciscoes. Even before the population crashes of the 1940s, '50s, and '60s, fisheries people struggled with the appropriate naming of individual cisco species. A catastrophic result of the endangerment of some of these fishes has been their interbreeding with similar and more populous cisco species, creating a muddle of genes. If this process continues, the already fine lines between some of the 14 freshwater species in the genus Coregonus will disappear. Unfortunately, many other fish of this genus, including the houting (*Coregonus oxyrinchus*), kiyi (*Coregonus kiyi*), Atlantic whitefish (*Coregonus huntsmani*), Opeonga whitefish (*Coregonus* sp.), and Squanga whitefish (*Coregonus* sp.) also are threatened or endangered.

Also commonly called a chub or mooneye, the 10-inch kiyi is long and sleek yet robust from the side, but from the front appears somewhat compressed or flattened, like a plate on edge. The snout is not unusually long and is fairly blunt. The meaty body is accented

Commerical fishing must be controlled for the many endangered fishes of the Great Lakes—including the kiyi—to survive.

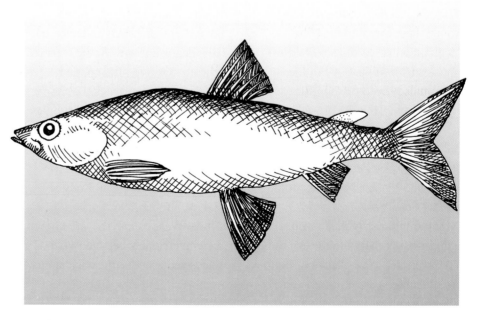

Kiyi
North America

by a mild hump on the back between the head and the dorsal fin. It has a substantial, but not bulbous, belly. The pectoral fins just behind the gills and the pelvic fins on the belly are triangular and somewhat pointed, the dorsal fin on the back and the anal fin just behind the anus are square, and the tail fin is moderately forked (a sign of a strong swimmer). Like all salmonids the kiyi also displays a small, fleshy adipose fin between the dorsal and tail fins. The body is uniformly a silver color, with darker tones on the back and lighter to white tones on the belly. The sides also show pink or purple iridescence in bright light. The dorsal and tail fins are dark and other fins are clear.

Kiyi spawn from November to January in water that is from 300 to 500 feet deep and only a few degrees above freezing. Little is known about how many eggs females produce, or whether the parents offer the eggs protection or time to hatch. Unfortunately, the kiyi is a slow-growing fish and does not approach adult size until its third or fourth year. Females tend to be slightly larger than their male counterparts and also live a few years longer on average (about ten years). Kiyi feed primarily on planktonic crustaceans (*Mysis*) in Lake Superior.

—*William E. Manci*

WESTERN KLIPSPRINGER
(Oreotragus oreotragus porteousi)

Status: Endangered

Class: Mammalia
Order: Artiodactyla
Family: Bovidae
Subfamily: Bovinae
Tribe: Neotragini

Description:
Weight: 22-40 lb (10-18 kg)
Shoulder height: 18-23 in (45-60 cm)
Diet: Leaves, twigs, grasses
Gestation period: 210-220 days
Longevity: 12-15 years
Habitat: Rocky outcroppings and thick bush
Range: Nigeria

Plains Antelope

The klipspringer is a small antelope that prefers to dwell amid rock outcroppings and other rugged terrain; these outcroppings occur in the middle of vast plains. But the klipspringer is also found in other mountainous terrain and has been found at altitudes of up to 1,500 feet (400 meters).

Klipspringers tend to live alone or in pairs (a mother with a kid), and are most active at dusk, preferring the shade and shelter of the rocks by day. They will occasionally graze on grass, but they browse on whatever is available, including herbs, plants, and fruits. Klipspringers are never far from a water source, even though they appear not to drink water regularly.

The klipspringer has a coarse, brittle blue-gray coat. This coat provides a thick cushion against bruises as the animal hops about its rocky environment. The male has small, parallel horns that are about 6 inches (15.2 centimeters) in length. One of its most distinguishing features is its manner of walking and climbing. A klipspringer stands on its tiptoes, on narrow cylindrical hooves, seeming to be in danger of tipping over. But its sense of balance is remarkable, and its climbing ability is unequaled.

Hide and Seek

The klipspringer's habitat above surrounding plains allows it to view and sense danger approaching. It has the ability to make a loud whistling noise to alert others. This animal is also known to stand frozen in place for long periods to avoid detection, and its coloration acts as camouflage, allowing it to blend into the background.

A klipspringer's most common

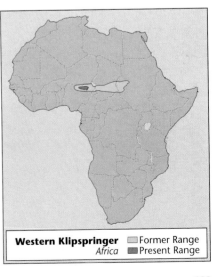

Western Klipspringer □ Former Range
Africa ■ Present Range

The narrow hooves of the klipspringer seem too small to support its own weight. Oddly enough, this antelope is an excellent climber with superb balance. This antelope's agility saves it from such predators as the python, which might otherwise pose a threat to the klipspringer.

predator is the leopard, with an occasional pursuit by a caracal or jackal. Even pythons—when given a chance—will go for a klipspringer; however, the animal is so agile it is difficult for a python to ambush it.

Klipspringers are found over much of southern and eastern Africa south of the Sahara, and are still found in reasonable numbers over their entire range with one exception. The Western klipspringer, a subspecies, is found only in north central Nigeria. Because of the encroachment in that country by humans, along with heavy hunting, political unrest and civil wars, the Western klipspringer (like much of the other Nigerian wildlife) has severely declined.

Captivity

Klipspringers do reasonably well in captivity; however, they do take careful management. There are currently no animals existing in captivity, although a number of European zoos and some American zoos have had some success with them in the past.

Unfortunately, there is no group of Western klipspringers available at this time for captive breeding. A disaster in the wild could wipe out this subspecies entirely. Current population estimates of the species place them at less than 2,500 individuals.

—*Warren D. Thomas*

KOKAKO
(Callaeas cinerea)

Status: Threatened

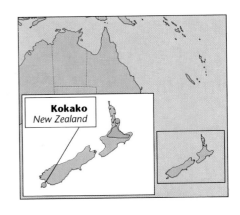

Kokako
New Zealand

Class: Aves
Order: Passeriformes
Family: Callaeidae

Description:
Length: 15 in (38.1 cm)
Weight: 6.9-9.5 oz (195-265 g)
Clutch size: 2-3 eggs
Incubation: 25 days
Diet: Mostly leaves, berries, some insects
Habitat: Evergreen forests
Range: North, South, and Stewart Islands of New Zealand

A Loud, Clear Call

A gray shape sails out of a tree and glides across a small opening in the forest. A bit of sunshine reveals the bird: it is bluish gray with a darker wing and tail. Just a glimpse and then it slides back into the shadow. Landing near the base of a tree, it hops quickly from branch to branch, using the branches as ladder rungs to climb the tree, as a jay does. But New Zealand has no jays. Well up into the forest canopy the bird stops to call. It gives a loud, pure note again and again. People have called it the "organ bird" and the "bell bird."

The kokako has patches of earthy brown accenting its wing, lower back and rump, and its belly. A black lore and eye ring highlight an otherwise plain blue-gray face.

From the jaw, between cheek and chin, protrudes a bare, fleshy, bright blue wattle. People sometimes call it the wattle-bird.

Of three wattle-bird species, the kokako is one of two still alive. The huia (*Heterolocha acutirostris*) became extinct early in the 1900s, the last live one reliably recorded in 1907. The kokako has also declined, but not yet with such finality.

When the first humans found New Zealand, the kokako inhabited forests all across North, South, and Stewart Islands. Polynesian explorers arrived about 950 A.D. and they brought rats (*Rattus exulans*) and dogs (*Canis familiaris*) with them. Great Britain claimed the islands and established a settlement in 1840. For 30 years the British and the Maoris, descendants of the first Polynesian settlers, fought bitterly. The wars ended in 1870, but New Zealand had changed forever.

A Habitat Changes

No terrestrial mammals lived on New Zealand. The Maori people hunted moas as a main source of their meat. Moas were a unique order of flightless birds. Some species were chicken-sized, but others stood 10 feet (3.3 meters) tall and weighed perhaps 300 pounds (140 kilograms). The

The future of the kokako is relatively positive. It is expected to survive, although in reduced numbers. Today wildlife specialists are working to preserve its habitat and control exotic predators.

Maoris consumed the moas into extinction. British colonists achieved the same results with other birds, but through different means. They established a Western culture based on industry and agriculture. But they brought more than sheep and cattle to raise. Hunters and fishers organized "acclimatization societies" to import game animals (fish, birds, and mammals) for the purpose of establishing recreational hunting and fishing—the kind the British were accustomed to, that is. Other groups and individuals imported other wildlife, ranging from daffodils and pines to song birds. Many of these exotic species succeeded. Their populations grew explosively, but their success came at the expense of native wildlife.

Many New Zealand birds lost their ability to fly because the absence of predatory mammals and reptiles made life on the ground much safer. When the predators arrived, the birds were defenseless. European rabbits (*Oryctolagus cunicularis*) were released on New Zealand as a potential food for people. Humans, however, could not eat rabbits fast enough to keep up with their population growth. Weasels (*Mustela erminea*) were imported as a natural control for the rabbits. The weasels were released in about 1890, and soon many New Zealand birds began to decline rapidly. Undoubtedly, the weasels found flightless birds to be easy prey compared to the rabbits they were meant to eat. Rats (*Rattus* sp.) and feral house cats (*Felis sylvestris*) proved deadly, too.

Deforestation

The British cut the native forests partly for the lumber and partly to open the land for sheep grazing. Exotic plants—imported as crops or just for their appearance—escaped cultivation and became nuisance species responsible for degrading much New Zealand habitat. What the plants did not degrade, the exotic animals did. Within a century of British colonization, New Zealand had lost many of its unique life forms to extinction. Many others were seriously imperiled.

Recovery Efforts

During the 1960s, New Zealand wildlife officials began a bold program of recovery. They aggressively trapped cats, rats, and weasels and successfully eliminated them from a few small coastal islands. They then captured seriously endangered birds and released them onto islands where exotic predators could not reach them.

The kokako was one bird that showed a rapid decline after weasels arrived. Cats and rats had no doubt already damaged the population, and the weasel was just one predator too many. South Island lost its kokakos in the early decades of the 1900s. The last few live kokakos were seen there in the 1950s and 1960s. Kokakos on North Island yet survive, but only in scattered pockets of native forests. Their absence in forests dominated by exotic plants testifies to the impact exotic plants have on native birds.

The kokako will probably survive, although in reduced numbers. Wildlife specialists are working to preserve habitat, improve habitat quality, suppress or eradicate exotic predators, and educate people about this problem.
—*Kevin Cook*

KONYE
(Konia eisentrauti)

Status: Threatened

Class: Osteichthyes
Order: Perciformes
Family: Cichlidae

Description:
   Length: 3.5 in (9 cm)
   Reproduction: Egg layer
   Habitat: Open water
   Range: Lake Barombi-Mbo, Cameroon

In the Hands of People

The west African crater lake called Barombi-Mbo in the country of Cameroon is the only stronghold of the cichlid species commonly called the konye. This small and relatively infertile but deep freshwater lake is only about 1.5 miles in diameter (2.4 kilometers), yet is the primary source of food for the village of Barombi on its northern shore. Fishermen jealously guard their right to fish the lake and, unfortunately, the konye and a total of ten other threatened and endangered cichlid fishes are sought by them as food.

Given that the konye can be found only in Lake Barombi-Mbo, clearly the species is vulnerable to natural or man-made problems or to prolonged over-fishing. However, the desire on the part of the Barombi villagers to maintain exclusive fishing rights on the lake may work to the advantage of the konye and other cichlids. Because the

villagers have been able to maintain a workable balance between their "required" catch and the natural supply of fish and have resisted over-fishing, government officials are hopeful that this balance can be continued. Along with measures to prevent pollution in the lake as well as the introduction of harmful non-native fishes like the large and aggressive predator, Nile perch (*Lates niloticus*), conservationists wish to continue the ban on fishing by other villages and educate the people of Barombi as to the delicate balance of the ecosystem they currently exploit.

Despite their seemingly endless physical and behavioral differences, cichlids possess many similar physical characteristics. All cichlids present a fairly flattened and more round appearance than other streamlined and torpedo-like fishes. Most have broad, hardened mouth parts that are used to scrape algae from surfaces or crush hard food items. In addition to teeth on the jaws, these fishes have hundreds of teeth on a plate-like bone at the base of the mouth and throat to hold and process food items; these teeth within the throat are called pharyngeal teeth. After food is swallowed, cichlids have a long gut to further process and absorb nutrients. The length of the gut is often over two-and-one-half times the length of the fish.

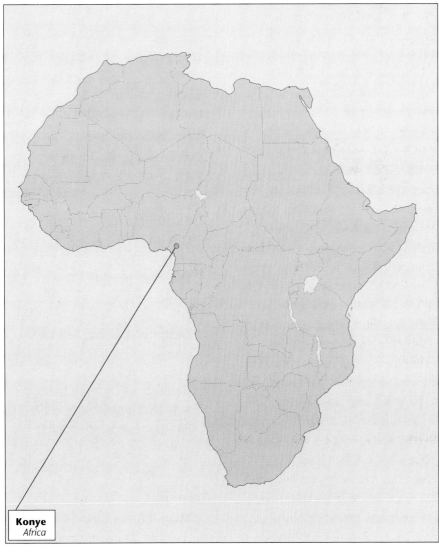

Konye
Africa

A distinctive characteristic of the konye as well as all other cichlids is the long, spiny, protective dorsal fin on the back that can extend from just behind the head all the way to the tail section of the body; the dorsal fin segment near the tail usually is longer than the segment near the head. In many cichlids, the segment near the tail carries a dark blotch called a tilapia mark. The konye's dorsal fin does not carry a tilapia mark.

The konye is somewhat different in appearance than other cichlids that live Lake Barombi-Mbo. It has a dramatically sloping face and forehead and a horizontal mouth rather than one that is upturned. Body color patterning is very distinctive with a row of large dark blotches down the back, a row of connected dark blotches on the sides from the cheeks to the base of the tail fin, and lighter patches below and behind the eye and on the snout. This patchwork covers a lighter background that is slightly darker on the back and lighter on the belly. The body and gill covers are well scaled. The cheeks have some scales but the rest of the head is nude.

The konye eats various kinds of plant material and insects (mayflies). Using filtering devices on the gills called gill rakers, the konye can remove floating algae from the water as it passes through the mouth cavity and out past the gills. Other plants are scraped from rocks or parts are torn from a stem. Some konye are known to eat fish eggs.

The konye engages in a form of parental care called mouth brooding. After eggs are laid and fertilized, one or both of the parents picks up the eggs and protects them within their mouth cavity during the incubation period that lasts from a week to ten days. Parental care continues beyond the hatching date as the juvenile fish swim free, outside the nearby parent's mouth. At the first sign of danger, the parent opens their mouth and the newly hatched fish scurry inside, where they are protected from attack. The konye produces relatively few young, only about 60 per female per cycle. Clearly, this type of parental care is a step in ensuring the survival of the few young that are produced.
—*William E. Manci*

KORRIGUM
(Damaliscus lunatus korrigum)

Status: Endangered

Class: Mammalia
Order: Artiodactyla
Family: Bovidae
Subfamily: Bovinae
Tribe: Alcelaphini

Description:
Weight: 330-375 lb (150-170 kg)
Shoulder height: 43-51 in (110-130 cm)
Diet: Grasses, leaves, and twigs
Gestation period: 225-240 days
Longevity: 12-15 years
Habitat: Scrub thorn bush to semi-arid grassland
Range: Senegal to western Sudan

Senegal
Since the late 1960s, drought has been an almost constant reality for the people who live in Senegal, Africa's westernmost nation. Yet wildlife virtually thrives here primarily because a wide range of vegetation is available. Senegal has large areas set aside to protect elephants, lions, and other animals, but poaching is still a big problem. It is in this nation where the korrigum is found.

A Hartebeeste
The korrigum, also called the Senegal hartebeeste, is part of the genus *Damaliscus* of smaller hartebeestes with lyre-shaped horns. It has the typical brownish tawny coat, with black or dark flashings on the hip, shoulder, and face. Both the male and female are armed with horns, with the male having much heavier horns than the female.

In its habits the korrigum is principally a grazer, found in open grasslands to scrub areas. It is occasionally found in ones and twos, but is most often seen in herds of from 15 to 20 individuals. Unfortunately, the korrigum is thought to be a nuisance to the people of Senegal and Sudan. Searching for food, it comes into the fields and livestock grazing lands of farmers. These intrusions have increased during recent severe droughts. Naturally, the local human inhabitants do not take kindly to such intrusions by wild ungulates (even-toed, hoofed animals) like the korrigum.

As with other hartebeestes, the korrigum relies on its ability to run away from danger in order to escape predation. Not only are these animals fast but, like other hartebeestes, they have a great deal of stamina and can outrun many predators. Korrigums sometimes

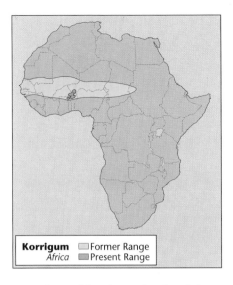

Korrigum
Africa ☐ Former Range ■ Present Range

associate with other animals of the plain, such as local gazelles and even cape buffalo at times.

The area of Africa in which the korrigum is found is heavily utilized by people. Civil strife has also disrupted the lands in their range. Severe drought and poaching have combined to further bring the korrigum population down to an alarmingly low level. Thus, the korrigum is considered to be a severely endangered animal. The species still exists in small pockets, although their range was once from Senegal through western Sudan in an almost unbroken stretch. Their numbers now total less than 5,000, scattered in some half-dozen separate populations.

The korrigum and its relatives, the topis and the tsessebes (or sassabies), have been kept in captivity, but only on a limited basis—they do only moderately well in a captive environment. At this time, no captive population exists to support the wild korrigum population. With its numbers dwindling, and its habitat afflicted by drought and political unrest, the korrigum's future appears dim.
—*Warren D. Thomas*
See also Antelopes and Hartebeestes.

KOUPREY
(Bos sauveli)

Status: Endangered

Class: Mammalia
Order: Artiodactyla
Family: Bovidae
Subfamily: Bovinae
Tribe: Bovini

Description:
Weight: 1,543-1,985 lb (700-900 kg)
Shoulder height: 67-75 in (170-190 cm)
Diet: Grasses, leaves, twigs, and shoots
Gestation period: Unknown
Longevity: Unknown
Habitat: Open forest
Range: Southeast Asia

Forest Ox

The kouprey, or the giant Cambodian forest ox, is a remarkable animal. It is one of the largest cattle forms found in Southeast Asia. Its distribution is from Kampuchea (formerly Cambodia) into Laos, Vietnam (although this is questionable

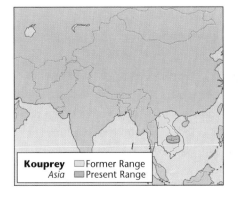

Kouprey
Asia ☐ Former Range ■ Present Range

today), and Thailand.

The kouprey is an interesting-looking animal. It has a dew lap (a fold of skin that hangs from the nape of the neck) that is quite large. Bulls are dark in color, with white leggings and yellowish horns. The horns have ribbed rings at the base and curve out, down, and then up again in a corkscrew fashion. The tips are frayed. Cows and offspring are lighter in color, and the horns are more lyre-shaped.

Koupreys will inhabit any low rolling hill country if it is covered with patches of dense, deciduous forest, open forest, or monsoon forest, along with some open grassland. They are grazers and, when necessary, do some browsing among plants and trees as well. Koupreys are often found in the wild in the company of eld deer, sambar deer, or hog deer. They are also seen mixed with herds of banteng. When they are not with other animals, koupreys are found in herds of 20 or more, which usually consist of one or two adult males and the rest females and their young. The herd, as is common with wild cattle, tends to be led by an old female.

Kouprey herds do not have a highly structured social organization, in that they split up and come back together again, which may be a reaction to the available food supply. All-male herds are found occasionally, but old bulls commonly appear to be solitary. The mating period is sometime during April, with young being born in December and January. The female and her young usually remain by themselves. The female leaves the herd to give birth, and tends to stay by herself for a month or so and then returns.

The kouprey used to roam the open forest, grazing in the land that boasted an abundance of the grasses, leaves, and twigs that made up its diet. Now these areas have been drastically changed by human beings.

This is quite different from the behavior of the gaur or a banteng, where the female with a newborn calf will remain with the herd.

Changed Habitat

The local human population has burned the land in which the kouprey roams in order to clear fields for their own needs. Unfortunately, they also tend to do this at the time when the grass is young and tender shoots are abundant, so not only is the kouprey's range reduced, but its food source is destroyed as well. This has had a devastating effect on the animal.

Today, political conditions have produced civil unrest and warfare over the entire range of the kouprey. Experts doubt whether any pure-bred koupreys still exist in the wild at all. Crude estimates place the wild population at between 100 and 300 individuals. But some animal experts question whether this is a genuine population, or one that is a hybrid resulting from crossbreeding with feral cattle, bantengs, gaur or even zebras. In 1937, one live animal—a male—was obtained and taken to a zoo in Paris, where it lived for a number of years. However, a mate was never found, and no others were ever brought into captivity. There have been several expeditions to try to bring more animals out of the wild; however, they have all failed.

Because the kouprey population was probably low to begin with, the constant hunting pressures and destruction of the kouprey's habitat have only made its situation worse. Since there are no captive animals, there is no population to fall back on to replenish the species. If pure captive populations could be obtained and successfully managed, it is possible that the kouprey could survive into the future. Otherwise, its future does not look good.

—*Warren D. Thomas*
See also Banteng and Gaur.

636

KULULU
(Sarotherodon steinbachi)

Status: Threatened

Class: Osteichthyes
Order: Perciformes
Family: Cichlidae

Description:
Length: 5.1 in (13 cm)
Reproduction: Egg layer
Habitat: Shallow inshore waters
Range: Lake Barombi-Mbo, Cameroon

Patrolling the Shallows

The crater lake called Barombi-Mbo in the West African country of Cameroon is the only home of the cichlid species known locally as the kululu. This modest and relatively sterile but deep freshwater lake is only about 1.5 miles (2.4 kilometers) in diameter, yet is the principal source of food for the village of Barombi on its northern shore. Fishermen protect their right to fish the lake and, unfortunately, the kululu and a total of ten other threatened cichlid fishes are sought by them as their best source of high-quality protein.

Because the kululu can be found only in Lake Barombi-Mbo, this species is considered vulnerable to many natural or artificial catastrophes or to sustained over-fishing. However, the desire on the part of the Barombi villagers to maintain exclusive fishing rights on the lake may work to the benefit of the kululu and other cichlids. Because

the villagers have been able to maintain a viable balance between their "required" catch and the natural supply of fish for many decades and have resisted over-fishing, Cameroon is hopeful that this balance can be maintained. Along with measures to alleviate pollution in the lake and prevent the invasion of harmful non-native fishes like the large and aggressive predator, the Nile perch (*Lates niloticus*), conservationists look to continue the ban on fishing by other villages and educate the people of Barombi as to the fragile equilibrium of the ecosystem they currently utilize.

A distinctive trait of the kululu as well as all other cichlids is the long, spiny, defensive dorsal fin on the back that can extend from just behind the head all the way to the tail section of the body; the dorsal fin portion near the tail usually is deeper than the segment near the head. In many cichlids the segment near the tail carries a dark blotch called a tilapia mark.

Despite a multitude of distinct physical and behavioral variations, cichlids posess many similar physical attributes. All cichlids present a fairly flattened and more

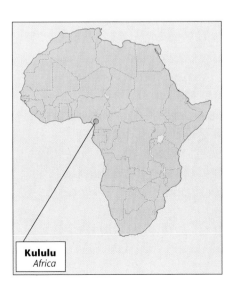

Kululu
Africa

round look (like a plate on edge) than other more streamlined and torpedo-like fishes. Most have broad, hardened mouth parts that are used to scour algae from surfaces or crush hard food items. In addition to teeth on the jaws, these fishes have hundreds of teeth on a plate-like bone at the base of the mouth and throat to hold and prepare food items for digestion; these teeth within the throat are called pharyngeal teeth. After food is swallowed, cichlids have a long gut to proficiently process and absorb nutrients. The length of the gut is often over 2.5-times the length of the fish.

Other than its physical characteristics common to other chichlids, the kululu is fairly nondescript. The adult kululu has no markings on the body but does display a beautiful uniform pearly yellowish coloration, with shades of gray-blue on the back and cream on the belly. This visual feeder has large eyes and is completely scaled except for the gill covers and portions of the face, chin, and throat.

The kululu has been observed engaged in an activity called mouth brooding. After eggs are laid by a female and fertilized by a male, one or both of the parents (depending on the species) picks up the eggs with the mouth and guards them in a chamber in the mouth cavity where oxygenated water is pumped past them. The parent incubates the eggs until they hatch, after a period of one to two weeks. Even after the fish hatch, the free-swimming offspring continue to rely on the parent for protection. At the first sign of a predator or some other threat, the offspring race to the parent, where they immediately re-enter their parent's mouth. This protective behavior significantly increases the chances that offspring will survive to adulthood.

The kululu is not choosy when it comes to food items. Decaying organic matter, sponge spicules, floating algae called diatoms, plant hairs, and terrestrial insects all have been found in the stomach of this fish. The kululu is observed shoveling sand and food mixture into its mouth, removing appropriate items with its pharyngeal teeth, and spitting out the sand. The pharyngeal teeth are eventually worn down by this activity.
—William E. Manci
See also Fissi, Konye, Myakamyaka, Leka keppe, Otjikota tilapia, and Unga.

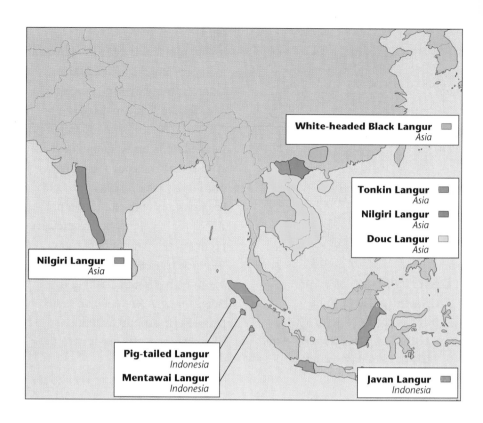

White-headed Black Langur
Asia

Tonkin Langur
Asia

Nilgiri Langur
Asia

Douc Langur
Asia

Nilgiri Langur
Asia

Pig-tailed Langur
Indonesia

Mentawai Langur
Indonesia

Javan Langur
Indonesia

LANGURS

Class: Mammalia
Order: Primates
Family: Cercopithecidae
Subfamily: Colobinae

Langurs are part of the vast monkey family, and are found in Asia. Monkeys are a complicated animal group to classify as there are so many categories into which they may be divided. Within the langurs, there is more than one species group and some 16 species exist overall.

Like other colobine monkeys (such as the colobuses of Madagascar), langurs have a highly specialized digestive tract that permits them to eat large quantities of leaves (explaining their other common name, "leaf monkey"). Leafy vegetation is hard to digest, so langurs have what is called a sacculated stomach. The stomach contains large quantities of bacteria that break down cellulose—the principal nutrient in leaves. Theirs is similar to the digestive system of cows and other members of the cattle family. When they are not eating, langurs spend much time resting in order to digest their food. Langurs are generally considered to be a more "primitive" primate than other New World monkeys and apes.

BLACK-SHANKED DOUC LANGUR
(Pygathrix nigripes)

RED-SHANKED DOUC LANGUR
(Pygathrix nemaeus)

Status: Endangered

Description:

Weight: Approximately 15-22 lb (7-10 kg)
Head-body length: 21-25 in (53-72 cm)
Tail length: 23-27 in (56-76 cm)
Diet: Leaves, fruit, and flowers
Gestation period: About 165 days
Longevity: Unknown
Habitat: Tropical rain forest; gallery and monsoon forest
Range: Southeast Asia

Langurs of Southeast Asia

Douc langurs live in the lush tropical rain forests of Laos and Vietnam. Reports that they have also been seen on Hainan Island across the Gulf of Tonkin near China have not been confirmed.

Doucs are among the larger monkeys, with no difference in size between the sexes. They are beautiful primates, split into two subspecies: the red-shanked douc which lives in central Vietnam and eastern Laos, and the more southerly (and less common) black-shanked douc. Their fur follows a well-defined pattern that features many hues: brown, yellow, orange, white, black, and gray.

Although the douc langur has a four-footed walking style on the ground, it is almost completely arboreal, transporting itself through the forest by frequent leaps. These leaps are as long as 15 to 18 feet (5 to 6 meters), with the arms stretched above the head, and the hind limbs making initial contact with the landing point. These monkeys live in groups of roughly 3 to 11 individuals, with a ratio of at least one male to two females. Females mature sexually at four years and males at five years of age.

The red-shanked douc langur (also known as the Cochin China monkey) has a distinctive coat. It is white and black, with an orange band that sometimes separates these colors between the throat and the chest. The face is also white, fringed with orange, and having a speckled gray crown.

The black-shanked douc langur differs primarily from the red-shanked variety in color; there is more black speckling on the gray forearm and black shank. Its facial skin is blue, with a reddish-yellow tinge to the muzzle.

Because of the political instability in the region, the status of these langurs in the wild is not well known. The population of the red-shanked langur is thought to be more numerous than the black-shanked variety (although some biologists do not separate these two subspecies). However, Vietnam now has a national conservation strategy with a few reserves to better protect these monkeys.

Years of warfare took their toll on both douc langur populations. Bombing and chemical defoliants (substances that kill natural

Douc langurs are among the larger monkeys, split between two subspecies: the black-shanked and the red-shanked douc langurs seen below.

vegetation) ruined large sections of langur habitat. Those douc langurs that survive number less than 25,000, and continuing habitat destruction and severe hunting are likely to keep them endangered unless action is taken.

Red-shanked doucs have been captured and bred in the United States and Europe. In 1985 there were reportedly 58; that number is undoubtedly higher now. But more surveys are desperately needed, particularly in war-torn Laos, where the survival rate of douc langurs is not known.

JAVAN LANGUR
(Presbytis comata)

Status: Endangered

Description:

Weight: 13-19 lb (6-8.6 kg)
Head-body length: 17-24 in (43-60 cm)
Tail length: 22-33 in (55-83 cm)
Diet: Leaves, fruit, buds, flowers, seeds, stems.
Gestation period: Unknown
Longevity: Unknown
Habitat: Tropical rain forest
Range: Java

Restricted to Western Java

The paws of the Javan langur or Javan leaf monkey, also known as

the grizzled sureli, are blackish. The crown is black or brown, and the rest of the upper side of its body is pale gray, speckled with black or brown. The animal's underparts are whitish in color. This rare species is restricted to western Java, where only small areas of evergreen forest remain.

The Javan langur is known for its extraordinary leaping ability. Like other langurs, it dwells in small groups dominated by a single male. It is probably territorial, but not enough study has been done to know more about its specific habits. The current population size of the Javan langur is unknown, but since much of its range has been deforested for timber and agriculture, it is, no doubt, endangered. Unfortunately, the pressures of Java's increasing human population make it virtually impossible to create any new reserves for the protection of this monkey.

There are two existing reserves, one at Ujang Kulon/Gunung Honje, and the other at Gunung Halimun, where the largest populations live. The protection

afforded inside these two reserves, however, needs upgrading. Extinction is a strong possibility unless something is done to preserve this langur's habitat.

MENTAWAI LANGUR
(Presbytis potenziani)

Status: Endangered

Description:

Weight: 12-16 lb (5.5-7 kg)
Head-body length: 17-23 in (44-58 cm)
Tail length: 20-25 in (50-64 cm)
Diet: Probably leaves
Gestation period: Unknown
Longevity: Unknown
Habitat: Rain and mangrove forests
Range: Mentawai Islands near western Sumatra, Indonesia

Unique Island Fauna

The Mentawai langur, or

The Nilgiri langur is also known as John's leaf monkey. Because India's rain forests are so poorly studied and protected, this primate's habitat has been drastically reduced.

Mentawai leaf monkey, has a small ridge-like crest on the crown of its head. Its upper parts and tail are blackish, the pubic region is yellowish-white, and its brow, cheeks, chin, throat, upper chest and sometimes the tip of the tail are whitish. The rest of its underparts and sometimes its collar are reddish orange, brown or occasionally whitish-orange.

This monkey is an important member of the unique primate fauna found on the Mentawai Islands. It is best represented on the island of Siberut. Although very little has been learned about the Mantawai langur's ecology, one research team in the 1970s documented that these langurs live in small monogamous groups (that is, one male and one female bond).

Deforestation and hunting are the regular culprits in this langur's decline, except on the island of Siberut. That entire island has now been designated a Biosphere Reserve by UNESCO. Unfortunately, the langurs on the other islands are deliberately poisoned, as they are considered a pest by banana growers. In addition, logging and harvesting of rattan are degrading what is left of this langur's habitat.

There is currently a plan to expand the 25-square-mile (65-square-kilometer) Teitei Batti Game Sanctuary for several species of primates. If successful, they may all have a chance at survival. The IUCN estimated that less than 25,000 Mentawai langurs remain.

NILGIRI LANGUR
(Trachypithecus johnii)

Status: Threatened

Description:
Weight: 21-30 lb (9.5-13.6 kg)
Head-body length: 20-30 in (51-76 cm)
Tail length: 28-38 in (71-97 cm)
Diet: Mostly leaves
Gestation period: Unknown
Longevity: Unknown
Habitat: Evergreen and riverine forest; deciduous woodland
Range: Southern India

Leaf Monkey
The Nilgiri langur has blackish-brown fur with a gray-

speckled, short-haired rump. The gray coloration will sometimes extend to the thighs and tail. It has a purple face with white sideburns.

This langur has suffered at the hands of poachers for years, and is now confined to isolated patches of the forest. It is almost entirely arboreal, and is an excellent leaper. It appears to live in small, single-male groups.

Widespread deforestation has drastically reduced India's moist evergreen forest. Although logging is selective at present, other projects, such as hydroelectric plants, new roads, and railroads, pose serious threats to the habitat of this langur.

PIG-TAILED LANGUR
(Simias concolor)

Status: Endangered

Description:
Weight: 15 lb (7 kg)
Head-body length: 20 in (51 cm)
Tail length: 6 in (15 cm)
Diet: Leaves, fruits, and berries
Gestation period: Unknown
Longevity: Unknown
Habitat: Tropical rain forest, secondary forest, occasionally mangrove forest
Range: Mentawai Islands, Southeast Asia

Simakobu
The pig-tailed langur is also known as the Simakobu. It is a medium-sized monkey with a stocky build and a short tail that is almost devoid of hair. This langur is unique among the leaf-eating monkeys because of its short, pig-like tail.

There is little difference in body size between the sexes; both males and females have a blackish-brown coat speckled with pale spots on the nape, shoulder, and upper back; the facial skin is black, bordered with whitish hairs, and one in four individuals are cream-buff mixed with brown.

The social organization of this langur is simple, usually consisting of an adult pair with up to three young. In some areas, however, there are larger groups with up to four adult females. While there is little information on reproduction, births have been observed during June and July. The family groups tend to be territorial, and when they meet another group, the males start giving loud but brief ritual calls to mark their borders.

The pig-tailed langur is extremely inconspicuous. It moves and feeds quietly, and vocalizes little. It is extensively hunted by the local Mentawai people, who have taken to hunting the simakobu on Saturday in order to provide ritual meat for their Sunday sabbath. Their modern hunting method is effective; they now use air rifles loaded with poisoned pellets, replacing their traditional bows and arrows. Although the use of air rifles is banned, the law is not enforced. Furthermore, there is no protected reserve of any kind. The only defense this langur has is concealing itself and keeping quiet or, if necessary, making a speedy retreat along the ground.

This unique species is ranked by the IUCN's Action Plan for Asian Primate Conservation (1987-91) as one of eight most highly endangered primates in Asia. Less than 10,000 individuals remain, and no section of its population is really safe from harm. It is the only member of its genus, making it even more irreplaceable. This langur has been under tremendous pressure both from hunting and from commercial exploitation of the forests for logging and conversion of the land for agriculture.

TONKIN LANGUR
(Trachypithecus francoisi)

Status: Endangered

Description:
Weight: 13 lb (6 kg)
Head-body length: 20-27 in (51-68 cm)
Tail length: 32-36 (81-91 cm)
Diet: Mostly leaves
Gestation period: Unknown
Longevity: Unknown
Habitat: Tropical monsoon forest
Range: Northeastern Vietnam, south-central China

Six Subspecies
Also known as Francois' leaf monkey, there are six known subspecies of this langur (all distinct and all endangered). In some areas these subspecies live together but do not interbreed, a behavior which may eventually reclassify them as a separate species. Members of the genus *Trachypithecus* are also known as

brow-ridged langurs.

The most seriously endangered subspecies, *Trachypithecus francoisi leucocephalus*, is reduced to a mere 400 individuals in the Chinese province of Guangxi.

The Tonkin langur's coat is glossy black, with white from the end of its mouth to its ears. It has a pointed crest. There is not a great deal of information available about these primates in Vietnam, although with forest cover reportedly reduced from 44 percent in 1943 to 21 percent at present, it is probable that this species is in trouble. Rapid increases in human population have made this situation worse. Vietnam does have a National Conservation Strategy, but no primates are adequately protected.
—*Sarah Dart and Gregory Lee*

ASHY-HEADED LAUGHINGTHRUSH
(Garrulax cinereifrons)

Status: Threatened

Class: Aves
Order: Passeriformes
Family: Muscicapidae
Subfamily: Timaliinae

Description:
  Length: Unknown
  Weight: Unknown
  Clutch size: 3 eggs (single nest)
  Incubation: Unknown
  Diet: Insects
  Habitat: Wet forests
  Range: Sri Lanka

Hard to Find
Dark birds in dark forests can be hard to find. When those dark birds are also scarce, the combination helps to explain how 132 years could pass between discovering a bird and finding the first nest.

The ashy-headed laughingthrush was first described as a species in 1852. A plain-colored bird, it has dark reddish brown upperparts and noticeably paler, grayer underparts. Its head is gray and its beak black. Reliable size measurements, like its length or weight, have never been made, but the species was reported to be larger than the red-vented bulbul (*Pycnonotus cafer*) but smaller than a common myna (*Acridotheres tristis*)—roughly nine inches (23 centimeters) long. A denizen of forests in Sri Lanka's wet zone, the ashy-headed laughingthrush once occupied both lowland and montane forests up to 5,000 feet (1,524 meters).

Until 1984, no one had seen and reported this bird's nest. That year, some observers discovered a single nest about 40 miles (64 kilometers) southwest of Colombo, Sri Lanka's capital city. The nest was in dense undergrowth beneath tall trees that grew on a steep hillside. There were three eggs inside. More than one bird gathered leaves and sticks, depositing them in a tree fork about 15 feet (4.6 meters) above ground. Rain interfered with access so the discoverers could not follow the progress of the nest on a daily basis. All three eggs eventually disappeared and predation was suspected. Apart from discovering the first known nest of a species, however, this observation was important for revealing helpers at the nest. At least three birds were seen to help build the nest. Nest helpers are known from other bird families, notably the jays and crows; but laughingthrushes are a type of babbler.

Through the years ornithologists have variously classified babblers as a discrete family and as a subfamily of the Old World flycatchers (*Muscicapidae*). A 1990 reclassification names the laughingthrushes as a subfamily of the Old World warblers (*Sylviidae*), but there is no agreement yet on the correct system of classification. The relationships among these small songbird groups are not clear-cut and obvious. Subtle differences of anatomy and behavior can be interpreted more than one way.

About 50 species make up the laughingthrush genus Garrulax. Some species are good singers and so create some demand in the cagebird market. This group, however, occurs only in Asia, with individual species inhabiting portions of India, China, Southeast Asia, or the East Indies. The ashy-headed laughingthrush is unique to the wet zone of Sri Lanka.

Rain Inhibits Observation
A small system of mountains in south-central Sri Lanka radically affects distribution of rainfall on the island. From May to September the monsoons blow from southwest to northeast. Beginning over the Indian Ocean, the monsoons gather much moisture. As the winds come ashore, they sweep up the mountains, cool the air, and dump rain. This particular wedge of Sri Lanka receives up to 200 inches (508 centimeters) of precipitation each year. The foothills and montane forests of the wet zone are dense with lush vegetation as a result. Access can be severely hampered by weather, which

643

The ashy-headed laughingthrush was first described in 1852. Yet it was 132 years later before the first nest was found. These dark birds live in equally dark forests where they are difficult to spot. Combined with the bird's scarcity, this partially explains why it was so hard to locate.

further explains how the nesting of a small, dark bird can go unrecorded for more than a century.

The ashy-headed laughingthrush inhabits the forests of the wet zone, where it behaves much the same as other babblers. It moves close to or onto the ground in small troupes. Noisy birds, they stay in touch as they move by "babbling"—making small chattering sounds and call notes. Sri Lanka's forests have grown quieter over the years, as the ashy-headed laughingthrush has steadily declined.

Agriculture in the Forest

Sri Lankan forests have been replaced by plantation crops such as tea and coffee, plus eucalyptus and other trees. The ashy-headed laughingthrush has shown no ability to accept secondary forests or agricultural lands. Some primary forest has been set aside such as the Morapitiya Forest Reserve where the nest was found in 1984. Protecting the forest has not been as easy as setting it aside. Poor people desperate for cooking and heating fuel cut firewood in the reserve. Simple firewood cutting is severe enough to damage the primary forests. The cutting has degraded the primary forest and, consequently, threatens the ashy-headed laughingthrush. Preserving the laughingthrush depends on saving the forests of Sri Lanka. Preserving the forests may require an inexpensive fuel substitute so that people do not have to continue cutting firewood.
—*Kevin Cook*

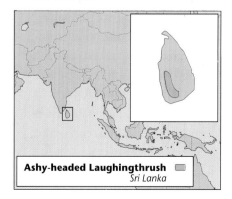

Ashy-headed Laughingthrush
Sri Lanka

LECHWE
(Kobus leche)

Order: Artiodactyla
Family: Bovidae
Subfamily: Bovinae
Tribe: Reduncini

Description:
Weight: 154-287 lb (70-130 kg)
Shoulder height: 36-43 in (90-110 cm)
Diet: Grasses, leaves, twigs, and shoots
Gestation period: 210-240 days
Longevity: 15-18 years
Habitat: Open woodland, swampy lowlands
Range: Southern Zaire, Northern Botswana, Zambia, Namibia

Water Lover

The lechwe is accurately described as a water-loving antelope. It lives in swamps and open forest, and is rarely found more than a few miles away from a source of water. Its preferred habitat is a shallow, inundated flood plain next to a river and close to a swamp, particularly if it has high stands of papyrus reeds and semiaquatic grasses.

There are three different subspecies of lechwe considered here: the black lechwe (*Kobus leche smithemani*) from northern Zambia, the kafue lechwe (*Kobus leche rafuiensis*) from southern

Zambia, and the red lechwe (*Kobus leche leche*), which ranges from southern Zaire through Angola, Namibia, Botswana and Zambia.

The lechwe uses water to escape predators, and it feeds on many of the water-loving plants. When spied on dry land, a lechwe has an awkward gait while running and, therefore, is not particularly fleet of foot. This is probably due to its long, narrow hooves, which are ably adapted for running through marshy wetlands. Lechwes tend to be active before sunrise and in the early morning, and then again in the late afternoon toward sunset. Lechwes are preyed on by lions and leopards on occasion, and in swampy areas they can be eaten by crocodiles.

The lechwe is fairly sociable in its habits and is found in small herds of 15 to 20, even more on occasion when these herds can merge into larger groups. Like many other antelope species, the males are often found in their own bachelor groups.

The rut season occurs in October, but only a few males defend territories and mate. Maintaining a territory against

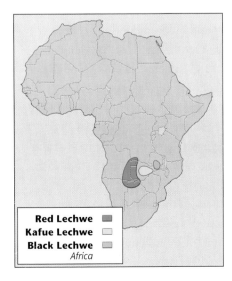

Red Lechwe
Kafue Lechwe
Black Lechwe
Africa

The kafue lechwe (Kobus leche rafuiensis) is found in southern Zambia. All three subspecies of lechwe have a coat of long hair that ranges in color from bright chestnut to black, with white underparts, depending upon the subspecies.

other males involves posturing, threats and chasing rivals, with a fight breaking out occasionally. Females, however, move freely within the mating ground or territory and mate with the dominant male.

Lechwes eat almost entirely semiaquatic grass and are specialized grazers; however, they will nibble on some leaves and twigs. The young may be born at any time during the year, but the predominant time for the calf season is between mid-July and mid-August. After a gestation period of seven to eight months, the females give birth and then stay

The red lechwe (Kobus leche leche) ranges from southern Zaire through Angola, Namibia, Botswana and Zambia. It is the only subspecies that still occurs in more than one population.

see as many as 5,000 lechwes killed in a three-day period. A significant proportion of females were killed, and the population dwindled so rapidly that eventually this practice was banned.

Of the three different types of lechwe, all have succumbed to essentially the same pressures: severe hunting, intrusion by people, and the subsequent destruction of lechwe habitat. The black lechwe in Zambia ranges in a restricted environment: there is only a single population of less than 40,000 individuals (and declining). This alone makes its wild status extremely vulnerable. There is a small captive population —just one effort to breed this animal—now underway in Spain. However, the success of that group is not known at the present time (there are reportedly 10 or 15 individuals).

The kafue lechwe is also restricted to one population, this one in Zambia. They number only 25,000 or so, and their group is also declining. The third subspecies, the red lechwe, is the only one that occurs in more than one population over its wild range, but it too is declining, not increasing. The red lechwe currently numbers an estimated 37,000. The total known captive population of kafue and red lechwe combined does not exceed 100 individuals at the present time. Despite these low numbers, the red lechwe appears to do reasonably well in a captive breeding environment. If these programs can be sustained, the lechwe may yet survive the pressures of the late twentieth century.

—*Warren D. Thomas*
See also Antelopes.

hidden with their young for the first two or three weeks. The females leave their young, go out and forage, and then come back and suckle in the early morning and late afternoon. It is at this time that calf mortality is at its highest,

when they are unprotected and found by predators.

One of the most flagrant causes of this species' decline is hunting. Up until 1957 (when a law was passed to discontinue the practice) there was an event known as a lechwe drive or chilas, held at the time of high flooding in the Kafue flats of Zambia. At these times, literally thousands of African hunters gathered with their spears and dogs and guns, and hunted the lechwe. It was not uncommon to

LEKA KEPPE
(Sarotherodon lohbergeri)

Class: Osteichthyes
Order: Perciformes
Family: Cichlidae

Description:
Length: 4.7 in (12 cm)
Reproduction: Egg layer
Habitat: Inshore areas and river pools
Range: Lake Barombi-Mbo and Kumba River, Cameroon

Escapee from the Lake

As with several other threatened and endangered cichlids, the crater lake called Barombi-Mbo in the African nation of Cameroon is the sole residence of the cichlid species called the leka keppe; a few individuals were located in a small outlet stream called the Kumba River. The leka keppe is the only Lake Barombi-Mbo cichlid to escape to the Kumba River. This escape required a hair-raising ride across a lake outlet sill, over a high waterfall and into a gorge, then through some rapids to the river.

Lake Barombi-Mbo, a small and relatively infertile but deep freshwater lake, is about 1.5 miles (2.4 kilometers) in diameter, yet is the primary source of food for the village of Barombi on its northern shore. Fishermen defend their right to fish the lake but, to the detriment of the leka keppe, this species and a total of ten other threatened and endangered cichlid fishes are sought by the village inhabitants as food.

The leka keppe can be found only in Lake Barombi-Mbo and the adjacent river and therefore is vulnerable to any of a number of natural or artificial catastrophes or to prolonged over-fishing. However, the insistence of the Barombi villagers to maintain exclusive fishing rights on the lake may work to the advantage of the leka keppe and other cichlids. The townspeople have been able to maintain a functional balance between their food needs and the natural supply of fish for many decades, and have resisted over-fishing. If harmful non-native fishes like the destructive Nile perch (*Lates niloticus*) can be kept away from the lake, conservationists look to continue the prohibition on fishing by other villages and educate the people of Barombi as to the delicate balance of the ecosystem that they currently depend upon.

Similar Features

Despite their endless subtle physical and behavioral variations, cichlids exhibit many similar physical characteristics. All cichlids display a fairly flattened and more round appearance (like a plate on edge) than other streamlined and torpedo-like fishes. Many have broad and almost parrot-like mouth parts that are used to scrape algae from surfaces or crush hard food items. In addition to teeth on the jaws, these fishes have numerous teeth on a plate-like bone at the base of the mouth and throat to hold and process food items; these teeth within the throat are called pharyngeal teeth.

A distinctive characteristic of the leka keppe as well as all other cichlids is the lengthy, spiny, protective dorsal fin on the back that can extend from just behind the head all the way to the tail section of the body; often, the dorsal fin segment near the head. A dark blotch in the dorsal fin segment near the tail of many cichlids is called a tilapia mark. However, the leka keppe's dorsal fin only rarely carries a tilapia mark.

This fish is silvery gray as an adult, with a prominent stripe from just behind the gill covers to just slightly forward of the base of the tail fin. A dusky spot is positioned slightly closer to the tail fin and follows the same line as the stripe. The lower jaw and face also have dark markings. The fins follow the coloration of the body with the exception of the anal fin just behind the anus and genitals, which shows a hint of red and orange. The body is well scaled; some portions of the head, chin, and throat are scaleless. The eyes are well developed for visual feeding, and teeth in the jaws are somewhat flexible to prevent breakage.

The leka keppe probably

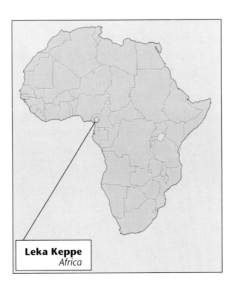

Leka Keppe
Africa

engages in an activity called mouth brooding; no observations in the wild have been recorded, but aquarium specimens perform this behavior. After eggs are laid by a female and fertilized by a male, one or both of the parents (depending on the species) picks up the eggs with its mouth and guards them in a chamber in the mouth cavity where oxygenated water is pumped past them. The parent incubates the eggs until they hatch, after a period of one to two weeks. Even after the fish hatch, the free-swimming offspring continue to rely on the parent for protection. At the first sign of a predator or some other threat, the offspring race to the parent where they immediately re-enter their parent's mouth. This protective behavior significantly increases the chances that offspring will survive to adulthood.

The leka keppe feeds on algae, sponge spicules, microscopic plankton in the water column, stems of rooted aquatic plants, and parts of terrestrial plants that fall into the lake.

Some of the other cichlid fishes that are listed in this series include the fissi (*Sarotherodon caroli*), kululu (*Sarotherodon steinbachi*), myakamyaka (*Myaka myaka*), Otjikota tilapia (*Tilapia guinasana*), and unga (*Sarotherodon linnellii*).

Westerners who are accustomed to plentifully stocked lakes all over North America may have a hard time accepting the fact that many species are jeopardized in other parts of the world.
—*William E. Manci*
See also Fissi, Kululu, Myakamyada, Otjikota tilapia, and Unga.

LEMURS

Class: Mammalia
Order: Primates
Family: Cheirogaleidae (Dwarf Lemurs)
          Indriidae (Indri, Woolly Lemurs)
          Lemuridae (True Lemurs, Ruffed Lemurs, and
            Gentle Lemurs)
          Lepilemuridae (Sportive Lemurs)

The island of Madagascar has been separated from the African mainland for more than 35 million years, creating a unique situation where primates have evolved in a different environment from their neighbors, free from many of the predators and competitors present on the mainland. Madagascar is the world's fourth largest island, approximately 1,000 miles (1,600 kilometers) long and 360 miles (580 kilometers) wide. Lemurs evolved in Madagascar and are found nowhere else in the world, except for the tiny Comoros Islands, where two species are found (although they were probably introduced there by humans a few hundreds years ago).

Madagascar's geographic isolation allowed many other species to develop separately from their relatives on the mainland. Madagascar is like a global nursery: it has five percent of the world's total species. Seventy-five percent of the plant and animal species now on Madagascar are found nowhere else. More than 1,000 species of orchids, and one half of the globe's chameleon species, are found here. This diversity is amazing considering that this island is just half the size of Alaska.

Madagascar is ecologically unique and contains several different habitat types. The high central plateau has been virtually deforested, but in the coastal lowlands there are many distinct vegetational types remaining, ranging from tropical rain forests in the east to dry tropical forest in the west. There are even dry, arid zones in the south and southwest of the island.

New growth is continually burned to encourage the sprouting of grass for cattle grazing. All of this spells disaster for animals that depend on Madagascar's lush forests for survival.

Madagascar has two national parks and 34 nature reserves that are supposed to protect forests. The World Wildlife Fund paid off $3 million in debt on behalf of that country in exchange for the teaching of ecology in Malagasy schools.

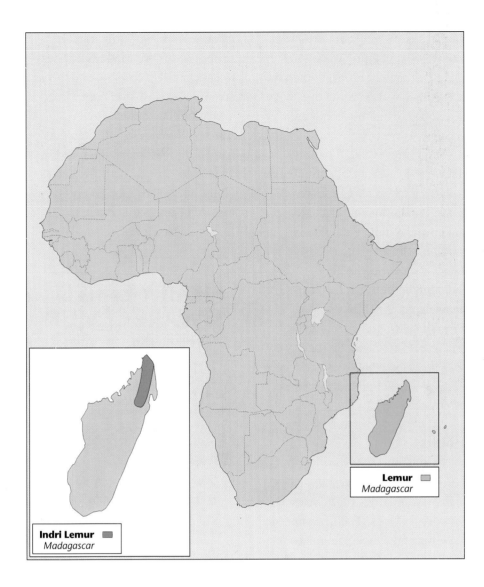

Indri Lemur ▨
Madagascar

Lemur ▨
Madagascar

the habitat of these Malagasy primates. The introduction of cattle and goats, as well as the newer factor of hunting, caused the extinction of at least 14 species. Deforestation has also contributed to their demise. If deforestation on Madagascar continues at its present rate, all forests there could be gone in just 25 years. The human population has more than doubled in 30 years. Since people depend on agriculture for their livelihood, which requires clearing the forests, the competition between humans and lemurs continues. But the Malagasy government is showing signs that it wants to preserve certain areas for wildlife. There is hope for the lemurs and other species.

COQUEREL'S DWARF LEMUR
(Mirza coquereli)

Status: Threatened

Description:
Weight: 10.5 oz (300 g)
Head-body length: 8 in (21 cm)
Tail length: 13 in (33 cm)
Diet: Insects, fruit, flowers, small vertebrates, and the secretions from Homopteran larvae.
Gestation period: 90 days
Longevity: 15 years
Habitat: Dry deciduous forest along rivers and ponds; rain forest in the Sambirano region
Range: West and northwestern Madagascar

Five Species
Dwarf lemurs are found in both the tropical rain forests of eastern

Prosimians
The primate order is divided into two major groups: simians (consisting of the apes and monkeys), and prosimians (namely, the lemurs and a few smaller nocturnal creatures from Africa and Asia). Prosimians are considered more "primitive" than monkeys, with smaller brains relative to their body size. Their faces are not nearly as expressive as simians. These prosimians are mostly nocturnal, relying primarily on their sense of smell (many species have elongated snouts).

The other principal difference between lemurs and monkeys is in their teeth. The front teeth on the lower jaw project forward to form a dental comb, which they use in grooming fur and scraping gum off trees.

Aside from lemurs, there are few other mammalian species on Madagascar. They are intelligent arboreal primates whose soft fur, long tails, distinctive snouts, large bug eyes, and nocturnal activity inspired their name—lemur is Latin for "spirit of the dead."

Lemurs diversified into more than 40 species. Lemurs have retained numerous primitive characteristics, while at the same time developing many features similar to the monkeys and apes of Africa and Asia. When people arrived on the island approximately 2,000 years ago, it changed forever

Because lemurs, including the dwarf lemur, live on the island of Madagascar, they have evolved much differently from the primates of the African mainland. Lemurs are one of very few mammalian species on the island and are part of the primate group known as prosimians.

Madagascar and in the dryer forests to the north, west and southwest. The dwarf lemurs represent just one branch of the lemur family, with five species. Two are considered endangered or threatened.

One of these is Coquerel's dwarf lemur, distinctive because of its long, hairless and membranous ears. The fur on its back is brown or gray-brown, sometimes with rosy or yellowish tinges. On its front, the gray color of the downy

hairs is visible beneath the yellowish, or slightly russet, tips. The tip of the tail is darker than the rest of its fur. Protruding eyes have developed to aid this nocturnal species.

This lemur is found in only three protected areas, distributed in isolated pockets along the west coast. Population numbers are unknown, and there are wildly varying estimates of its density. It eats a wide variety of food, including insects, spiders, frogs, chameleons, small birds, fruit, flowers, buds, gums from trees, and insect secretions. In the dry season, cashew nut trees and cashew fruits are important sources of protein.

Habits

This lemur spends the day in nests made from leaves, branches, and vines. It builds these nests in the forks of trees. The nests appear to be occupied by single males or by females with offspring. In some areas, adults defend the region close to their home range. Males tend to range farther than females into neighboring areas. Mother dwarf lemurs carry their infants around in their mouths, like large cats do. But for the first few weeks, infants remain in the nests.

In one area of Madagascar (Ambanja), these dwarf lemurs have been seen to nest in "villages"—that is, several nests are clustered together in a small area. During the first part of the night, these lemurs forage and groom. In the second half of the night, they engage in social activities such as play, mutual grooming, and vocalizing.

It is certain that habitat destruction is a major threat to this

creature's future. Farm animals reared in western Madagascar need to have grass to feed on, and this is acquired by slash and burn agricultural techniques that seriously jeopardize this lemur's habitat. It does, however, breed well in captivity. There are some 62 individuals in zoos and primate research centers that range from San Francisco to Paris.

HAIRY-EARED DWARF LEMUR
(Allocebus trichotis)

Status: Endangered

Description:

Weight: 2.6-3 oz (75-80 g)
Head-body length: 5.5 in (14 cm)
Tail length: 6.5 in (16.5 cm)
Diet: Unknown, possibly nectar, insects, fruit
Gestation period: Unknown
Longevity: Unknown
Habitat: Lowland rain forest
Range: Northeastern Madagascar

Rare Primate

Imagine a primate that could fit in the palm of your hand. A dwarf lemur could, and yet this tiny mammal—no bigger than a large mouse—belongs to the same scientific order as monkeys, chimpanzees, gorillas, and human beings. Its tail is longer than its entire body.

This lemur is extremely rare, both in the wild and in captivity, and its population numbers in the wild are unknown. Until 1989 this lemur was known only from museum collections, and it was thought to be extinct. Experts consider it to be the rarest of all lemurs. Very little can be said about its habits. Local peoples have reported seeing several individuals sleeping in the same tree hole. The locals call this species *tsidyala*, which means "mouse lemur of the big forest."

The fur on the back of the hairy-eared dwarf lemur is pale brown, fading to a white or cream color underneath; its ears are short but have pronounced tufts of long hair, which give this lemur its name. It has a long tongue that suggests that it eats nectar from wild flowers. In captivity this lemur has consumed insects, fruit, and honey.

Creature of the Night

The hairy-eared dwarf lemur is nocturnal, sleeping in tree holes during the day. When it wakes up at dusk, it has been noted to be a keen jumper. There is some evidence that it may hibernate (as some other dwarf lemurs do) during the dry season of June to September. In May lemurs develop a considerable layer of fat all over their body which may serve them well during hibernation.

A recent estimate stated that between the years of 1950 and 1985 some 444 square miles (111,000 hectares) of rain forest had been cleared each year, and most of this has been lowland forest. If felling of trees continues at this rate, extinction seems inevitable for this dwarf lemur.

GENTLE LEMURS
(Hapalemur sp.)

Status: Threatened To Endangered

Description:

Weight: 2.2-5.2 lb (1-2.36 kg)
Head-body length: 11-16 in (28-40 cm)
Tail length: 16 in (40 cm)
Diet: Bamboo and reeds
Gestation period: 135-150 days
Longevity: 12 years in captivity
Habitat: Reed beds
Range: Madagascar

Three Species

Three species of gentle lemur are recognized: the gray gentle lemur (*Hapalemur griseus*), the broad-nosed or greater bamboo (*Hapalemur simus*), and the recently-discovered golden bamboo (*Hapalemur aureus*). All species eat mainly bamboo (the stalk, the leaves, and the shoots) or reeds. They appear to be active both day and night; however, in the midday sun they seclude themselves at the base of bamboo trunks. All have fur ranging in varying shades of gray brown and without distinctive markings. They have powerful sex scent glands, differentiating them from true lemurs. These lemurs prefer to stay in small groups of from two to six individuals, and communicate with a variety of high-pitched calls.

Gray Gentle Lemur

(*Hapalemur griseus alaotrensis*)

There are three subspecies of gray gentle lemurs, including the Alaotran (*H. griseus alaotrensis*) and the Western (*H. griseus occidentalis*). The Alaotran gentle lemur is so named because it ranges only amid the swampy reed beds surrounding Lake Alaotra in eastern Madagascar. There is no bamboo near this lake, so this lemur feeds instead on reeds and on the buds and pith of papyrus.

The gray gentle lemur has a gray-brown coat. It has been reported that it never descends from the trees to the ground, yet it can swim quite well; females with infants clinging to their backs have been seen crossing canals over 50 feet (15 meters) wide.

This lemur is most commonly seen in groups of three and four, but as many as 30 to 40 individuals have been seen together during the wet season (February). Females give birth in January and February, and the infants cling to their mother's back from birth onwards until they become mature.

The annual burning of the reed beds around Lake Alaotra is a serious threat, and so is the local practice of catching the lemurs for food as they flee from the flames. People are steadily taking over this lemur's natural habitat without regard to consequences. The lake is being drained to make way for rice plantations, and the papyrus and reeds are cut for use in making mats and fencing. Sadly, this subspecies is not found in any protected area. While its population size is unknown, it is probably small and diminishing. Only one female exists in captivity at Duke Primate Center, which, at the time of this writing, is attempting to find a male for breeding purposes.

Meanwhile, there are proposals to transform Lake Alaotra into a reserve to protect endangered lemurs and birds.

The Western gentle lemur ranges in rain forest along the west coast of Madagascar near lakes Bemamba and Sambirano. The western gentle lemur occurs only in two small, isolated populations. It is slightly smaller and lighter in color than the other gentle lemurs. It is active during the day, foraging either on the ground or in low-level vegetation, usually in groups of between one and four individuals. Its total population is not known, but since its range is so restricted, it cannot be numerous. There are none in captivity.

Deforestation by fires to make way for livestock in western Madagascar is contributing greatly to the demise of this lemur.

Golden Bamboo Gentle Lemur

(*Hapalemur aureus*)

The golden bamboo lemur of southeastern Madagascar was only discovered in 1987 and, due to habitat destruction, is one of the most threatened primates there. It lives in small patches of rain forest and eats only bamboo. It appears to tolerate the high level of toxins found in bamboo shoots that would be lethal to most mammals.

This lemur has a black face with golden yellow eyebrows, cheeks and throat; and underparts are yellow. On its back are found gray-brown guard hairs over pale orange fur. Both sexes look similar. It lives in small family groups of adult pairs with immature offspring. It is reported to be active at dawn and dusk, and possibly during the night. It is estimated that only 200

to 400 individuals exist total, and only four exist in captivity. Legislation prohibits trade in this lemur, but its natural habitat of bamboo has been so decimated that it is unlikely that it will survive into the twenty-first century.

Greater Bamboo Gentle Lemur

(*Hapalemur simus*)

Also known as the broad-nosed gentle lemur, this species' population is down to only 200 to 400 individuals, probably less numerous than the golden bamboo variety. Slash-and-burn agriculture, and the transformation of bamboo fields into rice paddies are the main threats to this lemur's existence. One pair lives in the Paris Zoo; unfortunately, none of their offspring have survived. Little is known about this lemur, except that its coat is gray to gray-brown, with lighter underparts, and that it is larger and more heavily-built than the other gentle lemurs. An area of 50,000 hectares around Ranomafana has been proposed as a national park. Perhaps a sanctuary will protect this lemur.

INDRI (LEMUR)
(Indri indri)

Status: Endangered

Description:

Weight: 15.5-22 lb (7-10 kg)
Head-body length: 27-48 in (70-120 cm)
Tail length: Rudimentary
Diet: Young leaves, shoots, fruit
Gestation period: 137 days
Longevity: Unknown
Habitat: Coastal rain forest
Range: East coast of Madagascar

Largest Lemur

The indri is the largest member of the lemur family. Its name has an amusing origin, as *indri* means "There it is!" on Madagascar. An early zoologist misunderstood a local guide back in the 1700s, and

The indri is also known as the babakota, which means "the father of man" or "the ancestor."

the name stuck.

The indri has a thick, silky, black-and-white coat with white patches, making the animal difficult to see in the wild. There is, however, a great deal of variation in color between individuals. Occasionally, an indri may be almost totally black (or, more rarely, totally white). The indri's rump is almost always white (possibly useful in courtship displays), and its tail has been reduced to a stump. Overall, its appearance is quite striking, and it is nicknamed the "ape of the prosimians."

This lemur has powerful and flexible hind quarters that enable it to propel itself many feet when jumping from tree to tree. It performs these leaps in vertical fashion, and it is known as a vertical clinger and leaper. This ability to make spectacular leaps is misleading; the animal still spends most of its time relatively quietly, foraging for food or resting.

The indri lives in family groups of up to five members: a monogamous pair consisting of one male, one female, and their offspring. Each group occupies a precise territory of between 35 and 74 acres (14 and 30 hectares). The entire family emits periodic dog-like barks and mournful howling, which intensifies when a territorial boundary is crossed by another animal. These vocalizations seem to be a peaceful substitute for real combat.

Mothers take great care of their infants. They give birth every two or three years, and carry the infant in front for the first four or five months. Thereafter, the infant rides on the mother's back, and sleeps with her for the first year.

Unknown Population

The population size of the indri is not known. It is found in four reserves on Madagascar, but these areas are small and isolated from other blocks of forest. The indri is heavily threatened by destruction of its habitat, which occurs even in areas where it is protected because of lax law enforcement. More funding is needed to provide guards that can patrol these reserves. It is considered taboo among certain local groups to hunt this species, but it is still declining in numbers. This lemur has never been successfully kept in captivity, as it does not survive long when caged. The indri's notably slow rate of reproduction only increases its vulnerability to extinction.

RUFFED LEMURS
(Varecia variegata)

Status: Endangered

Description:
Weight: 7-10 lb (3.3-4.5 kg)
Head-body length: 24 in (61 cm)
Tail length: 24 in (61 cm)
Diet: Fruit, leaves, nectar, and seeds
Gestation period: 90-112 days
Longevity: 19 years in captivity (one specimen)
Habitat: Rain forest
Range: Eastern coastal Madagascar

Moves on All Fours

The ruffed lemur is the largest of the true lemurs, and is certainly one of the most striking. It has thick, beautifully colored fur, a prominent muzzle that is black and pointed, golden eyes, and tufted ears. This lemur moves on all fours, and its legs are longer than its arms.

There are two subspecies: the black and white ruffed lemur (*V. variegata variegata*), and the black and red (*V. variegata rubra*); both are endangered. The black and white variety shows a great deal of variation in its coat color and pattern, but individuals have a basic black-and-white patchwork look. They are found in the rain forests on the eastern side of Madagascar and on Nosy Mangabe Island.

The black and red ruffed lemur is more uniform in color, with deep orange-red fur on its back and sides, and black fur on its legs, tail, head, and underside. This lemur is restricted to the forest of the Masoala Peninsula.

The ruffed lemur lives in the upper parts of the forest in families headed by a male and female pair. There is a noticeably high rate of twin births.

Vocalization

Ruffed lemurs give incredibly loud, raucous calls to coordinate group movements and define territory. There is one report of the female black and white ruffed variety defending her group's territory. Ruffed lemurs appear to be most active early in the morning and at dusk.

The black and white species is found on five reserves, but the black and red is not protected anywhere. There are no estimates of population numbers, but numbers are definitely declining, and the species is threatened both by forest destruction and by hunting. There are, however, more than 700 of these lemurs in captivity, where they breed very well.

SPORTIVE LEMURS
(Lepilemur sp.)

Status: Threatened

Description:

Weight: 17.5-28 oz (500-800 g)
Head-body length: 10-11 in (25-28 cm)
Tail length: 10-12 in (25-30 cm)
Diet: Leaves and foliage, some fruit and bark
Gestation period: 120-150 days
Longevity: 8-9 years in captivity
Habitat: Moist forests or dry, deciduous forests.
Range: North and northwestern Madagascar

A Boxer

The sportive lemur was given its common name because, when it is threatened, it raises its hands like a boxer in order to punch its attacker. Zoologists have divided the sportive lemur into seven species, but they are all similar in coat color and overall anatomy. Sportive lemurs are found in all forested regions of Madagascar, from the evergreen forests of the east coast to the hot, dry forests of the southwest. They are also called "weasel lemurs."

Although it is nocturnal, the sportive lemur does not eat insects, but lives entirely on plant foods. It

eats tough foliage that is nutritionally quite poor, which means it must spend long periods of time in an inactive state, so that it can digest this food and conserve energy. These lemurs are also unique among primates in that they will eat their own feces, much as rabbits do. This is a way of recycling material to maximize all available protein.

During the day, a sportive lemur will sleep in a tree hollow, a forked branch, or in a tangle of vines, thus keeping out of the intense daytime heat. This lemur is medium-sized, slightly smaller than the typical lemur. Its preferred method of moving through the trees is a combination of vertical clinging and leaping; while on the ground it hops like a rabbit.

Solitary Creatures

These animals appear to be especially solitary. The largest groups consist of females with immature offspring. Both males and females defend small territories, although males' territories may overlap to some extent with the territories of two or

The striking ruffed lemur is the largest of the true lemurs. Like most of the wildlife on Madagascar, this primate's population has been reduced by forest destruction and hunting.

three females. Personal space is guarded jealously and, as with gibbons, vocalizing is an important method of warding off strangers. Their method of keeping watch over their space is through visual surveillance—another unique behavior in primates—in which lemurs will stare at one another for long periods of time.

The Nosy Be

The gray-backed sportive lemur (*Lepilemur dorsalis*) is also known as the Nosy Be sportive lemur, or apongy, among the local Malagasy people. It is one of the least widely distributed of the sportive lemurs. Its upperparts are medium to dark brown, and its underparts are of a lighter brown. Its face is dark, and its ears are small. It is found in only two areas: the Sambirano Region of northwestern Madagascar and the island of Nosy Be. Its total population is unknown.

Few studies have been made of this lemur, but it is probably one of the rarest sportive lemurs. Its numbers are being reduced in tandem with forest clearing operations within its range. There are none in captivity, but it is found in two reserves: Mamon Garivo on the mainland and Lokobe on Nosy Be. Neither of these reserves is safe from harm. On Nosy Be, not only are trees cut down to be later turned into canoes, but the land is also cleared for coffee and rice plantations. Captive breeding of these lemurs appears to be difficult.

Northern Sportive Lemur

Another variety, the northern sportive lemur (*Lepilemur septentrionalis*), has gray upper parts, is darkest on the crown, and becomes lighter toward its pale gray rump. There is a darker median stripe along its crown and back, and its underparts are gray. The species is nocturnal, solitary, and leaf-eating. During the day, tree holes or bundles of foliage are used as resting places; these nests are generally 20 to 32 feet (6 to 8 meters) off the ground in live trees. At night, adults roam solo, with only mothers and young associating together.

Malagasy law protects these lemurs from hunting and unauthorized capture, but unfortunately enforcement is almost impossible. Logging, burning, and overgrazing are still permitted on the only reserves for this species. No animals of this group exist in captivity, and captive breeding has never been successful. With no protection, deforestation threatens to eliminate this animal forever.

TRUE LEMURS
(Lemur sp.)

Status: Threatened to Endangered

Description:

Weight: 4.4-8 lb (2.0-3.5 kg)
Head-body length: 15-18 in (38-45 cm)
Tail length: 16.5-25 in (42-64 cm)
Diet: Fruit, flowers, leaves, bark
Gestation period: 127-135 days
Longevity: Up to 18 years
Habitat: Evergreen forests
Range: Madagascar; Nosy Be and Nosy Komba islands; Mayotte in the Comoro Islands

The Size of a Cat

True lemurs are generally cat-sized, with a head and body length averaging 15 inches (38 centimeters) and a tail that is slightly longer than their body length. Their arms are shorter than their legs, and they usually move on all four limbs. All lemurs are arboreal, but their leaping ability varies from species to species, and some species spend some time on the ground. Lemurs are herbivorous, eating mostly fruit and seeds, flowers, leaves, and nectar. True lemurs inhabit all varieties of moist and dry forest, but not open country.

This genus is the most widespread of all the lemurs, consisting of six species—all of which need conservation efforts, mainly due to habitat loss. The ring-tailed lemur (*Lemur catta*) is probably the best known to zoo visitors.

Black Lemur
(Lemur macaco)

The black lemur is found in evergreen forests of north and west Madagascar. It is primarily tree-dwelling, and awake during daylight hours and dusk, although

The black lemur, like most lemurs, is a nocturnal animal that lives in evergreen forests. There are about 250 individuals in captivity.

some groups have been observed to forage at night. It forages in groups of from 4 to 15 animals, and they gather together in the evenings.

The males are uniformly black, while the females are red-chestnut brown, with darker faces and heavy, white ear tufts. Both sexes are born black, but females change color at about six months of age. The differences between the sexes are more marked in this lemur than in any other.

Two Subspecies

There are two subspecies: *L. macaco macaco* and *L. macaco flavifrons*. The former is considered threatened, and the latter is endangered. Population numbers are unknown, but they may be declining due to forest destruction and slash-and-burn agriculture. The black lemur does use plantations and secondary forest, and is dependent on undisturbed forest. This gives it a better chance of adapting to deforestation. However, when it is found raiding crops, it is chased and killed by farmers. Approximately 250 of these lemurs exist in captivity. The St. Louis Zoo and the Duke University Primate Center have the greatest numbers. A reserve on Nosy Komba Island is protected, but more areas should be considered for development.

Brown Lemur
(Lemur fulvus)

There are a number of lemurs classified as brown lemurs. These lemurs have an interesting social system, nicknamed "fission-fusion." This means that their society is much like that of chimps or spider monkeys, where

individuals travel in groups, but those groups constantly change in size and membership.

The population numbers and densities of the collared lemur (*L. fulvus collaris*) are unknown. The males tend to have a black neck, ears, face and crown, while these parts are gray in the female. Both sexes have pale orange cheeks, which are bushy in the male. Upperparts are a darkish brown or gray-brown, with a darker stripe down the spine. Underparts are

Brown lemurs have a very interesting social system where individuals travel in groups that constantly change in size and membership. This is much like the social systems of chimps and spider monkeys.

paler. Habitat destruction is its main threat. It is also widely hunted, and is occasionally trapped to sell to the pet trade. A captive breeding program with 37 individuals is underway at Duke Primate Center.

It is believed that the Mayotte lemur (*L. fulvus mayottensis*) was introduced to the island of Mayotte by people several hundred years ago. Its coloration is variable, and some zoologists have suggested that there is no distinction between this lemur and the brown lemur. Its upper parts and tail are grayish-brown, its cheeks and beard are white, its muzzle and forehead are black, and its underparts are creamy tan.

Forested Land

Mayotte is covered in large trees of secondary forest, which support this animal even though lemurs usually only thrive in older, more established and undisturbed ecosystems. It is thought that deforestation of the island during the 1970s greatly reduced the population, maybe by as much as half, leaving as few as 25,000 lemurs. The building of more roads means there are no longer any remote, inaccessible areas providing sanctuary for these lemurs. There are no protected areas on the island, and without strict enforcement of conservation measures, their future is in serious jeopardy. At present, there are roughly 80 Mayotte lemurs reported in captivity.

Sanford's lemur (*L. fulvus sanfordi*) is another subspecies of the brown lemur that lives in a restricted range in the far north of Madagascar. Its population has not been estimated, but numbers are declining as forests are cleared. The male and female of this species are easily distinguished: the upper parts of the male are brownish gray, while the underparts are paler gray or cream; the crown of its head and its bushy cheeks are brown, while the muzzle is black. The male's ears are tufted with white hairs, and the forehead and areas around and below the eyes are white.

The female has gray, sometimes gray-brown upperparts and paler underparts. She has a black muzzle, with the rest of the head a darkish gray; the female's ears are not tufted ears and she lacks bushy hair on the cheeks. Sanford's lemur has shown itself to be remarkably adaptable, often appearing to prefer life in a forest that has been tampered with by people. However, destruction of its habitat is still a problem, since it has such a tiny range, living only on the northern flanks of Mt. d'Ambre. Poaching is increasing, and bush fires and illegal tree felling are also a problem. Twenty-two animals are held in captivity, all at the Duke Primate Center, which is coordinating a captive breeding program of brown lemurs.

Unstudied Variety

Another brown lemur is the white-collared variety (*L. fulvus albocollaris*), which ranges between the Mananara and Faraony rivers. No studies have been done of this lemur, and therefore population density is uncertain. It is subject to the same threats as other lemurs: habitat destruction and local indifference to its importance. Some recommendations for helping the white-collared lemur are simple, such as posting more signs within the Manombo Special Reserve to indicate the limits of the sole protected area for this lemur. Preserving this primate's habitat is also vital.

There are just three white-collared lemurs in captivity at the Strasbourg Zoo in France.

Crowned Lemur
(*Lemur coronatus*)

The crowned lemur is found in the dry forests of extreme northern Madagascar. Population numbers are unknown, and its small range is declining due to logging, burning, and cattle grazing within the forests. It is usually active during the day (but sometimes at night as well), and has been seen in groups of up to ten individuals. These groups consist of several adults of both sexes. It is most often seen in the trees, but travels frequently on the ground. Males have medium-gray backs, lighter limbs and underparts, with whitish faces, a "V-shaped" orange marking above the forehead, and a black crown. The female underparts and head cap are lighter in color. Some 40 individuals exist in captivity, both in the United States and in Europe, most of whom were born in captivity. Unfortunately, these lemurs are still poached in Montagne d'Ambre National Park, where illegal deforestation also continues, and bush fires threaten the edges of the park. Further study of this lemur's ecology is needed.

Mongoose Lemur
(*Lemur mongoz*)

The mongoose lemur is one of only two lemur species found in both the Comoro Islands and mainland Madagascar. Despite this range, it has a limited distribution. More specific details about its total population are unknown. Its numbers are definitely diminishing because of habitat destruction, and it is only found in one protected area: Amkarafantsika. This reserve is not sufficiently well-managed to protect the lemurs within it. Some zoologists consider this one of the

The crowned lemur is one of the diurnal varieties, although it is also known to be active at night.

rarest of the true lemurs.

This lemur is tree-dwelling, and is active both day and night. It is usually seen in small family groups consisting of one adult pair and their offspring. The males are gray with pale faces, red cheeks and beards. The females have browner backs, dark faces, white cheeks and beards. Groups rarely encounter one another, but when they do there is much threatening display and vocalization. There are about 100 individuals in captivity, but the mongoose lemur has a poor breeding record—one more reason it is steadily becoming the most endangered of the true lemurs.

Red-bellied Lemur
(*Lemur rubriventer*)

The red-bellied lemur lives at medium to high altitudes in the rain forests of Madagascar's east coast. It is mostly diurnal, and exists in small groups. Its upper parts are chestnut brown; it has a dark face, and a black tail. The underparts of the male are dark reddish brown, while those of the female are whitish. Its fur is relatively long and dense, to keep it warm in the high mountains.

No accurate population numbers are available. However, it is clear that logging and agricultural encroachment continue to make the future of this lemur uncertain. At the moment, there are barely one dozen animals in captivity, with Duke Primate Center having the largest collection for breeding and research.

Ring-tailed Lemur
(*Lemur catta*)

The ring-tailed lemur is probably the best known member of this diverse species. There is little difference between the sexes, both having a characteristic and beautiful black-and-white ringed tail. The tail is not only used in visual recognition, but also acts as a kind of fan to waft pheromones for identification by scent.

This lemur is found in the dry forests and bush of south and southwestern Madagascar. It spends more time on the ground than any other lemur, and is diurnal.

The ring-tailed lemur face looks like that of a clown: its eyes, nose and mouth are black, while the rest of its face and its ears are white. Its back fur is soft dove gray, and its limbs and belly are lighter in color, while the extremities are white. It lives in multiple male groups ranging from 3 to 24 members. In ring-tailed lemur society, females are dominant.

Females remain in their birth groups all their lives, forming strong bonds, while males switch groups (sometimes several times) during a single lifetime. Some males live solitarily between groups. The mating season (March and April) is brief, lasting two weeks at most. The female is ready to mate when a slight swelling and flushing of the genitalia occurs. The female is only fertile for one day a year, resulting in all newborns arriving at the same time, 120 to 135 days later.

The infant ring-tailed lemur is about four inches (ten centimeters) in length, and is a miniature replica of its parents. After three days, it is actively scrambling all over its mother's body. Groups of mothers will all groom each others' offspring, while the fathers make themselves scarce. At two and a half years, these lemurs are fully mature, and can expect to live for 15 years.

Stink Fights

Ring-tailed lemurs sometimes engage in territorial encounters, and females do most of the threatening—mainly by running at each other and vocalizing. These lemurs have a complex means of chemical communication. Both males and females mark ranges with genital secretions during aggressive moments. Males also have what are called "stink fights," secreting a strong-smelling chemical from special glands on the chest. The males rub their tails across these glands, then get down on all fours and wave their tails at their opponent. This behavior is most common during the breeding season.

Satellite pictures have been

used to monitor the destruction of Madagascan forest, and these show the declining acreage at an alarming rate. Local farmers set fire to the forest in an effort to promote the growth of grass. Cattle are grazed, and trees are felled for charcoal production. In addition, dogs are used to hunt down ring-tailed lemurs.

Several steps are being taken to reduce the hunting problem. There are several protected areas within its range, and better management plans are under way to protect the

The red-bellied lemur exists in small groups. No accurate population estimates are available for this species, and only about twelve animals are in captivity. Captive breeding of this lemur is not yet strong enough to support the species, should it cease to exist in the wild.

lemurs from extinction. All of these steps, however, are difficult to enforce. Meanwhile, the ring-tailed lemur breeds well in captivity, and there are estimated to be around 1,000 individuals in zoos and other institutions.

WOOLLY LEMUR (AVAHI)
(Avahi laniger)

Status: Threatened

Description:
Weight: 1.5 lb (.68 kg)
Head-body length: 12 in (30.5 cm)
Diet: Leaves and buds
Gestation period: 120-150 days
Longevity: Unknown
Habitat: Rain forest and dry, deciduous forest
Range: Eastern Madagascar

Smallest of the Indrii Family

The woolly lemur is the smallest and only nocturnal member of the *Indrii* family. It has soft, light brown fur, with a white band above the eyes. It lives in family groups of two or three individuals, with a single offspring born in August or September. It sleeps during the day, usually in a forked tree branch. The woolly lemur appears to be monogamous, living in small territories.

There are two subspecies, the Eastern woolly (*A. laniger laniger*) that lives in the moist rain forest, and another (*A. laniger occidentalis*) that prefers the drier forest of Ankarafantsika. Both are threatened.

Like the indris, woolly lemurs are capable of some first-rate vertical leaping. This is even more noteworthy considering the wooly lemurs prefer to do this in the darkness of night!

The Eastern woolly is found in

The ring-tailed lemur looks a little bit like a raccoon—or a clown. It is probably the best known member of the lemur family. Fortunately, this species breeds well in captivity.

six protected areas of Madagascar; the western woolly in only two. There are no population numbers for either group, but they are surely declining for the same reason that other lemurs are being affected: destruction of their limited habitat. There are no woolly lemurs in captivity, and those that have been in captivity were unable to survive. Malagasy law protects all lemurs from capture and hunting, but this law has been virtually unenforceable.

—Sarah Dart, Thaya du Bois, Gregory Lee
See also Aye-aye, Zanzibar Bushbaby, Pygmy Loris, Sifakas.

LEOPARDS

Class: Mammalia
Order: Carnivora
Family: Felidae

The leopard (Panthera pardus) is a large, powerful, spotted cat found in Asia and Africa. The name leopard has also been used to describe two other, quite different cat species, the clouded leopard and the snow leopard. These cats differ in many ways from the ordinary leopard—particularly the clouded leopard, which is such a unique cat that it is the single member of its genus. The clouded leopard and the snow leopard have one important thing in common: populations of both cats are declining.

CLOUDED LEOPARD
(Neofelis nebulosa)

Status: Endangered

Description:

Size: 23.6-39.4 in (61-106 cm)
Shoulder height: 16-20 in (40-50 cm)
Tail length: 21-35 in (53-89 cm)
Weight: 35.3-50.7 lb (16-23 kg)
Gestation period: 86-93 days
Litter size: 1-5, normally 2
Diet: Birds, various mammals
Habitat: Forests in elevations to 8,200 ft (2,500 m)
Range: From Nepal to south-eastern China and the Malay Peninsula and on Taiwan, Hainan, Sumatra, and Borneo

A Distinct Genus

Most authorities consider the clouded leopard a distinct genus with only one species. The coat of this unusual animal is grayish or yellowish. It features large, gray markings that look a bit like clouds, and this is where the animal gets its common name. The markings, which have dark circles around them, cover the forehead, legs, and the base of the tail; the remainder of the tail is banded. Occasionally melanistic, or all black, individuals have been observed. This leopard has a long tail that makes up about half of its body length, and short, stout legs with wide paws. The upper canine teeth are relatively longer than those of any other living cat, enabling it to bite deep into its prey.

The clouded leopard is unusual because it combines characteristics of both the great and the small cats. The structure of its skull and its teeth are like those of the leopard (*panthera pardus*), but it purrs like a small cat and has very similar patterning to that of the marbled cat. The two species are often confused, although the clouded leopard is much bigger. In terms of its behavior, this cat is much more like bigger felids. For example, it does not groom itself nearly as much as small cats do, concentrating primarily on the nose and paws. In addition, its eating habits are those of a big cat: grabbing meat with the incisors and canines, and tearing it off the prey by jerking its head upward.

This cat lives in various kinds of forests, preferring mountainous, wooded regions. It is found in elevations up to 9,800 feet (3,000 meters) above sea level. Many scientists believe it to be arboreal, hunting in trees and springing on grounded prey from overhanging branches. This tactic is unique to the species. Other scientists consider it a more terrestrial animal, using trees only as resting sites where it builds nests by breaking up branches. The species is most active in cool morning or late-afternoon hours.

The clouded leopard is easily tamed and establishes close relationships with its caretakers. Zoos began to have success breeding the animal in captivity in the 1960s. Reproductive habits are known only from captive breeding efforts, where births have occurred from March through August. The gestation period appears to be 86 to 93 days. Young are about five to six ounces (140 to 170 grams) at birth and are fed by the mother until the age of five months. However, they do show interest in solid food after six weeks. By the age of just three months they have been observed killing live chickens using their large teeth.

The clouded leopard has a relatively large range, but wide destruction of habitat has played a major role in the animal's decline, particularly in Thailand and Malaysia. It has also been hunted

The clouded leopard will eat birds as well as various small mammals, from monkeys to cattle, and even porcupines. Its special teeth enable it to strike its prey without using its forelegs, helping it maintain balance should it choose to hunt birds or other arboreal creatures.

for its beautiful skin; international trade for its pelt has only recently been restricted. The clouded leopard is protected over most of its range and is present in numerous parks and reserves.

Fortunately, the clouded leopard is kept in most larger zoos and is known to breed fairly regularly in captivity. Together with strict protection of those individuals in the wild, the strong captive population can probably help sustain this unusual member of the cat family.

SNOW LEOPARD
(Panthera uncia)

Status: Endangered

Description:

Size: 39.5-51 in (100-130 cm)
Shoulder height: 23.5 in (60 cm)
Weight: 55.1-165.4 lb (25-75 kg)
Gestation period: 90-103 days
Litter size: 1-5, usually 2-3
Diet: Various mammals
Habitat: Woodlands, true forest
Range: High altitudes of the Soviet Union, China, Mongolia, India, Nepal, Pakistan, and Afganistan

One of the Big Cats

The snow leopard, also called the irbis or the ounce, shares the genus *Panthera* with other big cats. This genus includes other leopards (except for the unusual clouded leopard, which is the single species of its genus), tigers, jaguars and lions. The nomenclature of cats is almost always somewhat of a problem for scientists, and the use of the term Panthera is no exception. Some scientists prefer to place large cats in the generic genus Leo, while others simply do not consider these animals to be distinct from the genus Felis, which includes most of the smaller cats.

There are two ways in which members of the *Panthera* genus differ from those of the genus *Felis.* The larger cats have an

662

elastic ligament in the throat near the base of the tongue that allows them to roar but limits purring to times of exhaling. While the snow leopard possesses this ligament, it apparently does not roar. Smaller cats in general do not roar, although certain species, such as the black-footed cat (*Felis nigripes*), produce a full roar that is not as fierce as the lion or tiger, simply because of the size difference between the animals. The purr of a small cat is not interrupted when it exhales; rather it is capable of purring when both inhaling and exhaling. The other difference between *Panthera* and *Felis* is that members of *Panthera* have hair that extends to the front edge of the nose.

The snow leopard shares similar characteristics with its relative, the ordinary leopard (*Panthera pardus*), but it is different in many ways as well. For example, the shape of the skull is quite distinct. The snow leopard's eyes are also set in a high position on the head, allowing it to peer over rocks and remain virtually unseen as it hunts for prey. The color pattern of this cat is quite different also, as is its thick, long-haired coat—undoubtedly an adaptation for living in tremendously cold climates.

The ground color of the snow leopard varies from a pale gray to a creamy smoke-gray, and the upperparts are whitish. The coat is exceptionally thick and long. It is a medium-sized feline with a relatively small head.

This beautiful cat lives in the high-altitude regions of Central Asia, from eastern Turkestan to Kashmir and Sikkim in India, from Altai and Pamir mountains of China to southeast Tibet. There is some question regarding the species' former range, as it may have occurred from northern Iran and Turkestan east and northward to more of China, Mongolia, and more of the Soviet Union. Normally the snow leopard prefers to live and hunt in regions at a height of 5,900 feet up to 9,800 feet (1,800 to 3,000 meters). It lives between the tree line and permanent snow, descending into upper valley bottoms in the cold winter months. In the hot season, the snow leopard will move to mountain regions as high as 19,600 feet (5,970 meters).

The cat has been observed using caves and rock crevices for refuge or breeding. It is often active during the day, especially in the early morning and late afternoon hours. This graceful animal has been reported to leap as far as 16.5 yards (15 meters). It takes its prey by either stalking or ambushing it.

One study in Nepal found five to ten snow leopards in a region of approximately 100 square miles. The snow leopards in this group had home ranges of approximately 12 to 40 square miles (40 to 65 square kilometers). These ranges would overlap among individuals, although the animals kept well apart from each other. It is possible that a pair of snow leopards will share a single range. It seems that this cat is primarily solitary, but not unsociable.

Although the snow leopard does not roar, it does possess several vocalizations, including a loud moaning that is associated with mating. Births occur from April to June, both in the wild and in captivity. The young, in litters of from one to five, are born in rocky shelters lined with the mother's fur; the cubs weigh about 16 ounces (450 grams) and eat their first solid food at two months. By three months of age they begin to follow their mother, and are hunting with her by their first winter. Sexual

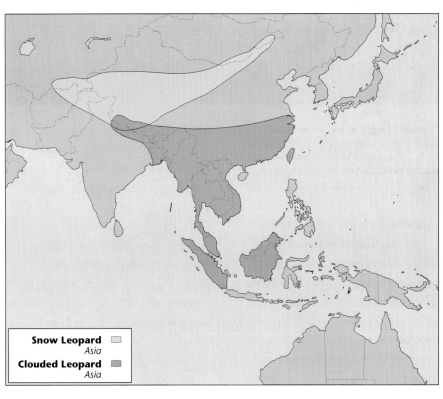

Snow Leopard ☐
Asia
Clouded Leopard ▨
Asia

The head, neck, and lower limbs of the snow leopard display solid spots, while the back, sides, and tail have large rings or rosettes that often enclose smaller spots.

maturity occurs at about two years.

Because of the remoteness of the snow leopard's range, habitat destruction has not played a major role in its decline. However, many of its prey species have been affected by changes to the environment, which has undoubtedly created a problem in some parts of this leopard's range, particularly in Nepal where there is an increased use of alpine lands for pastures. Nonetheless, the primary cause of this animal's decline is that its pelt has long been a favorite of fur trappers. The animal is protected in most of its range, but illegal hunting and trapping continue; as recently as 1985, furs were still being trapped and hunted for commerce. In China, the snow leopard continues to be hunted and is sold on the open market.

Another cause of decline is that the animal is considered a pest because it occasionally preys on livestock.

There are an estimated 3,000 to 10,000 snow leopards remaining in the wild, and another 400 in captivity. Fortunately, captive specimens breed regularly. The creation of reserves could conceivably ensure the future of the species in the wild.

—Elizabeth Sirimarco
See also Cats.

ASIATIC LION
(Panthera leo persica)

Status: Endangered

Class: Mammalia
Order: Carnivora
Family: Felidae

Description
Weight: Male, 330-551 lb (150-250 kg); female, 265-400 lbs (120-182 kg)
Head-body length: Male, 67-98 in (170-250 cm); female, 55-69 in (140-175 cm)
Tail length: Male, 35-41 in (90-105 cm); female, 28-39 in (70-100 cm)
Shoulder height: Male, 48 in (123 cm); female, 42 in (107 cm)
Gestation period: 100-119 days
Diet: Various animals
Habitat: Tropical forest
Range: Formerly western Iran to eastern India; today in the Gir Animal Reserve, India and vicinity

Close Relatives
In size and general appearance,

the Asian and African lions are very similar. Coloration can vary widely from a light buff and silvery gray to yellowish red and golden brown. The male has a beautiful mane that apparently protects the neck when lions fight one another. The mane darkens as the cat grows older, sometimes becoming black. The Asiatic lion is said to have a scantier mane than its African counterpart, as well as a thicker coat, a longer tail tassel, and more pronounced belly fringe. Some scientists do not think that these differences warrant full differentiation between the two lions, especially because of the wide variation among African lions in general coloration, length of mane, and other distinctions that occur between the Asian and African races.

Lions prefer grassy plains,

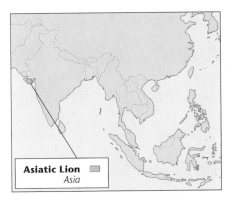

Asiatic Lion
Asia

savannahs, open woodlands, and scrub country; sometimes they are observed in semideserts and forests and have been found at elevations up to 16,500 feet (5,000 meters).

The lion can run for short distances at 30 to 40 miles per hour, but normally walks at about three miles per hour. Although this cat is not a great climber, it can readily enter trees by jumping; leaps of up to 39 feet (12 meters) have been recorded. The lion can be active around-the-clock,

particularly in places where it is safe from human harassment, but it appears to prefer twilight and nighttime. On average, the lion is inactive for more than 20 hours a day. Lions live in groups, called prides, that range in size from 4 to 37 animals.

Normally, the lion hunts by a slow stalk, creeping and freezing, taking cover from the landscape. It then leaps upon its prey. Because the lion only runs for short distances, if the prey is not captured within 150 to 300 feet (50 to 100 meters), it will usually give up. Small prey can be killed by a

A single male lion or a group of males will join a pride of females for an indefinite period of time to defend against the approach of outside males. Eventually, usually within three years, the males are driven off by a new group of males who take over the position within the pride.

blow from the lion's massive paw, while larger victims are seized by the throat and strangled. Sometimes the lion will suffocate an animal by clamping its jaws over the mouth and nostrils. Two lions, or even an entire pride may ambush prey. Because the majority of hunts end in failure, hunting as a group increases the chances of catching prey. A lion will eat anything it can catch, as well as eating carrion.

Social Organization

Prides are generally made up of a group of related females and their young, and are closed to strange females. There is a ranking system among the females of a group, and a female is the leader of the pride, even when males are present. Nonetheless, males always dominate with respect to feeding. Females do almost all of the hunting. There is often competition for food after a kill, and the pride can be seen quarreling among themselves over a catch.

Reproduction

Lions breed throughout the year in India, but in any pride, females appear to give birth at approximately the same time. Cubs follow the mother after about three months and are weaned by six or seven months. At 11 months they will begin to take part in kills, but are probably not capable of surviving on their own until at least 30 months. Sexual maturity occurs at about three or four years, but growth continues until about six.

As young male lions approach maturity, they set out on their own. By contrast, daughters may remain among the pride. Several adult males may group together, or males may remain solitary.

Lions have attained the greatest distribution of any animal except for people and their domestic animals. About 10,000 years ago the lion occurred in most of Africa, Eurasia, North America, and northern South America. It is thought to have disappeared from Europe as a result of the development of dense forests; it probably vanished from the Western Hemisphere as a result of the growing human population that took its toll on prey animals.

Today, the lion has continued to decline as a result of continued human expansion. The lion came into direct competition with human interests, primarily with respect to predation on domestic livestock, but in part as a potential threat to human life. As weapons improved, the threat to the great cat became severe. Up to the mid-nineteenth century, the Asiatic lion was still common from Asia Minor to central India. By 1940 it had been eliminated throughout these regions with the exception of the Gir Forest of western India. Through vigorous conservation efforts, the population there has survived; an estimated 180 cats are said to live there.

The Gir Forest covers about 309,000 acres, having shrunk from 786,000 since the 1880s. Each year, the nearby Gir Thar Desert advances into the forest by about one-half mile. Gir forest is the only large, forested area remaining in the region, and it has been increasingly used and cultivated by people in the twentieth century. Although the area is a sanctuary with legal protection given to animal populations within its boundaries, the rules are difficult to enforce. The fundamental problem

in the Gir forest is that the human population, and with it the livestock population, has grown significantly. As humans and domestic animals use ever-increasing portions of the forest resources, there is less available for the wild animal populations. All wildlife in the area are affected by the abuse and manipulation of the land.

Water seems to be available in the forest for the greater part of the year, and there is probably little competition for it. Unfortunately, natural prey species in the forest are decreasing as humans make greater use of other resources in the region, such as vegetation and natural cover. The lions have been forced to take domestic animals for food. In turn, humans kill the lions as threats to their livelihood. During the dry part of the year there is little cover for the lions, which also hinders their search for food.

Even if human and livestock populations in the area do not continue to grow, the present levels of land degradation will eventually destroy the Gir Forest. Overstocking is the primary source of the problem in the forest, and the answer lies in greatly reducing the numbers of domestic animals in the area. Since the 1970s, the Indian government has begun relocating families and farms that were once in the area. With strict protection of the forest itself, the Asiatic lion population, as well as other endangered species in the protected forest, may stabilize. The survival of the Asiatic lion is intimately linked to the survival of the Gir Forest; without the forest, the lion will disappear forever.

—*Elizabeth Sirimarco*
See also Cats.

667

LIZARDS

Class: Reptilia
Order: Squamata
Suborder: Sauria

Lizards are any of a large group of scaly reptiles that are related to snakes. They are the most abundant of all reptiles and are found throughout the world in tropical and temperate areas. They occur as far north as the Arctic Circle in Europe and as far south as Tierra del Fuego in South America, but are much more common in warmer areas. There are some 3,000 living species of lizards usually classified into 19 families.

There is a great deal of variety among the forms of lizards. Some are long and slender, some are stumpy and short-bodied, and some even have no limbs of any kind, much like a snake. External ear openings and eyelids are two major characteristics which distinguish most kinds of lizards from snakes. The body of these reptiles is covered with layers of scales that are separated from each other by thin, flexible skin. Scales also differ greatly among different species of lizards—some are rough while others are smooth and glossy with an enamel-like texture such as those found on skinks.

The tail is perhaps the most interesting feature of the lizard. It is useful to this reptile as a limb and helps to balance the body. Some species are able to run on their hind legs with the help of their tail. In some forms the tail is prehensile, meaning it is able to grasp or hook on to twigs as the lizard climbs. But a most amazing feature is the ability of some lizards to break off the tail when it so desires. Usually the break occurs at a fracture plane where a lizard has been attacked by a predator, and as the severed tail continues to move, the predator is often distracted and the lizard is able to escape. The lizard will regenerate a new tail, although it is generally shorter than the old one, but that can again be used for escape. Oddly enough, hungry lizards have been known to deliberately break off the tail to eat it.

Most lizards are active during the day, although some in warm regions are nocturnal. Because these reptiles are ectotherms, or cold-blooded animals, they must use their environments to regulate their body temperatures. For example, diurnal species will use heat from the sun to keep warm. They will bask in the sun, then move to a shady spot when they get too hot. To a limited degree, lizards can also raise their body temperature with slight muscle movements. In colder habitats, lizards generally will hibernate during the winter.

COACHELLA VALLEY FRINGE-TOED LIZARD
(Uma inornata)

Status: Threatened

Description:

Length: 5.9-9.4 in (150-240 mm) total length
Clutch size: 1-5 eggs
Diet: Primarily insects, but will take plant material
Habitat: Desert areas with fine, wind-blown sand deposits and vegetation that maintains insect populations
Range: Coachella Valley, Riverside County, California

Sandy Habitats

The Coachella Valley fringe-toed lizard (*Uma inornata*) lives only in sandy habitats on the floor of California's Coachella Valley. This is a particularly harsh environment, and the lizard seems to have a number of adaptations that allow it to survive there. Its critical habitat, or the range that possesses the physical and biological features essential for the conservation of the species, is made up of just 18.63 square miles (48 square kilometers) of private land and 1.08 square miles (2.8 square kilometers) of federally owned land.

Uma inornata was first described in 1895, and there has been much confusion about the species since this time. For many years, it was thought to be synonymous with the Colorado

Desert fringe-toed lizard (*Uma notata*) or the Mojave fringe-toed lizard (*Uma scoparia*). It was not until 1963 that the *Uma inornata* was permanently granted species status, but even as recently as 1980, certain researchers have still maintained that all three lizards were subspecies of *Uma notata*. Today, however, most biologists familiar with the genus consider *Uma inornata* a distinct species.

The Coachella Valley fringe-toed lizard is different from its close relatives in color. It is whitish to pale gray on the back, with patterns that resemble eyes formed by dark markings. The stomach is white, with one or several black dots on each side of the abdomen. There are grayish lines on the throat.

Scales

Scales of all lizards of the Uma genus are smooth and overlap evenly, giving the skin a soft, velvety texture. They are called "fringe-toed" because of a lateral row of long scales on the edge of the toes. These scales help the lizard live in its sandy environment by increasing the foot surface to help it move on and beneath the sand.

Other adaptations include its ability to run across the sand at relatively high speeds and literally dive into it. Once underneath the sand, it may move short distances, called "sand swimming," until it is completely buried. Its smooth scales reduce friction when it moves through the sand. The light, constantly wind-blown sand is an aid to the reptile, as packed sand would be impossible to penetrate. Numerous adaptations help keep sand out of the body openings and limit abrasion. *Uma inornata* can partially close its nostrils to keep

sand out, and if some does get in, it is trapped in a U-shaped nasal passage and blown out by a burst of air. The snout is shovel-shaped and blunt, spreading the sand as the lizard dives, and the upper jaw is longer than the lower, keeping sand out of the mouth. Fringed eyelids with a double seal and a loose flap that covers the ears are two other adaptations that protect this sand-diving lizard.

Sand-swimming protects the Coachella Valley fringe-toed lizard from predators, but it also helps the lizard reach cooler, underground areas in its harsh environment, where ground temperatures can exceed 160 degrees Fahrenheit (71 degrees Celsius). The activity of the *Uma inornata* is limited by temperatures. It is most active when ground surface temperatures are between 97 and 138 degrees Fahrenheit. As the seasons change, the difference in the behavior of the lizard reflects its preference for this specific temperature range. The *Uma inornata* may be active as early as February, but when temperatures are extremely hot from May through September, the

lizard is seldom active during midday, when it will spend time underground where temperatures are cooler.

Mating season begins in late April and extends to mid-August. The location and timing of egg-laying in the wild is not known, but more than one clutch may be laid in one year. Hatchlings have been observed from late August through the fall.

Decline

The primary reason for the decline in *Uma inornata* populations has been loss of habitat from urban and agricultural development and off-road vehicles. Until recently, this lizard existed with little interference from humans. Since the 1940s, however, the Coachella Valley has undergone dramatic development. In 1940, some 12,000 people lived in the area; by 1980 the permanent and

The Coachella Valley fringe-toed lizard has a number of adaptations that help it to survive in a harsh desert environment where ground temperatures are known to reach 160 degrees Fahrenheit (71 degrees Celsius).

part-time populations were estimated at more than 220,000. As the human population continues to grow, this lizard's habitat will become smaller and smaller.

In addition, humans have planted certain plants to act as wind breaks. Unfortunately, *Uma inornata* needs the wind to help the sand stay soft enough to burrow in. As wind breaks are built, more and more of its habitat becomes uninhabitable. Major highways in the area also may act as barriers between distinct populations of the Coachella Valley fringe-toed lizard, and at some point in time this may lead to weakened gene pools due to isolation of localized populations.

Advisory Committee

Serious efforts to help *Uma inornata* began in 1977 with a meeting of an advisory committee composed of scientists and resource managers dedicated to saving the species from extinction. This committee provided essential data which contributed to the lizard's official (U.S. Fish and Wildlife Service) threatened status. Since that time, efforts have been made to acquire a reserve that will provide critical habitat for *Uma inornata*. The Nature Conservancy has worked to acquire the private lands for such a reserve, and has negotiated to purchase 1,900 acres (769 hectares) at a cost of about $2 million. More acreage may be added at a later date. Management plans will be established to ensure the continued survival of the species. Because so many groups and individuals are dedicated to the conservation of the Coachella Valley fringe-toed lizard, its outlook for the future is excellent.

ISLAND NIGHT LIZARD
(Xantusia riveriana)

Status: Threatened

Description:

Length: 2.5-4.3 in (65-109 mm) snout-vent length
Clutch size: Mean of 3.76
Diet: Primarily insects, but will take plant material
Habitat: Areas in which rocks, dense vegetation, or other objects provide cover
Range: Channel Islands off the coast of California

Extinct on the Mainland

The island night lizard is a moderate-sized lizard, although it is considered large for its genus. It is quite different from its relatives that inhabit California's mainland. Fossils indicate that this particular species was extinct on the mainland as long as one million years ago, leaving relic populations on three of the Channel islands: San Clemente, San Nicholas, and Santa Barbara. Little obvious variation exists between the inhabitants of each island. There are slight differences in the scales, color, pattern, body size, and clutch size between populations.

Like other members of the family *Xantusiidae*, the island night lizard is very secretive and requires shelter. Rocks, cactus, or dense undergrowth are optimal, but these lizards will also hide beneath boards or debris if available. Cover protects lizards from predators and also allows them to regulate their body temperature. This species requires lower temperatures than most lizards and cannot tolerate temperatures much in excess of 100 degrees Fahrenheit (38 degrees Celsius). These lizards must be able to retreat from extreme surface temperatures on hot days, and the best cover for this purpose is provided by thick vegetation.

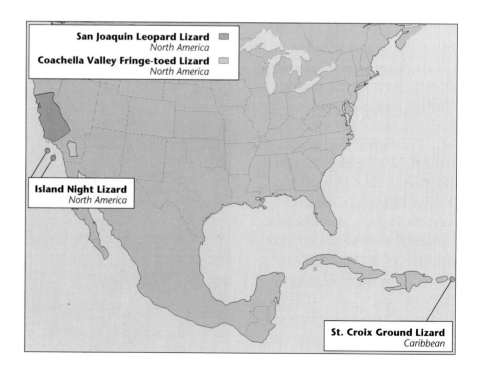

San Joaquin Leopard Lizard
North America

Coachella Valley Fringe-toed Lizard
North America

Island Night Lizard
North America

St. Croix Ground Lizard
Caribbean

The island night lizard begins mating in March, and gestation proceeds through the summer with the young appearing in September. Only about half of the adult female population is reproductively active in a given year. The mean brood size is 3.76, which leaves a potential of 1.88 young produced per female in the entire population. This is low when compared to other lizards. In addition, the species does not reach sexual maturity until the third or fourth year of life, which is quite late for a lizard of this size. The result is a low reproductive capacity. For this reason the island night lizard cannot withstand high rates of predation.

A variety of mammals and birds may prey on this lizard. Among these are the common raven, the burrowing owl, foxes, feral cats, and possibly rats. The lizard itself is omnivourous, feeding on a wide variety of insects and plant material. As captives, these lizards will cannibalize other small lizards, including other species of the family *Xantusidae*, indicating that in the wild they may cannibalize juveniles of their own species. The fact that they feed on a variety of food items may help them to occupy a wide variety of habitats.

Special Habitat

The Channel Islands provide a special habitat for this lizard. Predator densities are relatively low, and climactic conditions are relatively stable. This may be the reason this reptile has survived on the islands, and not on the mainland. The island night lizard has evolved a low reproductive potential and a long life span, but this pattern is sensitive to any

The island night lizard requires lower temperatures than most lizards. Its habitat must supply cover in the form of rocks or vegetation so the lizard may retreat from the sun on hot days.

disturbances caused by habitat destruction or the introduction of non-native species to the environment.

The largest population of the island night lizard is located in maritime desert scrub on the northwest coast of San Clemente island. No data exists on the status of the island night lizard prior to ranching activities and the introduction of animals such as feral cats on San Clemente island. However, it is possible to deduce the effects of such things on the lizard. Grazing and soil erosion have replaced shrub and vegetation with grassland, cactus, and bare ground, reducing the protective cover needed by the lizards. Rocky areas are now exposed to direct sun with the loss of original vegetation.

The effect of cats on the island night lizard population is uncertain. Although cats frequently feed on lizards, the lizard population does not appear to be adversely affected by cat predation in areas of optimal habitat, where lizards can still find cover. Cats also may not be sufficiently numerous to have a severe impact on the lizard.

Military operations on San Clemente have had a small effect on the lizards because of development in parts of the lizards' range. This affects only a small area, however. Goats and sheep released on San Nicholas island in the nineteenth century caused great habitat modification by grazing. Although the animals were removed after World War II, the habitat has not fully recovered.

Because the largest populations of the lizard occur in specific sites on San Clemente, the island has been designated as a critical habitat. Smaller areas on San Nicholas and Santa Barbara have also been cited as essential to the lizard's survival. The primary objective of this species' recovery plan is to restore and protect habitat that can support the populations. Additional information about the natural history and ecology of the lizard must be obtained to facilitate a recovery plan. The removal of exotic animals and plants, control of unnatural erosion, and revegetation with indigenous plants are all important goals. Once threats to the lizard have been removed, they must be properly managed to make sure the threat of extinction is gone.

SAN JOAQUIN LEOPARD LIZARD
(Gambelia silus)

Status: Endangered

Description:

Length: 9-15 in (23-38 cm)
Clutch Size: Unknown
Diet: Primarily insects
Habitat: Sparsely vegetated plains, alkali flats, grasslands, low foothills, canyon floors, large washes.
Range: Scattered localities in San Joaquin Valley, California

Leopard Lizards

The San Joaquin leopard lizard resembles the common leopard lizard, but has a blunter snout, which is why it is also known as the blunt-nosed leopard lizard. It has a spotted throat rather than the streaked throat typical of its relative. It has a slender, large body with a rounded tail and is generally gray or brown in color. The markings of the lizard consist of a series of light crossbars and dark spots. A female carrying eggs may have slightly different coloration or patterns on the sides of its body. Like other leopard lizards, the San Joaquin lizard is swift and agile, moving from one bush to another rather quickly in search of insects. It will also prey upon smaller lizards. In order to catch them, it will lie quietly in dark areas and then ambush them. The San Joaquin leopard lizard will initially stop dead in its tracks when danger approaches, then run for cover if threatened.

This lizard can be found in various places in California's San Joaquin Valley, including the Sierran foothills, eastern parts of the Coast Range foothills, and on the Carrizo Plain. It prefers areas with scattered bushes or low vegetation.

Development continues at a fast pace in California, and the environment is changing rapidly. This has left wildlife like the San Joaquin leopard lizard in a vulnerable position.

The primary cause for decline of this species is habitat destruction resulting from a great amount of development throughout its relatively small range. Agriculture and water control measures have also contributed to the vulnerability of this reptile. There is little hope for the survival of the natural flora and fauna of this arid region unless reserves are established.

The San Joaquin leopard lizard is protected by state law in California, prohibiting the capture, possession or sale of the species. The state is trying to provide protection for remnants of the habitat which exists on public lands and to preserve critical habitat on private lands through acquisition or agreements with owners. The species is also fully protected by the United States Endangered Species Act.

ST. CROIX GROUND LIZARD
(Ameiva polops)

Status: Endangered

Description:

Length: 1.3-3 in (3.5-8 cm)
Clutch size: Unknown
Diet: Small crustaceans, insects
Habitat: Beach areas and upland forests
Range: St. Croix, U.S. Virgin Islands; offshore islands and cays

Island Lizard

The St. Croix ground lizard is a small species of the genus *Ameiva.*

It has a light brown stripe in the middle of its back continuing down the tail, bordered by wide, dark brown or black stripes; below these are narrow parallel stripes of brown, black, and white. The tail has alternating rings of blue and black. The top of the head is a uniform brown. The chin, throat, chest, sides of the snout, and undersides of the forelegs are deep pinkish-red. The belly is light gray with lateral bluish markings.

The St. Croix ground lizard appears to prefer beach areas and upland forests, with the predominant plant species being the *Hippomane*, *Mancinella*, *Tabebuia heterophylla*, and *Exostema caribaeum*. Optimal sites appear to be those with both exposed and canopied areas, leaf or tidal debris, loose substrate, and crab burrows. Smaller lizards appear to exist in more exposed habitat, with the larger ones preferring canopied sites.

This species will actively prowl, root, and dig for prey. They appear to eat amphipods, a group of small crustaceans that are abundant along the beach. These lizards have also been observed taking small white moths from under forest litter and are known to forage out of sight beneath litter, or in shallow holes that they have dug. Foraging for food was the major activity observed in the St. Croix ground lizards, with heat regulation their next most frequent behavior.

Before land development in the Virgin Islands, this species was probably restricted to St. Croix and its offshore islands and cays. Early in the twentieth century, the St. Croix ground lizard was thought to be extinct, although it was reported to exist as late as the 1920s. By

1937, however, it was found in St. Croix's Christiansted Harbor and on Green and Protestant Cays, which are situated off of the north shore of St. Croix. In 1967, it was estimated that 200 lizards lived on Protestant Cay and approximately 300 on Green Cay; since 1968, the species has not been recorded on St. Croix. As of 1983, the two cays are the only sites where the species is known to exist. Population estimates in the 1980s suggested that there were between 360 and 43,000 individuals on Green Cay; the population on Protestant Cay is about 50 individuals. Although figures indicate an increase in population, biologists believe it is probably the result of improved census-taking rather than an actual increase in population. It appears, however, that the two cay populations are stable and will remain so if no significant changes occur at either site.

The decline of the species may correlate with the arrival of the small Indian mongoose (*Herpestes auropunctatus*) in 1884. The mongoose is responsible for reducing the numbers of various terrestrial animals on the Virgin Islands. Extensive real estate development of coastal areas may have also contributed to the decline of the ground lizard. The St. Croix ground lizard has been listed as an endangered species since 1977. A refuge on Green Cay was purchased that year that provides for the protection of 14 of the 18 acres of critical habitat. The remaining four acres on Protestant Cay are leased for private use. With the continued management of the Green Cay refuge, the St. Croix ground lizard has a good chance at recovery.

—Elizabeth Sirimarco

SPOTTED LOACH
(Lepidocephalichthys jonklaasi)

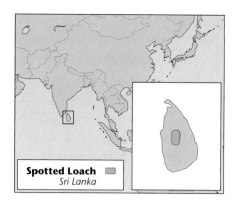

Spotted Loach
Sri Lanka

Class: Osteichthyes
Order: Cypriniformes
Family: Cobitidae

Description:
   Length: Unknown
   Reproduction: Egg layer
   Habitat: Streams and ponds.
   Range: Sri Lanka

At Home Out of Water

The spotted loach is a most unusual fish and is highly adaptable to changing environmental conditions. As a member of the genus *Lepidocephalichthys*, the spotted loach is capable of a very uncommon behavior. During times of drought, this species can survive in streambeds or basins that hold no water. As the spotted loach rests quietly in moist sand or mud, it can survive by swallowing air and forcing it through its digestive tract. Its intestine is highly veined with small blood vessels, much like a lung, and the spotted loach uses its intestine to absorb life-sustaining oxygen from the air it holds. After the oxygen is used up and replaced with the by-product, carbon dioxide, the gas is expelled and more air is swallowed. This process can continue for long periods of time, until the drought period has passed.

Despite its extremely adaptable nature, the spotted loach is under severe threat of extinction within its home range of Sri Lanka. Sedimentation caused by deforestation and pollution are challenges that this species cannot overcome. Sedimentation is particularly devastating because of its fouling of feeding and breeding sites and other profound changes that it imparts to otherwise pristine aquatic environments.
—*William E. Manci*

LOGPERCHES

Class: Osteichthyes
Order: Perciformes
Family: Percidae

Despite a difference in the common name, logperches are classified in the same genus Percina as several of the darters and should be included in this larger group. Logperches and darters share many common physical and behavioral "darter" characteristics. Only three genera are used to name all darters and logperches: Ammocrypta, Etheostoma, and Percina. The genus Etheostoma encompasses most of these brightly colored fishes. This highly diverse group of freshwater fishes contains a total of about 150 species, of which 24 darter species are considered vulnerable or endangered, and two logperches are so considered. Their diversity in North America is second only to the family Cyprinidae, a group that includes minnows and chubs. Dispersed across the Mississippi River system and rivers of the Great Lakes, Hudson Bay, Atlantic Coast, Gulf of Mexico, and rare occurrences on the Pacific Coast of Mexico, darters and logperches have achieved a continental distribution.

As a group, darters and logperches are distinctive in shape and size and are small relative to more commonly known fishes such as trout or bass; they reach a maximum total length of only two to eight inches. Their long, torpedo-like, slender bodies include two prominent dorsal fins on their backs as well as pronounced pectoral fins on their sides for steering and maneuvering. The first, or spiny, dorsal fin contains spines for protection against predators. The second, or soft, dorsal fin has no spines. Darters and logperches are generally brightly colored and display a wide variety of coloration patterns.

In spite of their small size, darters and logperches are closely related to some of North America's most popular game fish: the yellow perch, sauger, and walleye. They all are in the family *Percidae*. Unlike their relatives, the darters and logperches have small teeth and no gas bladder for buoyancy, or they have a gas bladder that is undersized relative to their bodies. This trait creates a tendency to sink and allows them to more effectively maintain their position within a stream.

The preferred environments of these fishes are the fast-moving, shallow, "rapids" areas of streams. This preference may have several advantages over the deeper pool areas. Unlike darters and logperches, larger fish (potential predators) tend to congregate in stream pools. Clearly, predator-free areas offer the best chance for survival. Additionally, stream riffles generally hold abundant supplies of food organisms, such as insects, that are poorly utilized by other fish until these organisms move downstream to pool areas.

Despite the advantages of river life, darters and logperches comprise the largest group of vulnerable and endangered fishes in the world. Darters and logperches cannot compete with the massive destructive power of reservoirs and flood-control projects, pollution, stream bank and watershed deforestation which cause siltation, and other activities that lead to the death of fish populations. All darters and logperches currently listed as vulnerable or endangered can attribute their status to these threats. Dam and reservoir construction is doubly damaging to

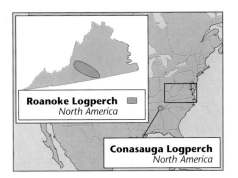

darter and logperch populations because they flood shallow river rapids (generally their preferred habitat) and prevent the downstream movement of populations to more suitable river areas after dam construction is complete. Removal of water from streams for urban and agricultural use also is blamed as a main cause for the decline of many of these species.

CONASAUGA LOGPERCH
(Percina jenkinsi)

Status: Endangered

Description:

Length: 5.9 in (15 cm)
Reproduction: Egg layer
Habitat: Stream riffles and pools over sand and gravel
Range: Upper Conasauga River, Tennessee and Georgia

Fish of the South

Restricted to an 11-mile (16-kilometer) stretch of the Conasauga River in southern Tennessee and northern Georgia, the Conasauga logperch is considered highly endangered. A member of the same genus as many of the darters, the

Conasauga logperch relies on high-quality flowing water and silt-free river bottom for its continued existence. The primary threats to the fish are agricultural and urban development in the Conasauga basin and the associated pollution. State and federal officials fear that a single event such as a chemical spill could wipe out all remaining individuals of the species. Additionally, a dam construction project slated for the lower Conasauga River could affect the Conasauga logperch and other upstream fishes. Often, after dam construction and reservoir develop-ment is complete, fishes such as common carp (*Cyprinus carpio*) tend to dominate the reservoir fishery. If destructive fishes like the common carp move upstream to the upper Conasauga River, the Conasauga logperch could suffer as a result of alteration of habitat caused by the common carp.

Fortunately, the U. S. Fish and Wildlife Service has designated the 11-mile stretch of the Conasauga River that is currently occupied by the Conasauga logperch as habitat that is critical to its survival. Hopefully this status, plus protection afforded by the Chattahoochee and Cherokee National Forests that surround upper sections of the Conasauga River, will be adequate until some individuals can be relocated to other suitable locations.

The Conasauga logperch is a large darter measuring almost six inches (15 centimeters) in total length. Despite its length, this fish is not as stout and robust as other darters and is, instead, very long and slender. This difference is accented by a very pointed, almost needle-like snout. Its coloration pattern is distinct, with alternating dark vertical bars and spots on the sides over a yellow background. The fins are primarily clear but are lightly spotted in patterns that suggest bands.

Not much is known about this fish's breeding and feeding habits, but based on the condition of eggs in collected specimens, the Conasauga logperch most likely spawns in the spring in gravel stream riffles and shallow rapids. Direct observations indicate that this species favors aquatic invertebrates such as insects as its principal foods. The Conasauga logperch uses its pointed snout to overturn stones as it seeks out its hidden prey.

ROANOKE LOGPERCH
(Percina rex)

Status: Endangered

Description:

Length: 5 in (13 cm)
Reproduction: Egg layer
Habitat: Riffles in moderate to large streams
Range: Upper Roanoke River basin, Virginia

A Land of Plenty

A resident of the most biologically diverse river system on the eastern seaboard of the United States, the Roanoke logperch claims the Roanoke River basin in southern Virginia as its home. This fish, along with several other species, is found only in the

The Roanoke logperch lives in the Upper Roanoke River basin of Virginia, a biologically diverse river system that is home to a number of other species.

Roanoke River system. Sharing all or part of the river with nearly 200 other fishes, it most often lives in close association with the orangefin madtom, a small catfish. Before cities like Roanoke and Salem began to spring up along the river, the Roanoke logperch could be found from its headwaters all the way to Albemarle Sound in North Carolina, where the river empties into the Atlantic Ocean. But people's insistence on dominating and over-exploiting natural systems has slowly put a stranglehold on the river's finite resources and forced this fish farther and farther upstream. Urbanization and the resulting deforestation have released tons of silt into the river; sewage has robbed the water of oxygen and choked the river with vegetation; toxic chemicals have rendered any remaining marginal habitat uninhabitable; and stream channeling to minimize flooding has turned sections of the river critical to spawning and feeding into worthless canals.

The presence of the Roanoke logperch is an excellent indicator of good water quality. This fish is a visual feeder that relies on hunting between small spaces and under pebbles to find its food and is therefore intolerant of silt, thick vegetation, and other impediments to the hunting process. If the Roanoke logperch is to survive in the wild, much greater care must be given to preserving high water quality in the Roanoke River and its tributaries. Given that the Roanoke River is used as a water supply for thousands of people who inhabit its banks, maintaining good water quality is important to people as well as to native Roanoke River fishes.

Typical Darter

This handsome darter possesses typical darter characteristics. A sleek torpedo-like body reduces drag in swift water, and large pectoral fins just behind the gills make maneuvering an easy task.

The blunt snout is used to overturn stones and rocks in search for food. The Roanoke logperch has two dorsal fins on the back, a forward spiny-rayed fin for protection against predators, followed by a somewhat longer soft-rayed fin for additional stability. Overall coloration is olive green with several dark saddle-like blotches on the back, dark vertical bars on the sides, a dark vertical slash across each eye, and a uniform lighter-colored belly. The spiny dorsal fin is a solid dark green with the exception of a prominent red band. The soft dorsal fin, tail fin, and pectoral fins are uniformly spotted, with dark green over a light green background that suggests bands or stripes. The anal fin just behind the anus and the pelvic fins just below the pectorals are a solid light green color.

This fish spawns in April by depositing fertilized eggs directly into sand or small gravel; the parents rely on well-oxygenated, silt-free water to prevent their offspring from being smothered in the nest. For this reason, all too often spawning efforts are unsuccessful.

Favorite foods of the Roanoke logperch are aquatic insects like midge, blackfly, cranefly, and caddis. Small crawfish and other invertebrate animals also will be consumed when the opportunity arises.

The increasing isolation in degraded habitat is the gravest problem for the Roanoke logperch. Not only does it interfere with its natural breeding habits, but it also affects the quality of the food it needs to survive. Many species face this same danger.

—*William E. Manci*

LORIKEETS

Class: Aves
Order: Psittaciformes
Family: Loriidae

Lorikeets look like many other parrots, but they do exhibit a major difference. Lorikeets have brush-like tongues that other parrots do not have. The unique tongue allows them to feed extensively on pollen and nectar. Many ornithologists claim this specialization is sufficient to recognize the lorikeets as a separate family from the parrots. The lorikeets include about 55 species.

Lorikeets probably originated in the New Guinea area because all the species occur in limited areas of the East Indies, Australia, and islands of the South Pacific. Several species inhabit only one or two small islands now under heavy pressure from human activities. At least two species are severely threatened. If more were known about them, they might be considered endangered.

BLUE LORIKEET
(Vini peruviana)

Status: Threatened

Description:

Length: 5.5 in (14 cm)
Weight: 1.1-1.2 oz (31-34 g)
Clutch size: 1-2 eggs
Incubation: 25 days
Diet: Nectar, pollen, small fruits
Habitat: Coastal and lowland forests and woodlands
Range: Cook Islands, Society Islands, and westernmost Tuamotu Islands

Nomads

Blue lorikeets gather in small flocks and wander nomadically, searching for trees in bloom. They grow only as long as an average ballpoint pen, yet they make a big impression.

Uniformly purplish blue above, blue lorikeets feature white across the cheek, chin, throat, and breast, appearing as if they were wearing a bib. A bright orange beak and yellow-orange foot and toe add a little contrasting color. The effect is of a little bird all dressed up in formal wear with nowhere to go. If this bird is going anywhere, it is slipping into the realm of extinction.

Blue lorikeets once inhabited at least two dozen islands of eastern Polynesia. Ornithologists cannot determine which islands they inhabited natively, and to which islands they were introduced. One early observer wrote that blue lorikeets are weak fliers, but their distribution across so many islands separated by ocean seems to argue otherwise. Unfortunately, these

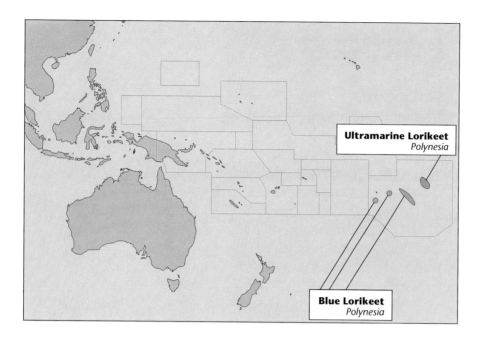

Ultramarine Lorikeet
Polynesia

Blue Lorikeet
Polynesia

birds have vanished from most of the islands where they were known to occur. As of 1990, they were found only on Aitutaki, Arutua, Bellinghausen, Rangiroa, Scilly, and Tikehau. Many islands have not been surveyed recently, if ever. Since many small islands and atolls are not inhabited by people and are seldom visited, they could be used to harbor blue lorikeets—if only in small numbers.

A Bird in the Tree

Completely arboreal, blue lorikeets even drink water that collects on tree leaves. Some lorikeets will bathe in ground pools and streams, and others bathe in rain or rainwater gathered on palm fronds. Because they eat the pollen of tree flowers, they must constantly move around to find fresh supplies. In the tropics where lorikeets live, flowers do not bloom seasonally as they do in temperate climates, but year-round. However, the flowers are usually are not very abundant in any one place. Thus, the birds must constantly move to find enough to eat.

Although pairs nest

individually, after the breeding season blue lorikeets flock in small groups. Many birds moving together can spread out to search a broader area. When one or more birds finds a new tree in bloom, their feeding activity attracts the attention of other birds.

Because blue lorikeets are so arboreal, they do not feed on ground-blooming flowers. People on the islands where blue lorikeets live have been cutting native forests for decades. Since the colonial era of the 1700s and 1800s, lumber, grazing, and tourism have become important. Tourism requires airports, hotels, and various other facilities, all of which demand space once covered by forest. The consequence has been less habitat for the blue lorikeet.

The habitat that remains has been degraded by the spread of rats. Both Polynesian rats (*Rattus exulans*) and black rats (*Rattus rattus*) climb trees, and both readily eat birds' eggs and nestlings. Other species may be affecting blue lorikeets as well. The swamp harrier (*Circus*

approximans) has been naturally extending its range through Polynesia, and the great horned owl (*Bubo virginianus*) of North America has been introduced to at least one island in the Marquesas, possibly to control rats. Whether the great horned owl has survived there or even spread to other islands has not been well documented. Both harrier and owl, however, do eat birds.

Cage Birds

Habitat has not been the only issue. As members of the parrot order, blue lorikeets have collector's value. Although never abundant in captivity, blue lorikeets were trapped and their nests raided. Small populations on small islands can be easily damaged by collecting. Ironically, lorikeets make difficult pets.

All lorikeets, including *Vini peruviana*, are now covered by the Convention on the International Trade in Endangered Species of Flora and Fauna (CITES). More than 130 nations have signed the treaty, which regulates the import and export of birds designated as protected. The treaty gives governments legal recourse to prosecute people who illegally trap wild birds.

The blue lorikeet's population was estimated at 680 pairs, or roughly 1,400 to 1,500 (counting non-breeding birds), in the late 1980s. These were optimistic figures. The total number of known birds is probably much lower. With so many unsurveyed islands, however, the actual total may be considerably higher. The only way to preserve blue lorikeets is to preserve their habitat, both in quantity and quality.

ULTRAMARINE LORIKEET
(Vini ultramarina)

Status: Threatened

Description:

Length: 7.1 in (18 cm)
Weight: Unknown
Clutch size: 2 eggs (known from one nest in captivity)
Incubation: Unknown
Diet: Pollen, nectar, small fruits
Habitat: Forests from coast to highest mountain ridges
Range: Nukuhiva, Uapou, and Uahuka of Marquesas Islands

Blue Bird

The ultramarine lorikeet is aptly named for its blue shades. The bird's shoulder, back, rump, and tail are colored somewhere between turquoise and lapis lazuli. A dark purplish blue covers the crown and nape, but the forehead is azure. The cheek, chin, and throat are basically white, but the feathers have dark blue bases with white tips, so the throat and breast look spotted. A dark purplish blue band across the lower breast highlights the whitish belly. A small but bright red beak is the only other accent to this bird's blue coloration.

Pollen and nectar comprise most of the ultramarine lorikeet's diet. An arboreal species, it specializes on tree flowers but also takes small fruits. Insects found in the crops of birds collected as specimens are believed to have been swallowed as the lorikeets lapped up pollen (and were

Lorikeets are in a different family than parakeets, but they share a similar appearance.

probably not hunted outright).

Several ultramarine lorikeets may band together outside the breeding season and travel in search of pollen. Unlike the blue lorikeet that stays at lower elevations, the ultramarine lorikeet wanders as high up the mountains as the pollen and nectar can be found. Perhaps some flexibility of diet or a lack of competing species explains why they range so much higher than blue lorikeets. Specific details about the ultramarine lorikeet, however, are not known.

Habitat destruction on Nukuhiva threatens the survival of many birds unique to that and other Marquesas Islands. The destruction of island habitat may have accelerated in recent decades, but it is nothing new. Island conquest and modification are deeply rooted in global history. The French originally fought for many South

Pacific islands in order to start plantations of coffee, cocoa, tea, tobacco, spices, and tropical fruits. These crops could be grown on islands where native islanders or indentured laborers could be employed cheaply to work them.

These colonial ambitions had two unforseen consequences. The Europeans carried diseases that devastated the islanders, and wholesale conversion of island landscapes from native plant communities to agriculture endangered many species. The French brought African and Oriental laborers to the Marquesas Islands to replace the islanders who died. But wild species cannot be so easily replaced.

On Uapou an estimated population of 500 to 600 ultramarine lorikeets in 1975 plummeted to no more than 240 birds in 1990. Only 70 of these lorikeets were known on Nukuhiva in 1990. An introduced population on Uahuka was steady at 400 to 500 birds. Introduced predators like rats and feral cats may pose some hazard to the lorikeet, and great horned owls (*Bubo virginianus*) introduced to Hivaoa like to eat birds. Introduced avian malaria may also be affecting native birds.

The birds of the Marquesas Islands need to be thoroughly studied. More information would help ornithologists learn how ultramarine lorikeets and other unique island birds might be able to coexist with humans with only slight modifications in human activities. The only way to guarantee ultramarine lorikeets any future at all is to plan for preserving their habitat while there is still time.
—*Kevin Cook*
See also Parrots.

PYGMY LORIS
(Nycticebus pygmaeus)

Status: Threatened

Class: Mammalia
Order: Primates
Family: Lorisidae

Description:
    Weight: Average 33 oz (950 g)
    Head-body length: 7-8 in
    (18-21 cm)
    Tail length: Vestigial
    Diet: Mainly fruit, plus insects,
    leaves, seeds, lizards, birds' eggs
    Gestation period: 193 days
    Longevity: Probably 12-14 years
    Habitat: Tropical forest,
    secondary forest and shrub
    Range: Vietnam

Unique Primate

In the jungles of Vietnam lives a small creature that is one of the most unusual primates in the world. It is the pygmy loris. It has thick brown, reddish brown, or gray fur, with a reddish brown stripe between its eyes from muzzle to forehead. This stripe continues and becomes brownish black as it extends toward the crown and between the ears.

In the primate order, there are simians (the apes and monkeys) and prosimians, consisting of such animals as the lemur, the bushbaby, and the pygmy loris. Prosimians are generally regarded as being more primitive than the apes and monkeys. Lorises are nocturnal, spending their day wound in tight balls hidden in dense foliage.

The face of the pygmy loris looks more like a marsupial.

Zoologists don't know much about their social behavior, but suspect that they are solitary. The pygmy loris uses urine to mark its territory. These animals, unlike some of their prosimian cousins, never leap. This gives them their other common name, "slow loris."

Although its status is unclear, the pygmy loris has suffered from the decades of warfare and habitat destruction that has been inflicted upon its native country. The greatest threat to its population growth at present is the clearing of more forest for agriculture. Although not often used for food, the pygmy loris is sometimes kept as a pet and can be seen for sale in markets in Hanoi, the capital city.
—*Thaya du Bois*
See also Lemurs.

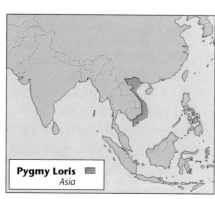

Pygmy Loris
Asia

SPANISH LYNX
(Lynx pardina)

Status: Endangered

Class: Mammalia
Order: Carnivora
Family: Felidae

Description:
    Weight: To 40 lb (18 kg)
    Head-body length: 2.5-3.5 ft
    (85-110 cm)
    Tail length: 5 in (12.5-13 cm)
    Shoulder height: 18-28 in
    (60-70 cm)
    Gestation period: 63-73 days
    Diet: Small mammals and birds
    Habitat: Bushlands and
    grasslands
    Range: Southwest Iberian
    peninsula

Endangered Lynx

The Spanish lynx is yellowish

red above and white below. There are round blacks spots on the body, tail, and limbs, and the triangular ears have pronounced tufts; the face has especially long whiskers. The fur tends to be long and thick, especially on the lower cheeks, giving it a bearded appearance—particularly in winter. Its tail is relatively short.

In general, lynx are nocturnal animals, and the Spanish lynx shares this characteristic. They tend to remain in one area, but will migrate if conditions require it. Lynx are excellent climbers, swimmers, and hunters. This particular species prefers open forests and thickets, and the diameter of its home range is between 2.5 to 6 miles (four and ten kilometers). Usually a lynx will stalk its prey to within a few bounds, or it might wait to ambush it. Generally, its diet consists of rabbits, but it will eat other small mammals and birds.

The Spanish lynx is generally treated as a full species separate from other lynx. It is the most endangered of all lynx, with a population estimate at just 1,000 to 1,500 individuals. While the species has occasionally been the victim of fur trappers and hunted as a predator of domestic animals, these are not the most ominous

Spanish Lynx
Europe

The lynx is a hardy cat, managing to withstand trapping, starvation, and habitat decline all over the Northern Hemisphere and still survive. In Siberia, where this lynx comes from, the maximum population density is five individuals per 38.6 square miles (100 square kilometers).

threats. Most damaging to its populations has been the decline of its prey species. For example, the Spanish lynx population was significantly diminished in the 1950s and 1960s when a disease called myxomatosis struck the rabbit population. As suitable habitat diminshes, both the lynx and the rabbit populations have continued to decline. The lynx has been known to breed in captivity, although there is concern that hybridization has occurred among

different subspecies of lynx. The Spanish lynx occurs in presumably growing populations at the Coto Doñana reserve. A study in 1983 marked 12 animals; just five years later, another study marked 25.
—*Elizabeth Sirimarco*
See also Cats.

681

MACAQUES

Class: Mammalia
Order: Primates
Family: Cercopithecidae
Subfamily: Cercopithecinae

Macaques are heavily built monkeys with tails that vary in size. Some have no tails at all, while others have tails that are longer than their body length. The male is larger than the female, often a great deal larger. They live in Southeast Asia, Japan, Gibraltar, and North Africa in a highly developed social system. Macaques have rigid dominance hierarchies, and those at the bottom of the system often lead stressful, unpleasant lives with less access to food.

There is some disagreement over the classification of macaques, with the number of separate species varying between 13 and 19. One problem is the identification of species on Sulawesi (formerly Celebes).

Existence for the macaque is fraught with such hazards as disease, stress, starvation, and almost constant fighting, and nearly 90 percent of the members of certain species die before they reach adulthood. Humans, however, have greatly increased the suffering of macaques. During the 1950s, up to 200,000 rhesus macaques a year were exported from India to the West for scientific research, particularly for the testing of vaccines. When this exportation ceased in 1977, Southeast Asia filled the gap in the market, starting up their own monkey trading, which brought in great financial rewards. These factors, along with habitat destruction and hunting, have greatly reduced the abundance of macaques throughout their range.

The macaque's coat is generally a dullish brown color, but its facial skin and rump may be bright red. Ischial callosities, the pads on the rump, are prominent. The macaque has well-developed cheek pouches for temporary food storage. The ears are bare, pointed, and protrude from the head. Some species exhibit swelling of the sexual organs in the mating season. Mostly macaques are seasonal breeders: they mate in the fall, and give birth in the spring, with an approximate five and one-half month gestation period. Females mature sexually at three and one-half years, and males at four and one-half years, but macaques do not become fully grown until six years in females and ten years in males. They may live to be over 30 years old.

Macaques live in groups which often include several adult males. Females generally spend their entire lives with their original family, but males leave at adolescence and then live either alone or in small groups of males as they attempt to work their way into established groups containing females. Communication is very intricate. Macaques use body language, vocalization, and facial expressions to "speak" to each other.

The macaque seems to be able to adapt to virtually any ecological situation, from tropical rain forest to artificial habitats to snow-covered winter landscapes. In general they are omnivorous, eating vegetables, insects, meat and marine animals. There is a famous colony of macaques that lives on the Rock of Gibraltar. It was fed by the British Army, and legend had it that if the macaques left the Rock, the British would lose Gibraltar!

BARBARY MACAQUE
(Macaca sylvanus)

Status: Threatened

Description:

Weight: 24-33 lb (11-15 kg)
Head-body length: 20-24 in (50-60 cm)
Tail length: Absent
Diet: Fruit, young leaves, bark, roots; sometimes invertebrates
Gestation period: Average 166 days
Longevity: 25 years in captivity
Habitat: Mid- to high-altitude forest, scrub and cliffs
Range: North Algeria, Morocco, Gibraltar

African Macaque

The Barbary macaque, also

Because they have no tail, Barbary macaques have been referred to as apes, although they are not apes at all.

known as the Barbary ape or rock ape, is the only macaque living in Africa.

Once widespread throughout North Africa, this macaque is now restricted to patches of scrub and forest in Northern Algeria and Morocco; there is also a small population in Gibraltar. Seventy-five percent of the wild population lives in the Middle Atlas, Morocco. Estimates of this macaque's population vary between 9,000 and 24,000. They breed very successfully in captive colonies, where over 900 exist. However, they are under increasing threat from a variety of factors, including capture for use as pets and being shot as agricultural pests. Human

encroachment has brought habitat destruction, and they have to compete for herbaceous foods with goats, sheep, and cattle. Macaques are still used for medical research, but most of the animals taken for this purpose are not from the wild, but are either from Gibraltar or are taken from captivity.

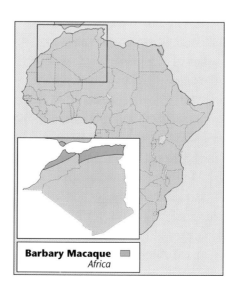

Barbary Macaque
Africa

LION-TAILED MACAQUE
(Macaca silenus)

Status: Endangered

Description:
Weight: 15 lb (7 kg)
Head-body length: 18-24 in (46-61 cm)
Tail length: 10-15 in (25-38 cm)
Diet: Omnivorous
Gestation period: 166 days
Longevity: 25 years in captivity
Habitat: Moist evergreen forest
Range: Southern India

Spectacular Sight
The lion-tailed macaque is a

Presently, logging has declined, but the most serious threats are development projects such as hydroelectric dams, railroads, and roads—not to mention human resettlements in the forest. More research on this macaque, and better protection of its habitat, are needed.

The lion-tailed macaque is rated at six in the IUCN's Action Plan for Asian Primate Conservation, which means that it is highly endangered. Less than 10,000 individuals remain, and no large section of its population is really secure. The most recent estimate places the species' numbers at around 3,000.

Lion-tailed macaques are being successfully bred at the San Diego Zoo. Some of the zoo's monkeys were received several years ago from the private zoo of Prince Rainier of Monaco.

spectacular-looking monkey with a black coat, and a gray ruff around its face. Its tail has a slight tuft at the tip. The ruff, as well as the macaque's stance, lends it the appearance of a lion. It is a shy animal that inhabits dense forests on the west coast of southern India. Although it occasionally descends

to the ground to play, or to splash about in water, it is basically an arboreal monkey. It moves through the trees in groups of between 10 and 20, with a dominant male acting as a "scout." This male carefully maneuvers through the forest canopy some distance ahead of the rest of the group, leading the way.

Extensive deforestation has reduced moist evergreen forest of southern India to a series of isolated patches. This is one of the world's least-studied rain forests.

YAKUSHIMA MACAQUE
(Macaca fuscata yakui)

Status: Endangered

Description:
Weight: 18-33 lb (8-15 kg)
Head-body length: 19-24 in (47-60 cm)
Tail length: 3-5 in (7-12 cm)
Diet: Fruit, insects, young leaves, crops, small animals
Habitat: Forest
Range: Yaku Island, Japan archipelago

Yaku Island Monkey
The Yakushima macaque is a subspecies of the Japanese macaque, or snow monkey. It is found only on Yaku Island, 37 miles (60 kilometers) south of Kyushu in Japan. It can be found

snuggled together in groups of four or five, trying to keep warm in the high mountains. It also has the northernmost range of any monkey, and its coat has adapted well to dealing with the harsh realities of life in a cold climate. Its fur is very thick, and it is pale in color. Its face and rump skin are naked and red-colored in the adult. It is not uncommon for snow to gather on its head but, thanks to its fur, it is able to survive the winter. Some lucky members of this species have learned that crouching in hot springs makes a welcome natural sauna on a freezing day. They take turns wading, single file, through the snow, searching for meager morsels of food such as seeds and pieces of bark.

In the summer months there is a lush supply of vegetation, and the Yakushima macaque spends the summer lazing around, grooming the rest of its group. The grooming ritual is important, both to eliminate parasites and also as a

way of maintaining friendly bonds. Males partake much less readily than females in the grooming ceremony, and are content to lie around waiting for the attentions of a subordinate male.

The young are born after a five- to seven-month pregnancy, the birth coinciding with the melting of the harsh winter snows. The

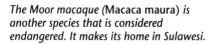

The Moor macaque (Macaca maura) is another species that is considered endangered. It makes its home in Sulawesi.

plentiful food supply in springtime allows the youngster to grow rapidly. However, it will be another year before it will leave its mother and take its first steps on its own.

A rough estimate of this monkey's population puts numbers at 3,000. A national park has been established on Yaku Island, containing about 450 monkeys. The future of the rest of these monkeys remains uncertain. They are regarded as pests when raiding orange plantations and are trapped in large numbers. Their natural forest habitat has been turned into conifer plantations, thus denying them their regular diet. If the present pattern of trapping continues, numbers will dwindle to a few hundred in several years. Steps that could be taken to alleviate the problem include surveying the population on the island in depth, and possibly declaring the Yakushima Macaque a National Treasure, which would automatically enhance its status.

Three other species of macaque are considered threatened or endangered:

MENTAWAI MACAQUE
(*Macaca pagensis*)
Status: Endangered
Range: Mentawai Islands
MOOR MACAQUE
(*Macaca maura*)
Status: Endangered
Range: Sulawesi
TAIWAN MACAQUE
(*Macaca cyclopis*)
Status: Threatened
Range: Taiwan
—*Sarah Dart*

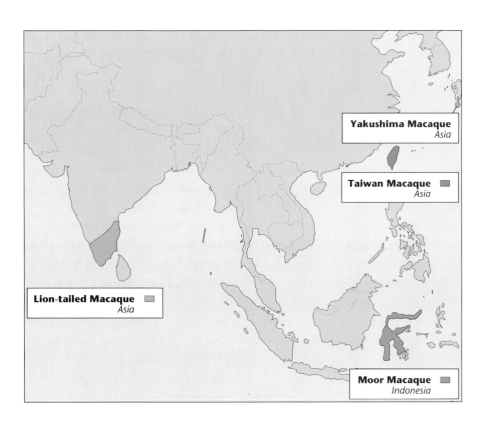

Yakushima Macaque
Asia

Taiwan Macaque
Asia

Lion-tailed Macaque
Asia

Moor Macaque
Indonesia

MACAWS

Class: Aves
Order: Psittaciformes
Family: Psittacidae

Macaws fly above the tropical forests of the New World. Their large size, bright colors, and long tails give them a stately appearance shared by few other birds. There are about 19 species in this group. Some species have enormous ranges that cover most of northern South America, but other species inhabit only single islands of the West Indies. Macaws have been extremely popular as pets since Europeans first began settling the Americas. Their popularity has not waned, although their habitat has. Many people find them more appealing as they become more rare. The illegal trade in macaws, with some specimens going for thousands of dollars, only increases their value. Many of the macaws are listed as protected species in the Convention on the International Trade of Endangered Species of Flora and Fauna (CITES), but quite often the damage has been done by the time law enforcement officials intervene. Several macaws have experienced at least slight population declines. Two species are severely endangered, and one of them may already be extinct.

LEAR'S MACAW
(Anodorhynchus leari)

Status: Endangered

Description:

Length: 29.5 in (75 cm)
Weight: Unknown
Clutch size: Unknown
Incubation: Unknown
Diet: Fruits of licuri palm and probably other fruits
Habitat: Dry shrub land
Range: Border of Bahia and Pernambuco in Brazil

Mysterious Bird

Everyone loves a good mystery, but the mystery surrounding an endangered species may carry greater significance than the usual tales of fiction. Nearly everything about Lear's macaw involves some mystery. It begins with the bird's identity and ends with its future.

Lear's macaw belongs to the same genus (*Anodorhynchus*) as the hyacinth macaw (*A. hyacinthinus*) and the glaucous macaw (*A. glaucus*). Largest of all the world's parrots, the hyacinth macaw probably has been popular in captivity since people first settled in South America. Even the ancient peoples of that continent liked to keep pet birds. When Europeans discovered the continent and began colonizing it, they sent hyacinth macaws back across the Atlantic Ocean. The great blue birds became immensely popular in zoos and private collections. The glaucous macaw closely resembles the hyacinth macaw but is 10 to 12 inches (25.4 to 30.5 centimeters) shorter. The last known sighting of a live glaucous macaw was in 1915. Ornithologists believe the bird to be extinct, but this is an unresolved mystery.

The Lear's macaw grows only slightly larger than the glaucous macaw. One theory says Lear's macaw is a hybrid between the hyacinth and glaucous macaw. This possibility has not been widely accepted, but it cannot be casually dismissed, either. One fact that argues against this hybrid theory is the range of Lear's macaw. It inhabits a dry plateau in eastern Brazil. The glaucous macaw lived much farther south, where Paraguay, Brazil, and Argentina converge. If hyacinth and glaucous macaws were interbreeding, then all their offspring were flying a thousand miles northeast and relocating in the same area.

A rich cobalt blue above and a greener blue below, the Lear's macaw sports a yellow ring of bare skin around the eye and a patch of bare yellow skin below the lore at the base of the beak. The glaucous and hyacinth macaws appear much the same. A powerful beak suggests the bird eats large seeds and fruits that it cracks open. Its exact diet remains unknown.

Virtually nothing about the natural history of Lear's macaw was known before 1978. Although the bird was described as a species in 1856, ornithologists knew only that the Lear's macaw occasionally turned up in shipments of the larger hyacinth macaws. They did not even know which country it inhabited. Then, in 1978, ornithologists found a small

The known population of Lear's macaws now occupies an ecological reserve originally established for other species, so further habitat loss is less likely to occur.

population of about 60 Lear's macaws living near some cliffs in Bahia, Brazil. They reported that Lear's macaw eats palm fruits and roosts at night in crevices and hollows on the cliffs.

Habitat loss through human activities might be a contributing factor in this bird's population decline, but heavy collecting for the pet trade is undoubtedly the leading cause of this species' disappearance.

The mystery of the Lear's macaw concludes with more questions. Can enough habitat be preserved and protected quickly enough to help the Lear's macaw survive? Can the illegal marketing of parrots be curtailed and enforced to keep the last few Lear's macaws in the wild? Can the Lear's macaw survive such a low population even if habitat is preserved and illegal trapping is stopped? Extinction would answer these questions with finality. Survival only grants the bird a little more time.

SPIX'S (LITTLE BLUE) MACAW
(Cyanopsitta spixii)

Status: Possibly Extinct

Description:
Length: 22 in (56 cm)
Weight: Unknown
Clutch size: Unknown
Incubation: Unknown
Diet: Unknown
Habitat: Palm groves
Range: Lowlands of Piaui and Bahia, Brazil

A Touch of Purple

Entirely blue, Spix's macaw looks like any other blue macaw until a second look reveals more detail. The back, wing, and tail shine with a bit of purple. The breast and belly carry a hint of green washed across the blue. A little pale gray lightens the cheek. The beak, foot, and toe are all black. Only the bright yellow eye adds any contrasting color. The uniform coloring lends the bird a different kind of beauty than the splashy yellows, greens, and reds of other parrots. This subtle beauty has long attracted the eye of people who treasure parrots.

No one has specifically studied wild Spix's macaws. They have been popular pets since their discovery in 1832, but their natural history remains almost completely

Lear's Macaw
South America

Spix's Macaw
South America

unknown. Their population has diminished so drastically that estimates of surviving numbers are no longer possible. Three Spix's macaws were seen in 1975. Some birds remain in captivity, but efforts to breed them have failed.

Many birds suffer because people do not consider them while planning plantations, airports, housing developments, and other commercial activities. Such activities either destroy or degrade habitat for many bird species. The Spix's macaw has disappeared because people paid too much attention to it. For centuries before Europeans colonized South America, people hunted and trapped it, both for food and as a pet. Europeans expanded the market for attractive tropical birds. Although the supply once seemed limitless, the Spix's macaw now faces extinction because trapping continued without restraint for too long.

During the 1970s, various observers reported that the habitat of Spix's macaw seemed safe from destruction. The species' habitat is scattered in patches, so some birds may yet survive.

—Kevin Cook
See also Parrots.

MADTOMS

Class: Osteichthyes
Order: Siluriformes
Family: Ictaluridae

Members of the family Ictaluridae *(catfishes), the madtoms play an important role in the overall ecology and balance of many aquatic systems. A fairly specialized group of fishes, they fill a vital niche as they "police" the bottom zones of streams. They were given the name "madtom" because their habit of swimming erratically in search of food is one characteristic that sets them apart from other catfishes.*

The name "catfish" conjures up an immediate image in the minds of most people. The most distinguishing features of this ancient group of fishes are the cat-like barbels, or "whiskers," that all catfishes exhibit. Barbels are not hairs, they are sensitive organs containing taste buds and other sensors that collect chemical cues from their surroundings. Catfishes have been enormously successful in adapting to a wide range of environments and colonizing all of the earth's continents except Antarctica; the madtoms are confined to North America.

Catfishes are not only diverse in their distribution but also in their various forms, and are categorized under several scientific genera. Other catfishes contained in this volume include the blindcats, cavefishes, those species given the common name "catfish," as well as others. They generally occupy warmwater environments and can tolerate high temperatures, low levels of oxygen, and other insults both natural and artificial. The madtoms are somewhat different in this regard. Catfishes occur in streams and lakes, caves and springs, and at both deep and shallow depths. When introduced to areas in which they do not naturally occur, they can thrive to the point where they become pests. The exotic walking catfish, Clarias batrachus, *of Florida is a perfect example of a species that has supremely adapted to a totally new environment. Native to Asia, the walking catfish was introduced to Florida and has displaced some of the less aggressive native fishes. This species is appropriately named; when state officials tried to poison some of the walking catfish from their new living quarters, they simply swam to the surface and walked on land while breathing air and moved to untreated waters, leaving the native fishes to die. Despite their success and adaptability, some catfishes and madtoms are in danger of extinction from human destruction of their habitat and pollution of their water.*

Catfishes share some common characteristics. The skin is scaleless, they have an adipose fin (fatty fin) on the back, some fins have spines for protection, and the anal fin just behind the anus and genitals is unusually long and wide. This feature helps keep the thin, wide mouth in contact with the bottom as the fish swims in search of food. Catfishes are in demand around the world as food fish. In the United States, the channel catfish is cultured on southern farms just like other livestock. The process, termed aquaculture, involves stocking of large ponds with small catfish and feeding them until they reach market size. Several species of *Clarias* also are raised for food in countries like India and the Philippines. None of the madtoms currently are in use in an aquaculture setting because of their small size.

CADDO MADTOM
(Noturus taylori)

Status: Threatened

Description:
Length: 2.4 in (6 cm)
Reproduction: Egg layer
Habitat: Shallow river areas over small rock
Range: Ouachita River basin, Arkansas

Damned by Dams
As the common name partially suggests, the Caddo madtom occupies the upper reaches of the Caddo River, Little Missouri River, and Ouachita River in southwestern Arkansas; the Caddo River and Little Missouri River are tributaries of the much larger Ouachita River. All three of these rivers have been subjected over the past several decades to massive dam construction projects designed to control flooding and supply water to nearby communities. Lake Ouachita, the reservoir formed by the construction of a dam on the main stem of the Ouachita River near the city of Hot Springs, has been particularly destructive to habitat preferred by the Caddo madtom. A river fish, the Caddo madtom requires shallow, flowing water to flourish. The Lake Ouachita project inundated many miles of this fish's prime habitat. Likewise, dams on the Caddo and Little Missouri Rivers have flooded habitat, restricted movement by the Caddo madtom up and down the river channels, and dramatically affected water quality below the dams by disrupting seasonal water flow and temperature patterns.

While removal of the dams and restoration of these areas is neither realistic nor practical, the maintenance of remaining prime and acceptable rivers stretches for the conservation of the Caddo madtom will be necessary to ensure the continued survival of this threatened species.

This small, unassuming fish presents a typical madtom profile with barbels on the face, a compressed and shallowly sloped head, a long keel-like adipose fin on the back between the dorsal fin and tail fin, and a long and wide anal fin just behind the anus used to lift the tail and maintain contact with the bottom during swimming and feeding. The Caddo madtom is dark brown on the back, speckled brown on the sides, and creamy on the belly. All fins are predominantly light and creamy colored, but the dorsal, anal, and tail fins show some dark banding near their edges.

Little is known about the reproductive or feeding habits of the Caddo madtom, but it probably spawns its adhesive eggs in the spring in crevices or other covered areas in flowing water. Most likely, a parent provides protection until the offspring hatch. It is safe to assume that the Caddo madtom consumes river-bottom insects and other invertebrate animals.

FRECKLEBELLY MADTOM
(Noturus munitus)

Status: Threatened

Description:
Length: 3.1 in (8 cm)
Reproduction: Egg layer
Habitat: Riffle and rapids of large rivers
Range: Eastern Louisiana to eastern Tennessee

True to its Name
Throughout its range in the southeastern states of the U. S., the frecklebelly madtom is under severe ecological pressure. As appropriate habitat is wiped out by human development, this small fish is forced to survive in higher densities or entire populations are

eliminated. Flood control and water supply projects are a high priority in the states of Louisiana, Mississippi, Alabama, Georgia, and Tennessee. Most of these projects involve the construction of dams and the modification of stream channels to stabilize seasonal water flow rates and reduce resistance to flow in the channel. The impacts of these activities on stream fishes like the frecklebelly madtom are devastating. Dams create reservoirs that flood stream channels and produce habitat that is unhealthful for these fishes. Also, much of this work, in addition to deforestation of the surrounding watershed and pollution from agricultural, domestic, and commercial sources, causes and promotes erosion and siltation in the rivers and further degrades vital living space and water quality. This madtom relies on clean flowing water that is free of pollution, silt, and debris to find

The frecklebelly madtom averages just over three inches (7.5 centimeters) in length and conforms closely to the "typical" madtom physique.

food, successfully reproduce, and thrive.

Principal river systems that support the frecklebelly madtom include the Pearl, the upper Tombigbee, and the upper Alabama Rivers. These are important waterways to both fish and people. Without a plan that takes into account the needs of both, populations of threatened species like the frecklebelly madtom will continue to shrink and eventually will be lost forever.

The frecklebelly madtom possesses the signature keel-like adipose fin on the back between the dorsal fin and tail fin, and barbels ("whiskers") like all members of the family *Ictaluridae*. This fish is aptly named as it displays large dark blotches and smaller freckle-like spots on its body over a much lighter-colored background. The flattened head of this scaleless fish can be used like a wedge to unearth small rocks and stones in its search for food in shallow stream riffles. Several of the fins, particularly the pectoral fins just behind the gills and the pelvic fins on the belly, are quite

stout and provide leverage as its moves bottom debris. The anal fin just behind the anus and the tail fin are pigmented in patterns that mildly suggest banding, and the dorsal fin is multi-colored as well. The small eyes are relied on little for sensory input; this fish relies on its touch, smell, and highly developed sense of taste.

The frecklebelly madtom is secretive and little is known about its feeding and reproductive habits. It likely spawns in the spring and deposits its adhesive eggs in well-oxygenated crevices and protected areas of the river. Some parental care of incubating eggs would not be considered unusual. The frecklebelly madtom probably prefers stream-dwelling insects and other invertebrate animals as its principal foods during its nightly feeding excursions.

NEOSHO MADTOM
(Noturus placidus)

Status: Threatened

Description:
Length: 2.4 in (6 cm)
Reproduction: Egg layer
Habitat: Under and around rock in shallow riffles
Range: Rivers in Kansas, Missouri, and Oklahoma

A Vanishing Midwest Fish
Throughout its range in the south-central states of the United States, the Neosho madtom is under severe ecological pressure. As appropriate habitat is wiped out

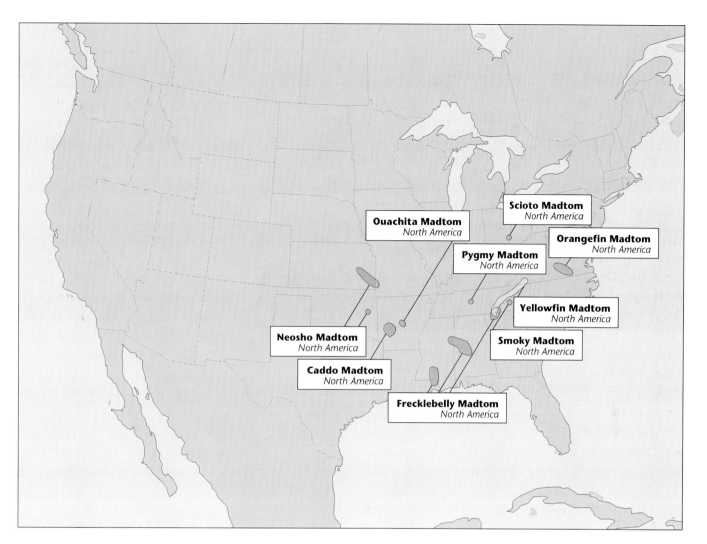

by human development, this small fish is forced to survive in higher densities or entire populations are eliminated. Flood control and water supply projects for domestic and agricultural use are a high priority in the states of Kansas, Missouri, and Oklahoma. Most of these projects involve the construction of dams and the modification of stream channels to stabilize seasonal water flow rates and reduce resistance to flow in the channel. The impacts of these activities on stream fishes like the Neosho madtom are devastating. Dams create reservoirs that flood stream channels and produce habitat that is completely inappropriate for these fishes, both behind the dam and downstream where temperature and flow

profiles are dramatically altered. Also, much of this work, in addition to deforestation of the surrounding watershed and pollution from agricultural, domestic, and commercial sources, causes and promotes soil erosion and siltation in the rivers and further degrades vital living space and water quality. The Neosho madtom relies on clean flowing water that is free of pollution, silt, and debris to find food, successfully reproduce, and thrive.

Principal river systems that support the Neosho madtom include the Neosho River, the lower Spring River, and the Illinois River of Oklahoma. These are important waterways to both fish and people. Without a plan that takes into account the needs of

both, populations of threatened species like the Neosho madtom will continue to shrink and eventually will be lost forever.

Appearance

The Neosho madtom has a "typical" madtom physique. It has the keel-like adipose fin on the back between the dorsal fin and tail fin, and barbels ("whiskers") like all members of the family *Ictaluridae*. Its barbels are somewhat shorter than other madtoms. This fish displays some dark blotches and smaller freckle-like spots on its body over a much lighter-colored background. The flattened head of this scaleless fish is used as a tool to wedge under small rocks and stones in its search for food in shallow stream riffles.

The Neosho madtom lives in river systems that are important to both fish and people. Unfortunately, the needs of humans usually come before those of wildlife.

Several of the fins, particularly the pectoral fins just behind the gills and the pelvic fins on the belly, are quite stout and provide leverage as it moves bottom debris. The anal fin just behind the anus and the tail fin are pigmented in patterns that mildly suggest banding, and the dorsal fin is multi-colored as well. The small eyes are relied on little for sensory input; this fish relies on its touch, smell, and highly developed sense of taste.

The Neosho madtom is secretive and little is known about its feeding and reproductive habits. It likely spawns in the spring and deposits its adhesive eggs in well-oxygenated crevices and protected areas of the river. Some parental care of incubating eggs would not be considered unusual. The Neosho madtom probably prefers stream-dwelling insects and other invertebrate animals as its principal foods during its nightly feeding excursions.

ORANGEFIN MADTOM
(Noturus gilberti)

Status: Threatened

Description:

Length: 5 in (13 cm)
Reproduction: Egg layer
Habitat: Rocky, clean river bottom
Range: Upper Roanoke River basin, Virginia

The Canary of Fish

The orangefin madtom only can be found in the upper reaches and tributaries of the Roanoke River in the state of Virginia, and is found in close association with an endangered darter, the Roanoke logperch. As such, the same human activities that threaten the Roanoke logperch threaten the continued survival of the orangefin madtom. Before cities like Roanoke and Salem began to spring up along the

river, the orangefin madtom could be found from its headwaters all the way to Albemarle Sound in North Carolina where the river empties into the Atlantic Ocean. But man's insistence on dominating and over-exploiting natural systems slowly has put a stranglehold on the river's finite resources and forced this fish farther and farther upstream. Urbanization and the resulting deforestation have released tons of silt into the river; sewage has robbed the water of oxygen and choked the river with vegetation; toxic chemicals have rendered any remaining marginal habitat uninhabitable; and stream channelization as a measure to minimize flooding has turned sections of the river that are critical spawning and feeding grounds into worthless canals.

The orangefin madtom is an excellent indicator of good or poor water quality. The presence or absence of this fish within a section of stream has been likened to the canary in a coal mine because loss of the orangefin madtom is one of the first indicators that water quality and habitat are deteriorating. Saving this fish from endangered status will require a commitment from many communities along the Roanoke River, particularly those near the headwaters, to "clean up their act." Federally mandated clean water legislation has improved the outlook for this and other Roanoke fishes by requiring thorough treatment of domestic sewage and further limiting discharge of hazardous and toxic materials, but more should be done.

Contrary to its common name, the orangefin madtom rarely displays orange fins. Rather, they are more yellow. It has a uniformly

The Ouachita madtom is found only in a small portion of the upper Saline River basin.

hued olive-brown back and sides and the belly is a pale yellow. The eyes are small and poorly developed and are used primarily to sense the presence or absence of light, as opposed to shape or form; taste is highly developed to compensate. This small catfish has protective spines on the dorsal fin on the back and on both pectoral fins just behind the gills. The fleshy adipose fin behind the dorsal fin extends the length of tail to the base of the tail fin, and gives the appearance of a keel on the hull of a boat. The head is very flattened and allows the secretive orangefin madtom to hide under rocks and in crevasses during the day. As with all catfish, the skin is scaleless.

During the breeding season in April, the orangefin madtom female searches for a protective and covered space in which to carefully deposit her gelatinous mass of fertilized eggs, usually no more than 75 per female. Depending on the water

temperature (warmer water reduces incubation time), the eggs hatch in two to three weeks. During the incubation period, the male guards the eggs from predators and fans silt off of the eggs with his tail fin to prevent smothering.

The orangefin madtom prefers to eat aquatic insects like mayfly, caddis, stonefly, and midge. This fish is not a visual feeder.

OUACHITA MADTOM
(Noturus lachneri)

Status: Threatened

Description:
Length: 2.7 in (7 cm)
Reproduction: Egg layer
Habitat: Shallow river pools
Range: Upper Saline River basin, Arkansas

Named for a Bygone Home
Today, the highly threatened

Ouachita madtom is found only in a relatively small portion of the upper Saline River basin (formerly occupying the Ouachita River as well), and is destined to be listed as endangered unless steps are taken to save this fish. As appropriate river habitat is wiped out by human development and activities, this small fish is forced to survive in higher densities or entire populations are eliminated.

The land around the Ouachita madtom's range is primarily agricultural. Flood control in the form of stream channelization to minimize resistance to high water flow also is a priority in the region, and the impacts of farming and flood control activities on stream fishes like the Ouachita madtom have been devastating. Much of this activity, in addition to deforestation of the surrounding watershed and chemical pollution from agricultural, domestic, and commercial sources, causes and promotes soil erosion and harmful siltation in the rivers and further degrades vital living space and water quality. The Ouachita madtom seeks clean-bottomed rocky streams and relies on clean flowing water that is free of pollution, silt, and debris to find food and shelter, successfully reproduce, and thrive.

The Saline River, a tributary of the Ouachita River, is an important waterway to both fish and people. Without a plan that takes into account the needs of both, populations of threatened species like the Ouachita madtom will continue to shrink and eventually will be lost forever.

The Ouachita madtom conforms closely to the "typical" madtom physique. It possesses the signature keel-like adipose fin on the back between the dorsal fin and tail fin, and barbels ("whiskers") like all members of the family *Ictaluridae*. This madtom can be distinguished from others by two obvious physical differences. Not only is the body of the Ouachita madtom uniformly dark (an unusual trait for a madtom), but the tail fin is quite different in shape and form. The tip is very rounded and the fin extends well onto the top and bottom of the tail, essentially joining with the adipose fin and the anal fin on the belly behind the anus. The flattened head of this scaleless fish is ideally shaped to use as a tool to wedge under small rocks and stones in its search for food in shallow stream riffles and pools. Several of the fins, particularly the pectoral fins just behind the gills and the pelvic fins on the belly, are quite stout and provide leverage as it moves bottom debris. The anal fin, paired pelvic fins on the belly, and dorsal fin on the back are almost entirely clear of pigment and the tail fin is dark like the body. The small eyes of the Ouachita madtom are relied on little for sensory input; this fish relies on its touch, smell, and highly developed sense of taste.

The Ouachita madtom is shy and little is known about its feeding and reproductive habits. It likely spawns in the spring and deposits its adhesive eggs in well-oxygenated crevices and protected areas of the river. Some parental care of incubating eggs would not be considered unusual. The Ouachita madtom probably prefers stream-dwelling insects and other invertebrate animals as its principal foods during its nightly feeding excursions.

PYGMY MADTOM
(Noturus stanauli)

Status: Endangered

Description:

Length: 1.6 in (4 cm)
Reproduction: Egg layer
Habitat: Stream riffles and rapids
Range: Tennessee

Smallest of the Bunch

As the name implies, the pygmy madtom is one of the smallest of the madtom group. This fish is extremely rare and at one time was thought to be extinct. Because it is extremely secretive and prefers to venture out of hiding to feed only at night, very little is known about this fish, the precise extent of its range, and specifics about its day-to-day life. The pygmy madtom is not well studied and was not even described until 1980. Most likely, and as is the case with most madtoms and other stream fishes, the pygmy madtom has been subjected to multiple insults that have robbed it of acceptable habitat and severely reduced its range. Human activities such as construction of dams for flood control and the generation of electricity are not uncommon in Tennessee. In addition to dams, stream channelization and modification to minimize flooding and pollution place severe burdens on fishes like the pygmy madtom who have adapted to conditions in clean, free-flowing rivers.

Appearance

Aside from its small adult size, the pygmy madtom is not particularly distinctive. It has the flattened head, long anal fin just behind the anus, and the keel-like adipose fin on the back between the dorsal fin and tail fin, and whisker-like barbels that characterize the madtoms.

The word pygmy means small, and the pygmy madtom is just that. At just 1.6 inches (4 centimeters), it is one of the smallest madtoms.

Presumably, the pygmy madtom dines under the protective cover of darkness and prefers to keep out of brightly lit stream areas during the daylight hours. Insects and other aquatic invertebrates probably are the food items of choice for this highly endangered fish.

SCIOTO MADTOM
(Noturus trautmani)

Status: Endangered

Description:
Length: 2.0 in (5 cm)
Reproduction: Egg layer
Habitat: Swift riffles over gravel and boulders
Range: Big Darby Creek, Ohio

On the Brink

With only 19 individuals located when it was first described by Taylor in 1969, the Scioto (pronounced sigh-O-toe) madtom remains one of the most endangered fishes in the world. It occupies a small section of Big Darby Creek in central Ohio, a tributary of the Scioto River, in a rural area just south of the state's capital city of Columbus. Today some experts think this fish is extinct. Fisheries scientists believe that, historically, the Scioto madtom never occupied a large range within the Scioto River basin. But today, as pressures on this fish's remaining habitat increase, the likelihood that a single catastrophic event could wipe out the surviving individuals

looms large. These pressures include destruction of habitat and food sources through soil erosion of the surrounding watershed and siltation that follows, and the ever-present threat of a pollution event, given the site's relatively close proximity to a major metropolitan area.

Little Is Known

Despite the fact that the fishes in Big Darby Creek are some of the most extensively studied in the state, almost nothing is known about the Scioto madtom's lifestyle and habits. This secretive fish is quite small, even for a madtom, and unspectacular in terms of its coloration. The olive or brown and mottled gray background color of the body, which tends to be darker on the back, is covered with many dark specks, spots and blotches; the belly is milky white and with no spots. A prominent dark patch is visible at the base of the tail fin and a cluster of spots forms a darker area at the base of the anal fin which is located just behind the anus. The dorsal fin on the back and the pectoral fins just behind the gills carry protective spines and are nearly pigment-free except for some light coloration that suggests banding. Likewise, the tail fin is lightly banded. The whisker-like barbels of this catfish are quite short, but the six barbels provide sensory coverage across the snout, mouth, and chin.

Aquatic insects and other bottom-dwelling invertebrates most likely are the favorite foods of the Scioto madtom. Breeding probably takes place in the summertime, with some protection afforded by the parents during egg incubation.

SMOKY MADTOM
(Noturus baileyi)

Status: Endangered

Description:
Length: 2.4 in (6 cm)
Reproduction: Egg layer
Habitat: Shallow stream riffles over rock
Range: Abrams Creek and Little Tennessee River, Tennessee

Extinct?

Presumably, the smoky madtom (so called because of the close proximity of its home range to the Great Smoky Mountains) can be located in its sole remaining habitat near the mouth of Abrams Creek, a tributary of the Little Tennessee River. Biologists are unsure if this unfortunate victim is still present in its native range or is extinct. For the past several decades, the smoky madtom has been under severe ecological pressure. As appropriate habitat is wiped out by human development, the status of this species has become increasingly unclear. In fact, no specimens of the smoky madtom have been found for many years, despite intensive searches.

Flood control and hydroelectric power generation are high priorities in Tennessee. These projects involve the construction of dams and the modification of stream channels to stabilize seasonal water flow rates and reduce resistance to flow in the channel. Tellico Lake and Fontana

Lake, both formed as a result of dams that were built across the Little Tennessee River, may have spelled the end of the smoky madtom. The impacts of these activities on stream fishes like the smoky madtom have been devastating.

The principal river system that supports the smoky madtom is the Little Tennessee River. This is an important waterway to both fish and people. Without a plan that takes into account the needs of both, populations of endangered species like the smoky madtom will continue to shrink and eventually will be lost forever.

This fish has a peculiar appearance, even for a madtom. It is much more tubular in shape, particularly around the head and abdominal region, than other fish in its genus. It has a very blunt snout. The smoky madtom is average in size. Coloration is unspectacular, consisting of a light-brown background and numerous dark spots over the head, body, and fins. These spots fuse to form dark regions at the base of the spiney dorsal fin on the back, in the area just behind the gill covers, in a stripe down the middle of the back, and at the base of the anal fin just behind the anus. The eyes are located high on the head and are used primarily to sense move-ment as opposed to recognition of shape.

The smoky madtom is highly secretive and little is known about its feeding and reproductive habits. It likely spawns in the spring and deposits its adhesive eggs in well-oxygenated crevices and protected areas of the river. Some parental care of incubating eggs would not be considered unusual. The smoky

madtom probably prefers stream-dwelling insects and other invertebrate animals as its principal foods during its nightly feeding excursions.

YELLOWFIN MADTOM
(Noturus flavipinnis)

Status: Threatened

Description:

Length: 4.3 in (11 cm)
Reproduction: Egg layer
Habitat: Medium-sized streams in pools and backwaters
Range: Northern Georgia to western Virginia

Driven from Tennessee

The upper Tennessee River basin in northern Georgia, eastern Tennessee and western Virginia is home to a unique-looking madtom, the yellowfin madtom. Like all madtoms, this fish lives in rivers

and, as is the case with many, the yellowfin madtom is threatened by human activities and development within its range. The yellowfin madtom relies on clean flowing water that is free of pollution, silt, and debris to find food, successfully reproduce, and thrive.

The principal river system that supports the yellowfin madtom is the upper Tennessee River. This is an important waterway to both fish and people. But dam construction activity, particularly from Chattanooga, Tennessee to Oak Ridge, Tennessee and from Oak Ridge to the Virginia border, has severely reduced the size of the yellowfin madtom range. As a result, almost all populations within the state of Tennessee have been lost. Most of the survivors live in a Tennessee River tributary, the Clinch River, in Virginia. Without a plan that takes into account the needs of both, populations of endangered species like the yellowfin madtom will

The yellowfin madtom relies on clean flowing water that is free from pollution, silt, and debris to thrive.

continue to shrink and eventually will be lost forever.

Appearance

At 4.3 inches (11 centimeters) in length, the yellowfin madtom is somewhat larger than other madtoms and displays an interesting pattern of pigmentation. A light-colored background is copiously covered with small spots from the snout to the base of the tail. A dark saddle-like blotch on the back over the fleshy adipose fin between the dorsal fin and tail fin, and a dark chevron at the base of the tail make the yellow fin madtom easy to identify. Brown coloration that suggests banding is present on the dorsal fin, tail fin, and anal fin on the belly just behind the anus and, as you might expect from its name, some of the fins show a hint of yellow. The head is flattened to allow access to crevices and other tight places, and the dorsal fin and the pectoral fins just behind the gills are spiny to provide some protection against predators.

The yellowfin madtom stays under cover during the day and hunts for food only at night; bottom-dwelling insects are the food of choice. This fish spawns in late spring and early summer by depositing adhesive eggs in a protected area and produces 100 to 250 young per year. Researchers have determined that it reaches sexual maturity after the first year and lives three to four years.

All the madtoms face the same problems as their catfish relatives: pollution, habitat encroachment, and the degradation of their ranges.
—*William E. Manci*
See also Blindcats, Cavefishes, and Catfishes.

SRI LANKA MAGPIE
(Urocissa ornata)

Status: Threatened

Class: Aves
Order: Passeriformes
Family: Corvidae

Description:

Length: Unknown
Weight: Unknown
Clutch size: 3-5 eggs
Incubation: Unknown
Diet: Insects, tree-frogs, lizards, occasionally fruits
Habitat: Primary evergreen forests
Range: Sri Lanka

Like the Jay

The Sri Lanka magpie is much like the jay in physique and character. It wears light blue body plumage accented by a rusty brown wing with black shoulders. The entire head, including the nape, chin and throat is earthy, almost chestnut brown, giving the bird a hooded look. A ring of bare skin around the eye is pinkish red as are the beak, foot, and toe. The

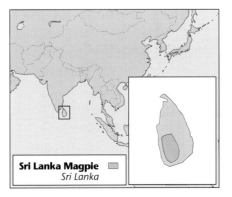

Sri Lanka Magpie
Sri Lanka

distinctive long tail is light blue with a white tip. Like other members of its family, the Sri Lanka magpie has strong legs that allow it to hop nimbly among the branches of the trees where it lives. Its home is the wet forest of Sri Lanka's foothills and lower mountain slopes.

Sri Lanka has two clearly defined life zones, one wet and one dry. Roughly circular, the island's southwestern quarter is the wet zone where as much as 200 inches (508 centimeters) of rain fall each year. The dry zone wraps around the other three quarters of the island. The term "dry" is relative because even the dry zone receives up to 75 inches (190.5 centimeters) of yearly rainfall. Mountains in south-central Sri Lanka account for the great difference. As the monsoons blow from southwest to northeast from May to September, the mountains obstruct the passing clouds, so the rain falls on their southwestern flanks. Little or no rain falls on the northeastern slopes. From September to May the monsoons switch direction and blow from northeast to southwest. Rain falls on the northeastern quarter of the island, but some also sneaks past the mountains to fall on the southwestern area. Because it receives rain year-round, this southwestern area supports a lush tropical rain forest. Many unique animals live nowhere else on earth except in that wet forest of Sri Lanka. Among them is the Sri Lanka magpie.

Habits

Ranging through the lowland forests up to 6,560 feet (2,000 meters) in elevation, the magpie works the forest trees from ground

The Sri Lanka magpie is one of many unique animals that lives nowhere on earth except in the wet forest of this island nation.

level to treetops. It eats any small animals it can catch, including large insects and small frogs. It will also eat fruits occasionally. Flocks of up to seven birds or so often move through the forest together. The Sri Lanka magpie sometimes wanders from the primary forest into gardens and parks, but it does not stay.

Sri Lanka's wet zone forests have been heavily cut by local people who need firewood and by agricultural developers who remove the native forest to cultivate plantations of coffee, tea, eucalyptus, and other crops. The magpie has shown no willingness to accept the plantations as habitat. No population estimates have been made, but the steady decline of habitat leaves no doubt that the magpie must be dwindling with the primary forest. The species no longer occurs in many areas where it was once found.

—*Kevin Cook*

MALEO
(Macrocephalon maleo)

Status: Threatened

Class: Aves
Order: Galliformes
Family: Megapodiidae

Description:

Length: 22-26 in (56-66 cm)
Weight: Unknown
Clutch size: 1 egg
Incubation: 78 days
Diet: Insects, spiders, millipedes, other invertebrates, and fruits
Habitat: Lowland forest
Range: Sulawesi, Indonesia

Life Replaces Itself

One of earth's most remarkable birds may be lost because people have forgotten a basic principle: given time, life replaces itself. The maleo may not have enough time for people to learn this lesson.

Since the beginning of agriculture, people who farm have understood that some portion of a harvested crop must be saved. The reserved portion becomes the seed to plant another crop next growing season. Ranchers well know that they must retain some animals as breeding stock and only sell off the extra. Wildlife management emerged as a profession in response to excessive killing of animals. Wildlife managers know that hunting and fishing must be restrained so that animal populations can sustain themselves. These fundamental management methods pertain to fishing, collecting specimens, hunting feathers, and gathering eggs.

The maleo looks much like a peculiar turkey. Its dull yellow beak is short and thick. An unfeathered, pale blue-gray structure known as a casque adorns the maleo's crown. The upperparts plus the chin, throat, and upper breast are a dull black. The belly is white. The maleo belongs to the family of birds known as the megapodes. The name "megapode" means "giant foot." Birds in the family have a very stout, well-developed foot and toe structure that is perfectly suited for life on the ground. Such a characteristic is not particularly remarkable, because many birds have stout legs and feet for a terrestrial lifestyle. The megapodes are amazing for their bizarre and unique nesting behavior. The maleo, in particular, nests more like a sea turtle than a bird.

Megapodes do not use the body heat of adult birds to incubate their eggs. Instead, their incubation depends on environmental sources of heat. Some megapodes build large mounds of vegetation. As the plant material decomposes, the process of decay releases heat that incubates the eggs laid inside the mound. The maleo uses heat from volcanos and sunshine to warm its eggs. When not breeding, the maleo inhabits primary lowland forests. For breeding, it leaves the forests for the sandy coastal beaches. Like sea turtles coming ashore from the ocean, the maleos throng to the beaches. After mating they dig pits up to three and one-quarter feet (1 meter) deep. They lay their eggs in the pits, then cover the eggs with sand.

Sulawesi (formerly known as Celebes) is a volcanic island. Pulverized lava forms black sand beaches. The dark sand absorbs energy from the sun during the day. That energy, stored as heat, keeps the maleo's eggs warm through the night. Maleos formerly nested in sandy open ground in forest clearings, where heat from volcanic activity and hot springs would keep the eggs warm. Egg collectors and hunters have virtually eliminated the inland breeding populations of the maleo. Now, dogs, pigs, and humans threaten to exterminate the last maleos by over-harvesting their eggs.

Dogs and pigs can sniff the beaches and find the eggs. When they do, they dig the eggs out and eat them. People watch the individual maleos and mark their nests with a stick in the sand. After the parent birds leave the nesting site, people go back to their sticks and dig out the eggs. To some extent, maleos can withstand predation. The incubation period lasts two and one-half months. When the chicks hatch, they struggle to the surface just like

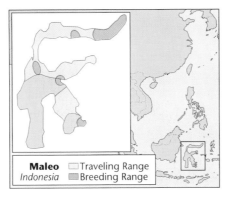

Maleo
Indonesia ☐ Traveling Range ▨ Breeding Range

baby sea turtles do. Once above ground, they run or fly to the forest for cover. The extra time in the egg allows the chicks to develop more fully than do other nestlings. The result is a chick that can fly soon after hatching. Of course, the chicks cannot defend themselves while still in the egg. People who collect eggs do not seem to be protecting them, either.

Sulawesi is part of the Republic of Indonesia, and Indonesian law protects the maleo against hunting and egg collecting. However, the tradition of egg collecting is strong among the local people. Either they have forgotten the principle that some crops must be saved to provide seed for next year, or else they flagrantly disregard the need to allow some maleos to survive.

Preservation

The International Council for Bird Preservation (ICBP) has been working with the people on Sulawesi for several years. The goal of the ICBP is to preserve the maleo as a species but still allow the Sulawesi people to collect some eggs. The entire maleo program has many facets. It involves regulating the number of eggs taken, incubating the eggs in captivity, excluding dogs and pigs from nesting beaches, and working with the Sulawesi government to allow rigorously controlled access to nesting beaches as a tourist attraction. Additional preservation steps aim to protect lowland forest where the maleos live most of the year when not nesting.

The effort to control egg collecting must succeed if the maleo is to survive.
—*Kevin Cook*
See also Micronesian Megapode.

Enthusiasts who gather the maleo's eggs must quickly learn to leave some behind, or the maleo will perish and the egg gathering will end.

IBADAN MALIMBE
(Malimbus ibadanensis)

Class: Aves
Order: Passeriformes
Family: Ploceidae
Subfamily: Ploceinae

Description:
  Length: 7-7.5 in (17.8-19 cm)
  Weight: Unknown
  Clutch size: 2 eggs
  Incubation: Probably 12-15 days
  Diet: Probably insects and some fruits
  Habitat: Zones between forests and savannahs
  Range: Southwestern Nigeria

Nesting

High in a palm tree hangs a peculiar structure. It is an elaborate nest, and flitting in the shadows of the palm fronds, a nest builder searches for more material. An Ibadan malimbe hops into the sunlight with a long leaf fiber in its beak. The bird's jet black cheek and throat offset the fiery red head, neck, and breast. A black belly, wing, back, and tail complete the contrast. It flies to the nest and busily weaves the fiber into place. Its stout, slightly decurved, black beak deftly works the fiber and draws it snug. Finished, the malimbe whisks off to another palm for another strand of fiber.

Nine species in the genus Malimbus make up the little group of weaver finches known as malimbes. They all live south of the Sahara Desert, and one species or another lives as far west as Senegal and as far east as Kenya. A few species range as far south as Zaire and Angola. The red-headed malimbe (*Malimbus rubriceps*) lives even farther south and is a common bird in southern Africa's dry shrub lands. The Ibadan malimbe, however, is different.

It was first discovered in a garden in Ibadan, Nigeria. Recognized as a species in 1958, the colorful little weaver sparked debate about its origin. Some ornithologists suspected it was a hybrid of two other malimbe species, but most are now convinced that the Ibadan malimbe is a full species. The Ibadan malimbe is, in fact, the only species of bird unique to Nigeria.

The Ibadan malimbe occasionally visits yards, gardens, and farmlands; but its preferred habitat lies outside towns and farms. This bird inhabits that zone where two major plant communities merge. Ecologists call such areas "ecotones" or "tension zones." In the malimbe's case, these plant communities consist of forest and savannah. A forest is a plant community where the trees

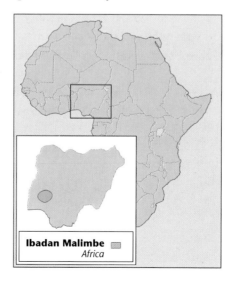

Ibadan Malimbe
Africa

grow tall enough and close enough together that their crowns intersect to form an overhead canopy. A savannah is a plant community where the trees grow far enough apart that their crowns do not mesh and grasses cover the ground beneath the trees. Some malimbes are forest species, some are savannah, but the Ibadan is neither. It inhabits the ecotone where the land has traits of both forest and savannah.

The agricultural potential of these areas has become increasingly important to the Nigerian people. Semidesert conditions limit agricultural development in northern Nigeria; mangrove swamps dominate coastal Nigeria in the south, limiting agriculture there. Inland from the coastal mangrove belt stretches a tropical rain forest. Although the rain forests are cut for lumber products and to open the land for agriculture, the soil is poor and unproductive. The land between the rain forest and the semidesert offers the best opportunity for livestock grazing and crop production. As the Nigerian population approaches 90 million people, the nation sorely needs a solid agriculture program just to provide adequate food for its people.

Converting the savannah to cropland and heavy grazing damage the landscape the Ibadan malimbe needs. Urban expansion compounds the habitat loss. Ibadan, a city with well more than a million people, continues to grow and sprawl, consuming malimbe habitat as it does so.

Always rare, the Ibadan malimbe disappeared from many of its native haunts during the 1970s.

Individuals and pairs were occasionally seen in secondary forest and urban gardens in Ibadan. Such sightings always stimulated hope that the Ibadan malimbe could adapt to a changing habitat. Those hopes faded as the bird was seen less often and in fewer places.

Ornithologists have urged that research be undertaken to find remaining Ibadan malimbe populations. Once found, the species can be studied so that recommendations for preserving its habitat can be made. If such action is not taken, the Ibadan malimbe will likely fade into extinction.
—*Kevin Cook*

RED-FACED MALKOHA
(Phaenicophaeus pyrrhocephalus)

Status: Threatened

Class: Aves
Order: Cuculiformes
Family: Cuculidae
Subfamily: Phaenicophaeinae

Description:
  Length: 18-20 in (45.7-50.8 cm)
  Weight: Unknown
  Clutch size: 2-3 eggs
  Incubation: Unknown
  Diet: Small fruits
  Habitat: Forest canopy
  Range: Sri Lanka

High Flyer
High above the forest floor, a bird races through the crowns of trees by hopping from branch to branch. Coming to a space too large to leap, it spreads its wings and glides across the span. The short, rounded wings hum as the bird sails back into the cover of the treetops. It quickly disappears, but a harsh "kok" says the red-faced malkoha is still there.

Aptly named, the bird has a large bare patch that encircles the eye and includes the lore, part of the cheek, and extends onto the side edge of the crown. The patch is bright red. Just below the patch, the lower cheek is white. A dark purplish brown color runs from the forehead over the crown onto the nape and sweeps around the neck to the chin and throat. The breast and belly are white, but the back, wing, and long tail are dark brownish black, or black with a little green or bluish sheen. A broad, white band runs across the tail tip. The greenish yellow beak is stout and slightly decurved. The wing is not well developed for flying; but the leg, foot, and toe are sturdy. No other bird in Sri Lanka looks anything like the red-faced malkoha.

The malkohas include a group of five species in four genera, all of which live in Sri Lanka, Southeast Asia, or Indonesia. The subfamily to which the malkohas belong also represents the yellow-billed cuckoo

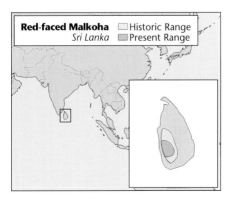

Red-faced Malkoha · Sri Lanka · ☐ Historic Range · ☐ Present Range

(*Coccyzus americanus*) and the black-billed cuckoo (*Coccyzus erythrophthalmus*). Both species occur over much of the United States, and they behave much like malkohas. They are birds of the forest canopy and are masters of "skulking about." The malkohas and North American cuckoos do not resemble each other superficially, but ornithologists long believed that similar anatomy and behavior indicate their relationship. A revised classification of birds proposed in 1990 separates the New World cuckoos into a separate family and leaves the Old World cuckoos and malkohas in one family. This system has not been widely accepted, but it has forced a reconsideration of the relationships among cuckoos.

The red-faced malkoha has wandered to India, but a population has never become established there. As a breeding species, the red-faced malkoha is a denizen of Sri Lanka's primary forests. These forests include lowland and montane stands within both the wet and dry zones. From May to September, monsoons blow from southwest to northeast across Sri Lanka. The monsoon winds blow rain-heavy clouds right into the mountains of south-central Sri Lanka. Too heavy to rise, the clouds dump their rain on the southwestern quarter of the island. From September to May, the monsoons switch directions and blow from northeast to southwest. During this time, the eastern and northern sides of the island get most of their rain. Some rain spills over to the southwest quarter and adds to the annual total. Receiving as much as 200 inches (508 centimeters) of rain every year, the southwest quarter is known as the wet zone. The other portions of the island receive 25 to 75 inches (63.5 to 190.5 centimeters) of rain each year. This broad area is called the dry zone, although it is not particularly dry by comparison to desert areas.

Forests occur in both the wet and dry zones. Those in the wet zone are tropical rain forests. The red-faced malkoha inhabited most of the forests in either zone. Agricultural development, especially plantations, and firewood gathering have devastated Sri Lanka's forests. The red-faced malkoha shows no willingness to occupy secondary forest or plantations, so as the forests have dwindled, so has the bird. Human development of the land has left many fragments of forest, particularly in ravines and along streams in the dry zone and a lower montane patch in the wet zone. Usually, considerations such as steep terrain or too much rainfall determine where the forests survive, because some areas are just not useful to people. The red-faced malkoha continues to survive in some of the remaining forest patches.

The future of Sri Lanka's forest birds probably depends on several factors. First, an alternative fuel source must be developed so that firewood cutting does not exceed a forest's capacity to replenish itself. Second, alternative farming techniques should be used to improve yields on existing farms and plantations, rather than converting all available land to agricultural production. Third, the remaining primary forests must be aggressively protected. Fourth,

good educational programs about wildlife and wildlife habitat must be initiated so that the people of Sri Lanka can learn and understand the importance of their forests and birds. Such measures must be undertaken if birds such as the red-faced malkoha are to survive.
—*Kevin Cook*

MARIANA MALLARD
(Anas oustaleti)

Status: Possibly Extinct

Class: Aves
Order: Anseriformes
Family: Anatidae

Description:
Length: 21 in (53.3 cm)
Weight: Probably 20-24 oz (560-672 g)
Clutch size: Probably 2-10 eggs
Incubation: Probably 28-30 days
Diet: Probably seeds of aquatic plants and invertebrates
Habitat: Wetlands
Range: Mariana Islands in the western Pacific Ocean

Imaginary Bird?
The Mariana mallard may never have existed. Or it might be a species teetering on the brink of extinction. Knowing what action to take to preserve the Mariana mallard requires understanding this bird. Interpreting the Mariana mallard depends on understanding ducks, and the mallard in particular.

Mallards (*Anas platyrhynchos*) live north of the equator on all continents and many islands. Various cultures began domesticating them 3,000 to 5,000 years before Europeans colonized North America. After several millennia of selective breeding, people have developed domestic strains such as the large Cayuga, Pekin, and Raouen ducks, the peculiar Chinese racer, and the tiny call duck. These strains of mallards are much like the different breeds of dogs. They are the common ducks of barnyards and ponds in city parks. This potential for variation may turn up in populations of wild birds. When variations occur predictably according to their geographic location, the populations that show those variations are called subspecies. The mallard also interbreeds with other duck species, and the offspring are called hybrids. The mallard is known to interbreed occasionally with more than a dozen other duck species. Knowing about this facet of mallard behavior helps explain the confusion about the Mariana mallard.

A Mystery
The status of the Mariana mallard has puzzled ornithologists for years. Ornithologists have considered the Mariana mallard as both a discrete species and as a subspecies of the mallard. Treating it as a subspecies, however, does not resolve a basic issue. The Mariana mallard was never abundant, but its small population showed two distinct forms. One form closely resembled the mallard, and the other form resembled the gray duck (*Anas*

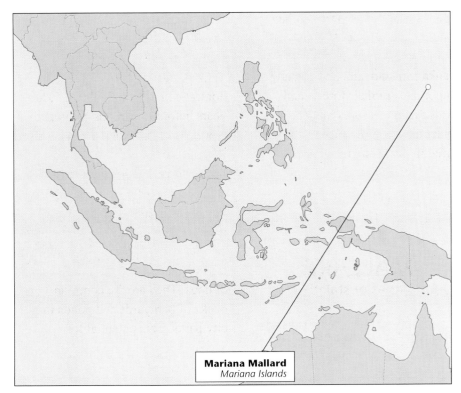

Mariana Mallard
Mariana Islands

In 1979 three Mariana mallards were trapped to begin captive breeding of the species. Two were kept, but they died in 1981 before they could produce offspring. Wild Mariana mallards have not been seen since the third bird, a male, was released after capture in 1979. And so, the mystery of the Mariana mallard expands from "What is it?" to "Does it still survive?" Was the Mariana mallard a subspecies, a hybrid, or a species in its infancy? If the species has indeed become extinct, no one will ever know. As of 1990, some habitat endured at Lake Susupe on Saipan. It is dense enough that some Mariana mallards could live there and escape detection. Perhaps this mystery bird yet survives and the story will someday become known.
—*Kevin Cook*
See also Ducks.

superciliosa). Most ornithologists interpreted the forms as evidence that the Mariana mallard was actually a hybrid between the gray duck and the mallard. However, neither the mallard nor the gray duck has been found in the Mariana Islands. If the parental species does not occur on the Marianas, then the Mariana mallard may represent the beginnings of a new species. The final outcome of this natural phenomenon may never be known, because the last wild Mariana mallards were seen in 1979.

History

The Mariana mallard historically occurred only on the islands of Guam, Tinian, and Saipan. At least 38 specimens were collected on Tinian and Saipan in the decade before World War II. Toward the end of the war, personnel of the United States Navy were stationed there. Records indicate military personnel shot the ducks, if only occasionally. Duck hunting has persisted on the islands despite the presence of the highly endangered Mariana mallard. Wetland destruction on these three islands has further jeopardized the species. Almost no habitat remains on Guam, and the Mariana mallard has been seen on that island only once since 1946. Only Lake Susupe on Saipan and Hagoi Marsh on Tinian still offer any suitable habitat for this species.

Mallards live on all continents and islands north of the equator. The Mariana mallard has been classified as both a separate species and as a subspecies. Within the small population of this bird are two distinct forms, an issue that further confuses ornithologists who try to classify this rare bird.

MANATEES

Class: Mammalia
Order: Sirenia
Family: Trichechidae

Manatees belong to an odd and unusual order of mammals called Sirenia, which includes the dugong and the extinct Steller's sea cow. The sirenia have been categorized as being more closely related to the elephants and hyraxes (animals similar to rodents) rather than to other marine mammals such as whales or seals. However, their relationship with elephants and hyraxes are distant enough that none of these three groups of mammals much resembles their common ancestor.

All sirenians are completely aquatic, and their body shape, structures, and behavioral adaptations are all oriented toward a life in water. While a cursory examination of a manatee might bring to mind the word "dumpy," the body is actually fairly streamlined. Manatees have nostrils placed on the top of the snout, allowing them to breathe without raising their heads above water level. Wide pectoral flippers help guide the manatee through the water and occasionally are even used to hold objects. A large tail flipper is used to push the manatee through the water. The tail fin is the simplest way to tell the two genera of Sirenia apart: in the manatees, the tail is a large, round paddle; while in the dugong it has two pointed lobes to its fluke, in much the same manner as a whale or dolphin tail.

All three species of manatee are under enormous pressures from human activities. This is partly due to the large amount of meat a single kill can provide to people. However, a greater threat to their existence is that they live in prime real estate, such as large rivers, bays, and coastal ocean waters. These areas are highly valued by humans, who use them as transportation routes, larders, sewers, and locations for housing and factories. The result is a constant degradation of the manatees' environment, and frequent interactions between manatees and human-made objects such as fishing nets, motorboats, and dams, usually means the manatees come out second best.

AMAZON MANATEE
(Trichechus inunguis)

Status: Threatened

Description:

Weight: 1,000 lb (450 kg)
Length: 9 ft (2.75 m)
Diet: Aquatic vegetation
Gestation period: About 360 days
Longevity: Unknown
Habitat: Major rivers and lakes
Range: Amazon basin of South America

Rain Forest Manatee

The Amazon manatee's primary habitat is the large rivers and adjacent lakes of the Amazon basin. It appears that this manatee is found only in fresh water. Although most of its range is in Brazil, it can also be found in parts of Colombia, Ecuador, and Peru.

The Amazon manatee differs from its two closely related cousins, the West Indian and West African manatees, in a number of ways. It is the smallest manatee, the largest just breaking 9 feet (2.8 meters) in length. It has light-colored patches on its underside. It is also the only manatee to lack nails on the front flippers.

As is true with many aquatic animals, little is known about the habits and ecology of the Amazon manatee. It is thought to live in small groups of four to eight, which would make it one of the more social of the manatees. Most other species tend to occur in pairs, usually a mother with her offspring. However, the Amazon manatee will occasionally be found in large groups, sometimes numbering in the hundreds. These groups are probably created by local ecological conditions such as food, temperature, or water levels, rather than any specific social need. Like the other species of manatees, it can communicate using high-pitched cries.

Giant Plant Eater

The Amazon manatee is

completely herbivorous. It feeds mostly on sea and river grasses, but will eat most aquatic plants and marine algae. It is even known to graze on shore vegetation that reaches out over the water. A manatee can eat over 30 pounds (13.6 kilograms) of vegetation every day. However, it appears that while a number of manatees may be capable of keeping a short stretch of water free of plants, the high productivity of tropical waters combined with the low productivity of manatees makes this idea unworkable in all but a few places. However, manatees could be used in conjunction with other methods, as manatees are maintenance-free and do not pollute the environment; as a matter of fact, it appears that manatee droppings can help to increase the productivity of waterways.

Fasting

The Amazon manatee also appears to be able to fast for long periods, perhaps over half a year. This ability enables it to survive long dry seasons, when water levels can drop over 20 feet (6 meters) and the manatee is forced to live in deep channels where vegetation is scarce. These channels may end up holding large numbers of Amazon manatees during the dry season. Once the rains begin and water levels rise, the manatees spread out again in smaller groups.

Because of the manatee's large size, tasty flesh, and slow movements, it has come under a fair amount of hunting pressure from local hunters and fishermen.

As with other tropical American animals, the Amazon manatee is also threatened by habitat

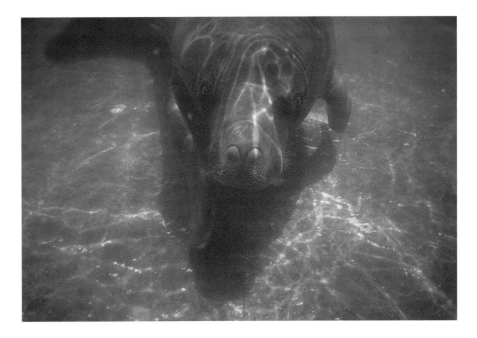

destruction. Heavy logging and clear cutting can degrade riverine habitat by increasing erosion, which increases the silt load of the water. This in turn affects the amount of sunlight penetrating the water, which can have an destructive effect on the aquatic plant life that the manatee depends upon for its survival.

Another problem facing the Amazon manatee relates to its own biology. The slow rate of reproduction in manatees means that reduced populations cannot replace their numbers without

Amazon Manatee ▪
South America

The manatee's tendency to gather in groups during the dry season has allowed people to kill large numbers in a relatively short period of time.

many years of protection from further causes of mortality.

Vast Range

The Amazon manatee's range, which is enormous and covers terrain that is isolated and frequently impassable much of the year, makes it almost impossible to adequately determine numbers or enforce regulatory laws. Since the rivers in which it lives cross international boundaries, different parts of the same population of manatees may face varying levels of legal protection and enforce-ment. Since the species appears to make seasonal movements, it is possible that some populations can appear to be under little stress, but periodically become faced with a more intense level of hunting and habitat degradation due to movements into new areas.

One of the most important tasks needed to save the Amazon manatee is determining population

705

numbers and range. Only then can a park or reserve be developed that will adequately protect a population of manatees. These reserves could be the only solution to the manatee's struggle to survive. A reserve will serve little purpose, however, if it is too small or the boundaries are incorrectly placed to incorporate the entire population range of these animals. To complicate this, manatees live in a habitat that is more difficult to manage than normal, dry land areas. A manatee's habitat can be immediately affected by what occurs elsewhere. Therefore, human activity such as mining, damming, or development upriver of a manatee reserve will have to be carefully managed to avoid any negative effects on the manatee population within the reserve.

WEST AFRICAN MANATEE
(Trichechus senegalensis)

Description:
Weight: 1,200-3,500 lb (500-1,500 kg)
Length: 10-13 ft (3-4 m)
Diet: Aquatic vegetation, leaves, fallen fruit
Gestation period: About 360 days
Longevity: Unknown
Habitat: Coastal areas, large rivers, lakes
Range: West Africa

Equatorial Africa

The West African manatee

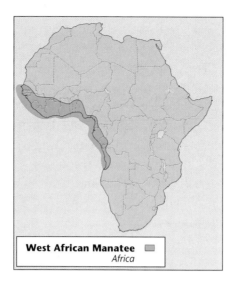

West African Manatee
Africa

looks remarkably like its close relative the West Indian manatee, and it is possible that the West African species descended from the West Indian species after it crossed the Atlantic some five million years ago. A close look reveals that the West African manatee has a comparatively shorter snub nose and more protruding eyes. Outside of those differences, however, even experts find it difficult to distinguish the two species. These two species may be even more closely related than the West Indian manatee is to the Amazon manatee, whose range it intersects.

The range of the West African manatee is spread out over the west coast of Africa on both sides of the equator. Extending from Senegal in the north to Angola in the south, this range encompasses at least 20 countries. Living both in salt and fresh water, the West African manatee may be found over 1,000 miles (1,600 kilometers) up the major rivers of West Africa, and possibly in Lake Chad as well. The manatees found in fresh water feed on many different kinds of aquatic vegetation. However, some saltwater populations appear to feed heavily on mangrove leaves, possibly due to a lack of other available vegetation. The manatees that are found in rivers appear to make long migrations upriver during the rains, and return downriver during the dry season.

Threats to the Manatee

During the dry season, manatees may get caught in lakes that become landlocked, and some manatees die when these lakes dry up. However, a bigger problem for manatees that regularly move up and down the rivers of Africa is the development of dams built for hydroelectric power, flood control, and irrigation. Manatees are regularly crushed by the devices used on these dams, and the manatee populations are blocked from moving along their normal river paths by these structures. Manatees trapped upriver from recently constructed dams may suffer when the dams alter water levels. While extensive damming is yet to be a problem in many countries, the need for cheap power, flood control, and water during the dry season and in times of drought make it certain that many more dams will be built, and that more populations of manatees will be affected.

The West African manatee is probably the most heavily hunted of the manatees. Some people along the coast specialize in hunting manatees. Traps are a common method of capture. Nets and hooks are also used, as are spears and guns. Accidental capture in fishing nets is another cause of death. These netted manatees are as likely to end up in the pot or the market as purposefully taken ones, and are welcomed as an important source of protein in many areas.

Lack of Knowledge

One of the greatest problems in preparing a conservation plan for the West African manatee is the lack of data concerning its numbers, location, and mortality. In most countries manatee surveys have never been performed, and the actual existence of the manatee in an area is frequently determined from anecdotal information. Some wildlife observations may be more than 50 years old, but represent the only published information concerning manatees for a given area. The lack of accurate numbers on the manatee population makes it difficult if not impossible to determine how quickly various populations are being reduced. However, there is a general consensus that populations are decreasing, in some cases radically, throughout the West African manatee's range. Older manatee hunters relate tales of greater catches in the past, and some areas that were once thought to contain manatees no longer appear to do so.

Despite the difficulty in documenting manatee population declines, a number of African countries that contain manatees have created legislation banning or limiting manatee hunting. Unfortunately, enforcing these laws is difficult at best, given the lack of resources and manpower among local police and conservation agencies. Add to this the acknowledged need for purposeful hunting to supplement the sometimes meager local food production, and the problems remain.

The West African manatee's survival is closely tied to the development of the countries that define its range. Drought, warfare, civil strife, and poverty create a social environment that taxes the importance of conservation—especially for areas that span many countries and require international action. Fortunately, many countries within the manatee's range understand the relationship between successful economic development and a healthy resource base, and have taken strong steps to preserve their natural resources, including their wildlife. However, without an equally strong enforcement policy and continued vigilance to maintain ecological systems within and between the countries of western Africa, large mammals such as the West African manatee are likely to become just another victim of human poverty and population pressure.

WEST INDIAN MANATEE
(Trichechus manatus)

Status: Threatened

Description:
Weight: 1,200-3,500 lb (545-1,590 kg)
Length: 10-13 ft (3-4 m)
Diet: Aquatic plants
Gestation period: 360-390 days
Longevity: Over 40 years
Habitat: Rivers, estuaries, shallow coastal areas
Range: Florida, the Caribbean, eastern Central and South America

Famous Siren

The West Indian manatee is probably the best-known member of this odd group of mammals. This is because of its existence around the southeastern coast of the United States, especially the state of Florida, where a good deal of observational work has been

The West Indian manatee, like other sirenians, is a vegetarian, eating mostly sea grasses and other aquatic vegetation. It appears to require at least occasional drinks of fresh water.

done in some of the clearwater streams of that state. Its odd and ungainly features have made it a minor celebrity among rare and threatened animals, and work on its behalf has led to an extensive conservation effort among both professional biologists and amateur naturalists.

The West Indian manatee has two distinct subspecies. The first is the Florida manatee, found around both the Gulf coast and the Atlantic coast of Florida and adjacent states, as well as the Florida Keys and coastal waters of the Bahamas. The second is the Antillean manatee, which is found down the Caribbean coast of Mexico through Central America, and along the Atlantic coast of South America to below the equator in Brazil. It is also found among many of the Caribbean islands, including Cuba, Haiti and the Dominican Republic, Puerto Rico, and Jamaica.

The West Indian manatee, like other sirenians, is a vegetarian, eating mostly sea grasses and other aquatic vegetation. It appears to require at least occasional drinks of fresh water. Ocean-going manatees frequently move into rivers for brief periods, and while at sea can be attracted by the freshwater output from a garden hose. However, some manatees are found near small islands far out to sea, and it is unclear how these individuals survive without any obvious source of fresh water.

Pressures on Populations

The West Indian manatee apparently has never been very common around Florida. The principal reason is that manatees are extremely temperature

West Indian Manatee
South America

sensitive. The waters around Florida present barely acceptable year-round temperatures for manatee survival. Manatees tend to migrate to warmer waters when water temperature drops to below 68 degrees Fahrenheit (20 degrees Celsius). Even so, every year manatee mortality is associated with water temperature drops during winter. Although manatees have been sighted during summer as far north as Chesapeake Bay on the Atlantic coast, Florida can be considered to be the manatee's northern extreme for year-round living.

Interestingly, some human activities have actually led to an increase in suitable habitat for the manatee. This is due to the release of warm water from power plants and factories into rivers and flood channels where manatees live. In winter, manatees often congregate in large numbers around these outlets, basking in the warm flow.

However, human activity has done more harm than good to the West Indian manatee. Hunting has been a constant threat to manatee populations. Although hunting has

been regulated in Florida since before 1900 and has been illegal since the early 1970s, people still occasionally poach the manatee, or cruelly use this large, slow animal for target practice. Entanglement in fishing nets and harassment by people have also led to manatee deaths. But by far the greatest single human-related cause of Florida manatee mortality today is collisions with motorboats. Of the approximately 1,200 manatees living in Florida waters, nearly 50 die from collisions every year. With the increase in human population in Florida and the subsequent increase in the number of power boats used in manatee waters, mortality is bound to increase—despite legislation to control boating and boat speeds in areas where manatees are known to reside.

The Antillean subspecies is also under pressure from human activity, despite its large range over the east coast of Central and South America. Although the population has this large range, they are not evenly spread across this area because not all of the coastline is suitable habitat for manatees. Much of it lacks protective shallow waters or ample vegetation. Another reason for the uneven distribution is poaching. Certain areas have been hunted more heavily than others.

Well Protected

The Florida subspecies is one of the better-protected species of rare animal in the world. Three important pieces of legislation were passed in the 1970s protecting the manatee: the Marine Mammal Protection Act, the Endangered Species Act, and the Florida

Manatee Sanctuary Act. These acts prohibit killing or bothering manatees. They also imposed restrictions on boat numbers and speeds in areas where manatees are common. There also are organizations such as the Save the Manatee Club that are involved in education, conservation, and lobbying for further legislation to preserve manatees. Rehabilitation facilities exist that care for injured and sick manatees and release them back to the wild once they become healthy.

People and a Changing Environment

Unfortunately, all of this effort may not be enough to save the manatee. While cold weather and boating accidents kill a number of manatees every year, the greatest long-term threat to Florida manatees is habitat destruction. Florida's human population has been one of the fastest growing in the United States, and is still growing rapidly. Most people live on or near the coast, and the beaches and warm waters attract more people every day. The result is extensive coastal development that threatens not only manatees, but most other forms of sea life along the coast. Salt marshes and sea grass beds are drained, dredged, or altered in some fashion by the construction of hotels, homes, and marinas. These areas are like nurseries for many kinds of sea life. Manatees also depend on these areas for food and shelter. Unless legislation is passed that restricts development along the more critical coastal areas, the manatee may still be edged out of existence.
—*Peter Zahler*
See also Dugong.

MANDRILL
(Mandrillus sphinx)

Status: Threatened

Class: Mammalia
Order: Primates
Family: Cercopithecidae

Description:
Weight: Males—55 lb (25 kg); female—25 lb (11.5 kg)
Head-body length: 27.5 in (70 cm)
Tail length: 3 in (7.6 cm)
Diet: Omnivorous, mainly vegetation
Gestation period: 168-176 days
Longevity: Up to 40 years or more in captivity
Habitat: Tropical rain forest, thick secondary forest, thick bush
Range: Equatorial Africa

A Baboon
The mandrill and its close relative, the drill, are large, forest-dwelling baboons. Both share the

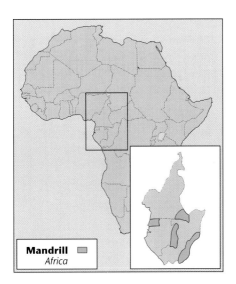

Mandrill
Africa

same environment—tropical rain forest—but the mandrill is larger and more brightly colored than the drill. The mandrill is currently regarded as vulnerable, while the drill is endangered because of habitat destruction and hunting.

The mandrill, while often classified as a baboon, looks quite different from other baboons. It is very large, thick-set in body, and fearsome-looking. The male is brightly colored, and several theories attempt to explain the reasons for this. The most probable explanation is that the colors are used as a way to signal their social and sexual status. When angered or agitated, the male's spectacular face of scarlet, white, yellowish-orange and cobalt blue, and its red, blue and violet rump all intensify in color. Because adult females greatly outnumber the males in their groups, it is assumed that great competition must exist among males to acquire females.

High Pitched Crowing
Mandrills congregate in single-male groups of from 15 to 50 individuals, called harem groups, which in turn often join with other groups. There can be a many as 100 to 200 animals living in close association with one another. Mandrills are noisy, emitting both deep grunts and high-pitched crowing calls. The complex vocalizations of the mandrill may help to maintain group solidarity in dense, darkly-lit forests where visibility is reduced.

A group of mandrills traveling in single file through the forests of western central Africa presents an easy target for native hunters, who have now managed to virtually

Primates generally exhibit strong nurturing behavior. Like human babies, mandrill infants need lots of care in the first few years of their lives in order to survive.

decimate the population. No valid estimates of mandrill numbers are available, but extinction is likely should populations continue to decline at the present rate.

Females are half the size of males. The female does not possess the same brightly colored features as her partner. Her coloring is less flamboyant, with a gray/black face and a brown and black rump. Mandrills usually give birth to one baby at a time. The female is ready to mate every 33 days, when a swelling is visible between the hardened pads of her rump (callosities) and her tail. Gestation time is not known, but it is thought to be similar to that of baboons (six months). The birth season runs from December to April.

The male mandrill has a very prominent muzzle, with bony swellings on either side of the nose. He also has large canine teeth. The female has altogether less exaggerated features.

Mandrills are well adapted to terrestrial life in the forest. They spend most of their time on the forest floor or at heights of less than five meters, and climb into the trees to feed and sleep. They move on all fours (i.e., they are quadrupedal), but they walk on their toes and fingers; their soles and palms rarely touch the ground.

Mandrills eat mainly fruit, leaves, buds, roots, fungus, ants, and termites. Sometimes they raid native plantations for crops and palm oil fruits, particularly when food is scarce or at the end of the dry season. When venturing onto local farms they run the risk of being shot by local farmers. It is thought that they are more strictly vegetarian than other baboons, but they have been observed eating small vertebrates, both in captivity and in the wild.

The largest remaining populations of this rare species are probably to be found in Gabon, the Campo Reserve in southern Cameroon, Rio Muni (Equatorial Guinea), and south western Congo. Habitat destruction and hunting are the main threats to the mandrill's future survival.

Drill

The drill (*Mandrillus leucophaeus*) is closely related to the mandrill, the main difference being its coloring and size. The drill is slightly smaller than the mandrill. Its overall color is olive brown with a grayish tinge, and it has a deep black face (surrounded by a white fringe), with no grooves on its muzzle. The male drill has a scarlet lower lip, and like the mandrill, the perineum and genital organs are brightly colored in blue, red and violet. The coloration of both females and infants is much less striking and is not present in the genital region. The male grows a patch of long hairs low on the

Mandrills live in groups of 15 to 50 individuals and are led by a single male. These "harem groups" will often form close associations with others, establishing a larger clan of up to 200 animals.

chest that conceals glands used for marking territory.

The drill lives in lowland rain forest, coastal forest, and on the banks of rivers in southeastern Nigeria, the island of Bioko, and western Cameroon. Although they thrive in similar ecological environments to those of the mandrills, drills are thought to be separated from them by the Sanaga River in Cameroon; thus they occur only from the Cross River in Nigeria to the Sanaga River in Cameroon. In Nigeria the drill is believed to be close to extinction; it is restricted to a small area only 185 miles by 155 miles (300 kilometers by 250 kilometers) in Cameroon.

Drills are semiterrestrial, and group sizes may vary from as few as 14 to as high as 200. Groups appear to consist of single male subgroups of roughly 20 individuals, which often join up

with other units, although solitary males have been observed. When females are ready to mate, a sexual swelling becomes noticeable. The length of gestation is probably 168 to 176 days, and the birth season probably ranges from December to April.

Diet

In common with their cousins the mandrills, drills eat fruit, seeds, fungi, leaves, ground plants, ants, termites, and small vertebrates. They have also been observed raiding native plantations for manioc and oil-palm fruits.

No estimates of the drill's population exist, but the numbers have declined throughout its range in the last few years. Sadly, it is thought to be threatened with complete extinction. The only area which is known to contain significant populations is Korup National Park in Cameroon. Surveys are urgently needed to establish whether the drill exists in any sizable numbers outside Korup, and to protect it against hunting. Drills are not only being shot while raiding crops, but are extensively hunted for their meat. Drills are especially vulnerable to hunting, because large groups can easily be tracked by listening for their loud cries.

About 60 individuals lived in zoos in 1985, but reproduction in these conditions has been mostly unsuccessful. Only about 25 percent of the animals breed. A successful breeding program is, however, underway in Hanover Zoo in Germany. This highly endangered primate is close to extinction in Nigeria and on the island of Bioko.
—*Sarah Dart*

MANGABEYS

Class: Mammalia
Order: Primates
Family: Cercopithecidae
Subfamily: Cercopithecinae

Mangabeys are large, slender monkeys, closely related to baboons. They are divided into two separate groups: one crested and mainly black (the Albigena group), and the other uncrested and mainly brown or gray (the Torquatus group). Mangabeys are generally restricted to the rain forest of west and central Africa, although two small isolated populations of crested mangabeys are found in East Africa.

The Albigena group prefers swampy forest and is almost totally arboreal. The Torquatus group is often found in primary and secondary forest, spending much of its time on the ground.

All mangabeys have tails that are longer than their bodies, and the females are smaller than the males. Infants are the same color as adults. They share certain habitats with guenons, but their large and extremely strong teeth allow them to eat hard seeds, which guenons cannot eat. They also eat fruit, leaves, mushrooms, grubs, insects, and small reptiles such as lizards and snakes. The mangabeys will also raid crops.

Mangabeys live in large groups of 10 to 25 animals, and move around using all four limbs (called quadrapedal). They are extremely loud and vocal, and the adult male in particular has a very dramatic long-distance call. The female's call, while not as dramatic, is also loud. Both single male and multiple male groups have been observed.

The female's menstrual cycle lasts about a month. Pregnancy lasts about six months, with no evidence of breeding during any one particular season. Gestation varies from 168 days to 177 days. Females are ready to reproduce during their fourth year; males, on the other hand, are not fully sexually mature until the age of six or seven. At age six their canine teeth are fully grown and their voice changes, with the "loud call" being heard for the first time.

COLLARED MANGABEY
(Cercocebus torquatus)

Status: Threatened

Description:

Weight: 22 lb (10 kg)
Head-body length: 26 in (66 cm)
Tail length: 17-30 in (43-76 cm)
Diet: Palm nuts, seeds, fruit, leaves, insects, small vertebrates
Gestation period: 164-175 days
Longevity: 30 years in captivity
Habitat: Primary rain forest
Range: Nigeria to Congo

Many Names

The collared mangabey is known by several names, including the white, red-capped, sooty or smoky mangabey. It spends most of its time on the ground, foraging in the leaf litter of the forest floor. Its coat is gray, but variations in coloring are found across its geographical range. For example, it has a white collar in Ghana and a red cap in Cameroon.

As with other members of the Torquatus group, this mangabey uses its fingers to bear its weight when walking. It has thumbs that function like our own, and a big toe which stands out from the rest of the foot.

Habitat destruction and hunting in equatorial Africa are causing major disruptions to the collared mangabey's way of life. Logging of commercially valuable timber and conflict with man over crop raiding in agricultural areas present additional threats to its existence. It does, however, breed well in captivity, with some newborns being second-generation captive births. It is also more adaptable than some of its primate cousins, showing an inclination to survive in areas that have been logged or converted to agriculture.

Congo has been logging its forests at a rate of 54,000 acres per year. Urban growth has created waste disposal and air pollution problems. Nigeria has already lost 70 to 80 percent of its original forest. It is this kind of abuse to the environment that threatens species such as the collared mangabey.

SANJE CRESTED MANGABEY
(Cercocebus galeritus sanjei)

TANA RIVER MANGABEY
(Cercocebus galeritus galeritus)

Status: Endangered

Description:

Weight: Males, 22.5 lb (10.2 kg); females, 12 lb (5.5 kg);
Head-body length: 17.6-23 in (44-58 cm)
Tail length: 17-30 in (43-76 cm)
Diet: Palm nuts, seeds, leaves
Gestation period: 164-175 days
Longevity: Unknown
Habitat: Rain forest
Range: Uzungwa Mountains of Tanzania; Kenya

Recent Discovery

The Sanje crested mangabey was only first described in 1981. No museum specimens exist, therefore, all information comes from live, wild animals. It is a subspecies of the crested mangabey (*Cercocebus galeritus*) and has many features in common with another subspecies, the Tana River mangabey (*Cercocebus galeritus galeritus*).

This mangabey lives in an extremely restricted area, and there are estimated to be less than three thousand left in total. It is protected in the Mwanihana Forest Reserve, but is threatened by habitat destruction due to timber extraction and charcoal production. If adequate forest management is not enforced in the very near future, there is grave doubt about the fate of this primate.

Tana River Mangabey

This subspecies is found only in small patches of forest that border a 37-mile (60-kilometer) stretch of the Tana River floodplain in eastern Kenya. This mangabey has a fawn and yellow coat, and the hair on top of its head stands up in a crest. Very little is known about this animal, except that it adapts

Females mangabeys are ready to reproduce during their fourth year of life, but males are not fully sexually mature until the age of six or seven. Above, a cherry-crowned mangabey (Cercocebus torquatus torquatus) holds her newborn.

remarkably well to environmental changes. However, as the woodland along the edge of its river is carved up by people, so this mangabey loses its food supply and the trees which form its natural habitat. The Tana River National Primate Reserve does protect some

713

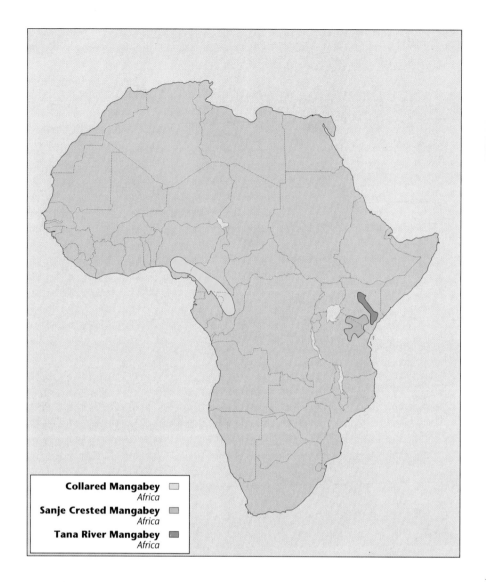

Collared Mangabey ☐
Africa
Sanje Crested Mangabey ☐
Africa
Tana River Mangabey ◼
Africa

MARGAY
(Felis wiedii)

Class: Mammalia
Order: Carnivora
Family: Felidae

Description:
Weight: 7-20 lb (3-9 kg)
Head-body length: 18-32 in (46-79 cm)
Tail length: 13-20 in (33-51 cm)
Shoulder height: 12-18 in (30-45 cm)
Gestation period: About 80 days
Diet: Birds, small mammals
Habitat: Forests
Range: From Mexico through Central and South America to Argentina; not recorded in Chile

of these monkeys, but this protection appears to be inadequate in securing its future. There are none in captivity. In the 12 years since the reserve was established, the population has decreased by 25 percent.

Precarious Future

The fate of these primates is truly in the hands of the Kenyan people and government. Because the mangabeys share this land with one of the fastest-growing human populations in the world, they are bound to experience more, not less, environmental stress.

Three-fifths of Kenya's land area is semidesert, forcing nearly all of its hungry population into the smaller, more tropical half of the country. As more people are squeezed together in what has become the most industrialized nation in East Africa, pollution increases. More land must be given up to grow food for millions of people. Water pollution from urban and industrial waste degrade topsoil. Even tourism in some of Kenya's game preserves has degraded habitat. What little is left of Kenya's forests (now three percent of the nation's land area) is disappearing at an alarming rate. All of these factors spell disaster for many species, including the mangabey.

—*Sarah Dart and Gregory Lee
See also Monkeys.*

A Lovely Animal

The beautiful margay is a yellowish brown above and white below. It has rows of length-wise dark spots that are paler in the center than at the edges. The margay is very similar in appearance to the ocelot, but is slightly smaller, is more slender, and has a proportionately longer tail. Both the margay and the ocelot have become victims of their beauty, for the most devastating blow to their decreasing populations is that they have been hunted for their furs.

The margay lives almost exclusively in forests. The animal is also know as a tree ocelot, as it appears to spend more time in trees than on the ground. It may even forage for food in trees. This cat is an agile climber and a natural acrobat, partly because of the special structure of its limbs. The feet are broad and soft, with movable metatarsals (the bones of the foot between the digits and the heel). The hind foot is more flexible than in any other felid, able to rotate a full 180 degrees. These adaptations help the margay move easily through the tall trees of its native Central and South America.

The margay has probably never lived north of Texas, although a single specimen was once taken from Texas prior to 1852. It is thought that the individual probably had wandered there, and did not represent part of a North American population. The distribution of the cat is quite wide, having been reported from Mexico to northern Argentina. The status of the margay throughout its range is poorly known, although it is considered more rare than the ocelot. Only in El Salvador is this mammal thought to be more common than the ocelot, and even there its status is still threatened.

Because of its arboreal habits, deforestation is probably more devastating to the margay than to the ocelot, which spends much less of its time in trees. In Ecuador, for example, it was reported that the best habitats for the species had virtually disappeared by 1981. The ongoing deforestation that plagues Central and South America will no doubt continue to reduce the margay population. In the past, a far greater concern has been the unregulated hunting of the margay for its spectacular coat.

The margay is predominantly a nocturnal animal. Its diet consists of small mammals and birds. Because it is a tropical animal, there is probably no particular breeding season.

Valuable

Until 1961, the margay's coat had little or no commercial value. During the 1960s, trade increased rapidly, with exports increasing from 42 in 1961 to 4,061 in 1966. Although the ocelot's coat is considered more valuable, it is difficult to distinguish between the two. The top price of a Brazilian margay pelt was about $10 in 1976, less than a quarter of the price for an ocelot fur. Nonetheless, 56,000 margay skins were counted in Brazilian warehouses in 1971; in 1977 margay trade involved no less that 33,000 skins.

Although these numbers are more than high enough to be alarming, they do not even take into account the many more pelts

20,000 margay skins were known to be involved in international trade; by 1985, the number had decreased to just 138.

The margay exists in a number of national parks and reserves, as well as in several large private ranches in Brazil and Venezuela. This cat is known to breed readily in zoos, which offer the species protection from extinction. Continued and strengthened enforcement of legislation to control exploitation of South American felids is necessary to ensure the survival of these beautiful and rare animals.
—*Elizabeth Sirimarco*
See also Cats and Ocelots.

that were no doubt poached and smuggled. Fortunately, exports of South American cats have decreased since the 1960s and 1970s, in part because of conservation legislation. But it has undoubtedly slowed because of the seriously depleted cat populations as well. The margay has also been taken from its environment for the zoo and pet trade, but this has had a far less significant impact on the animal than did the fur trade.

The margay is protected by law in most of its range; in Paraguay and Colombia, for example, it is illegal to hunt or trade the margay. Unfortunately, effective enforcement of such laws is difficult, and extensive illegal hunting persists. Smuggling operations continue to be highly organized and efficient. Protection has helped the margay in terms of illegal trade, however. In 1980,

MARKHOR
(Capra falconeri)

Status: Threatened

Order: Artiodactyla
Family: Bovidae
Subfamily: Caprinae
Tribe: Caprini

Description:
Weight: 176-243 lb (80-110 kg)
Shoulder height: 32-45 in (80-115 cm)
Diet: Grasses, leaves, bark, and shoots
Gestation period: 135-165 days
Longevity: 12-14 years
Habitat: Mountainous terrain
Range: Central Asia

Wild Goats
The markhor is one of the most striking members of the wild goat

family found in nature. The markhor dwells in the Hindu Kush mountain chain of Asia. It is spectacular in appearance. Males possess flattened, spiral-shaped horns and long shaggy hair on the neck, chest, and shoulders. Females are considerably smaller in size and possess much smaller horns.

For many years subspecies have been identified mostly by variations in their horns; however, this method has led to confusion over the true taxonomy of these animals. The classification used here recognizes four subspecies: Heptner's, or the Bokharan markhor (*Capra falconeri heptneri*); the flare-horned markhor, once known as the Astor or Pir Panjal markhor (*Capra falconeri falconeri*); the straight-horned markhor, which includes the Kabul and Sulaiman markhor (*Capra falconeri megaceros*); and the Chiltan markhor (*Capra falconeri chialtanensis*).

The markhor can be found on some of the alpine meadows, but for the most part it tends to dwell in the more inaccessible areas of the mountains that dominate Afghanistan, Pakistan, northern India, Uzbekistan and Tadzhikistan.

Living in small family groups of three to five, it is most active at dawn or at dusk. Bucks remain apart from the doe except during the rut or mating season. The markhor is preyed upon at lower altitudes by wolves, while their chief predator at higher altitudes is the snow leopard. For its diet, a markhor, like all goats, is an opportunistic feeder. It will eat nearly anything it can find, normally grasses, leaves, barks, and shoots.

Markhors as a whole do well in captivity, as demonstrated a number of years ago when

Bokharan markhor were imported through Russia. They have reproduced well enough that nearly 50 percent of the existing captive population can trace its lineage to the original pair. The offspring are precocious and frequently twins are born. The young will follow their mother shortly after birth.

Since 1945, markhor have been imported into North America in significant numbers. Virtually all the United States individuals have come from this original Russian source. Both zoos and private wildlife ranches maintain them.

Populations still found in the former Soviet Union are all now protected; however, there are still some diminishing populations there. Outside that land, most of the markhor are endangered due to severe habitat loss and uncontrolled hunting. This endangerment has been made worse by their nearness to the border of Afghanistan, where in recent years there has been considerable warfare.

Most Endangered

The most endangered of the four subspecies is the straight-horned markhor (*Capra falconeri megaceros*), which ranges in the northwest portion of Pakistan near the Afghanistan border. The straight-horned markhor may be the species' most spectacular member. It has an admirable set of horns that are exceedingly

The markhor is a dweller in high rocky crags and ledges, coming down to graze in winter and moving back up into the higher altitudes in the summer.

large—much larger and straighter than those of the other markhors. These horns rarely exceed 36 inches (14 centimeters), but they exhibit a much tighter twist than those of other markhors; these horns have as many as two or more complete spirals. This markhor ranges from the Khyber Pass at the Afghanistan-Pakistan border, southward into Pakistan west of the Indus River to just south of Quetta. The straight-horned markhor would probably do as well in captivity as other markhors; however, few have ever been brought into captivity, and never in sufficient numbers to establish a captive population. Today there are, at best, 30 individuals in three captive locations. This is a seriously endangered animal due to the intrusion and degradation of its habitat by people, and the hunting that inevitably accompanies settlement.

—*Warren D. Thomas*

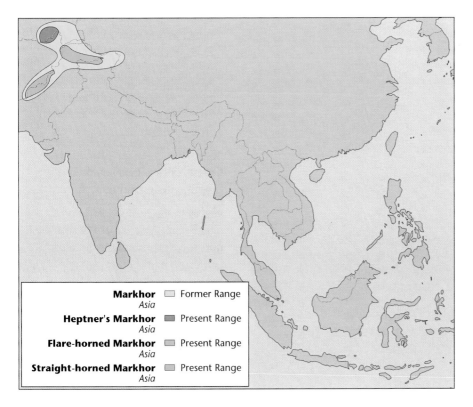

Markhor *Asia*	☐ Former Range
Heptner's Markhor *Asia*	■ Present Range
Flare-horned Markhor *Asia*	■ Present Range
Straight-horned Markhor *Asia*	■ Present Range

MARMOSETS

Class: Mammalia
Order: Primates
Family: Callitrichidae

Marmosets are the smallest of the South American monkeys, with body and tail lengths each ranging from just 6 to 18 inches (15 to 46 centimeters). They have long, soft, and very colorful fur, and tufted hair on their ears. Their tails are furry, and they sometimes have black or gray bands. Marmosets are unusual in that they have sharp, curved claws on all digits except the big toe, which has a broad, flat nail. These long claws enable marmosets to shin up tree trunks, to hide from predators.

Marmosets almost always stay up in the trees, traveling along large branches and sleeping in tree holes. They are found in several forest types, from tall primary rain forest in the Amazon Basin and the Atlantic coast of Brazil to semideciduous dry forest in savannah regions up through Bolivia and Paraguay. They prefer the lower levels of forest canopy, no higher than 62 feet (19 meters), although they will go up to the treetops, as well as to the ground to retrieve fallen fruits or to cross cleared areas of forest.

The marmoset's survival problems are linked with the rapid shrinking of South America's rain forests. While deforestation reduces animal habitat, it also destroys thousands of plant species that many animals rely upon for food.

Male and female marmosets look much the same—so much that it is hard to tell them apart. In their habits, they are very unusual in the primate order, because the male will carry the young (usually twin infants) and hand them to the mother only for nursing. Older siblings also help care for infants. In captivity, marmosets live in stable, monogamous family groups. Recent studies in the wild indicate that marmosets and their relatives, the tamarins, live in larger groups containing one breeding female and several males who mate with her.

As far back as the time before Columbus discovered America, marmosets have been popular as pets. In fact, when the original conquistadors returned to Europe, they brought marmosets back with them, and for a while it was fashionable for women to carry them inside their sleeves! Much later, they were found to be ideal for laboratory experimentation, which led to their large-scale exportation and eventually to their endangered status of today.

BUFFY-HEADED MARMOSET
(*Callithrix flaviceps caroli*)

Status: Endangered

Description:

Weight: 9.8-12 oz (280-350 g)
Head-body length: 7.6-8.4 in (19-21 cm)
Tail length: 10-11.5 in (25-29 cm)
Diet: Omnivorous
Gestation period: 130-150 days
Habitat: Remnant forests
Range: Southeastern Brazil

Dweller of Forests

The buffy-headed marmoset's ear tufts, cheeks, and the top of its head are ochre-colored, while its back is a patchy mouse color.

Marmosets can be distinguished from tamarins by their unusual teeth, or dentition. Tamarins have canines that are much larger than their incisors, whereas marmosets have enlarged incisors similar in length to their canines. These incisors are chisel-like, and adapted for boring or gouging holes in trees to retrieve gum, sap, and resin—all important parts of a marmoset's diet. Marmosets also eat fruit, flowers, nectar, spiders, frogs, snails, lizards, and insects.

The destruction of the Brazilian rain forest through logging and slash-and-burn agricultural techniques has led to the decline in numbers of this marmoset. Only a few thousand remain. Its range is very limited, and its future looks bleak unless drastic measures are taken to protect it.

BUFFY TUFTED-EAR MARMOSET

(Callithrix aurita)

Status: Threatened

Description:

Weight: 8-16 oz (230-453 g)
Head-body length: 8.5 in (21 cm)
Tail length: 11.5 in (29.5 cm)
Diet: Omnivorous
Gestation period: 130-150 days
Longevity: To 16 years in captivity
Habitat: Secondary forest
Range: Southeastern Brazil

Ear Tufts

The buffy tufted-ear marmoset has whitish, or buffy, ear tufts. Its forehead is ochre-colored to white, the front of its crown is tawny or pale buff, the sides of its face and its temples are black, and its back

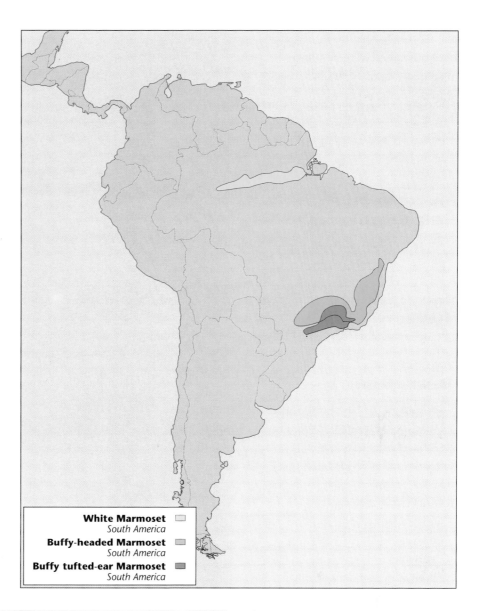

White Marmoset
South America
Buffy-headed Marmoset
South America
Buffy tufted-ear Marmoset
South America

is mouse-colored to dark brown or black. Its tail is black, and its underparts are black to ochre-colored.

In the Brazilian state of Minas Gerais, this marmoset has been observed to spend most of its time at heights of less than 16 feet (5 meters) above ground, in dense patches of bamboo and vines.

Marmosets move on all fours, with a jerky motion reminiscent of the squirrel. They are active during the day and are very sociable,

The buffy-headed marmoset lives in forests of southeastern Brazil, in the states of Espirito Santo and Minas Gerais.

719

making loud, penetrating calls to each other. Only the dominant male and female of the family reproduce; the other adult marmosets in the group do not mate.

WHITE MARMOSET
(Callithrix argentata leucippe)

Status: Threatened

Description:

Weight: 9.8-12 oz (280-350 g)
Head-body length: 7.6-8.4 in (19-21 cm)
Tail length: 10-11.5 in (25-29 cm)
Diet: Omnivorous
Gestation period: 130-150 days
Longevity: Up to 16 years in captivity
Habitat: Secondary forest, primary rain forest with broken canopy
Range: Brazilian Amazon, eastern Bolivia and northern Paraguay.

No Ear Tufts

Callithrix argentata is the only species of marmoset without ear tufts. In other words, it has bare ears, which distinguishes it from other marmosets. The white marmoset is a subspecies. Its coat is silver gray, and its tail is pale gold. This marmoset lives in the Amazon jungle of Brazil.

As humans increasingly encroach on its jungle habitat, so the future of this marmoset looks

more and more precarious. While only classified as vulnerable at present, it is likely to become endangered before the end of the century if measures are not taken immediately to protect it more stringently than is presently the case. Local human populations inevitably focus on short-term commercial rewards, with little concern for the fragile ecosystems within the rain forest. It is hoped that in the future, tourism will provide the revenue necessary to

A remarkable feature of marmosets, including the buffy tufted-ear marmoset, is that even after sexual maturity is attained, the young are still tolerated within the extended family group, and the varying age groups seem to have a harmonious existence.

justify preserving enough of the Amazonian rain forest to prevent the marmoset's habitat from being lost forever.
—*Sarah Dart*
See also Tamarins.